Hey Da

# The Wild Years

Thanks For all your support.

Dwight Worker

# THE WILD YEARS

## Dwight Worker

Feral World Press

ISBN-13: 978-1493702770
ISBN-10: 1493702777

v.3

## Dedicated to:

My brothers, Kenny, Wayne, Darrel, and Ron Worker. To my son Jesse Worker. To Greg Worker, Jason Worker, Mark Watson, and Susan Burk.

## Credits:

Cover design done by Terry Howe. Back photo by Eugene Beckes. Cover photo and other photos by Dwight Worker.

# CONTENTS

# The Wild Years

## Contents-2

I am not sure that these stories need to be read in any particular order. So if some particular story interests you more, go for it.

# Prologue

On July 21$^{st}$, 1998, I got hit by lightning in front of my sixteen-year-old son, Jesse. I remember sitting up and holding my wrist and shouting to my son, *"Are you okay?"* I looked at my arm, but I could only see out of my left eye. The hair was burned from my right wrist. Later my son told me that I had shrieked like I was dying.

Jesse answered that he was not hurt. We had been inside our tent during a thunderstorm in the Sangre de Cristo Mountains of New Mexico. Jesse had been lying on an insulated sleeping pad. I sat there dazed, but I seemed to be functioning. I staggered outside the tent. The lightning had hit a tree next to our campsite. I had been shocked by the jolt that spread along the ground.

On this trip out west, I had been showing my son where I had lived in the mountains of New Mexico. On this day I had given Jesse fly fishing lessons. Then we set up our camp next to the small mountain ranch I used to own here. We were at about 8800 feet in altitude. In 1974, while I was in prison in Mexico, the Internal Revenue Service auctioned off this ranch for back taxes. And the IRS was right. I had not paid my taxes.

Today had been a perfect day with my son. We had talked openly about everything. After two years of estrangement, he had moved back in with me. On this trip, we climbed Mount Wheeler, the highest mountain in New Mexico, rafted down the Rio Grande River, and spent a week of rough camping in the mountains.

Late that afternoon we had heard thunder from a storm rolling in over the mountain tops. We got into the tent. I gave Jesse the sleeping pad. After two years of sleeping on concrete floors in a Mexican prison, I had learned to sleep on anything. So we rested in the tent together.

Then my son said to me, *"Dad, why did you do what you did?"*

I knew this question was coming. I just didn't know when he would ask it. I also did not know how I would answer it. My son had just recently read the book *Escape* that his mother and I had written. This book was about my escape from Lecumberri Prison in Mexico. Jesse had also seen the movie that had been adapted from the book.

So now I had to finally answer to my son. But first, I have a warning to all future parents: If you are worried about what your children might find out about your past, then you had better not do it in the first place; for your children are going to find out.

*So, how do I answer my son?* I forgot all my rehearsed lines. I lay there wondering. Well, this is my moment of truth. Then I said "Son, I really think that for a few years, *I was out of my mind --- drug crazy.* I think it is a miracle that I am alive today. So I don't want you to make my mistakes. Think of some new mistakes to make then, but don't make mine. They've been done before."

We lay there, both of us thinking about what I had just said. Then Jesse sat up and looked at me. We spontaneously hugged each other. I don't know whether he saw my tears. We laid back down and talked some more. It was maybe the most heart-to-heart conversation I have ever had in my life. Surely so with my son. Those things don't necessarily come easily between men.

And then, as we were resting, through the tent flap came a blinding flash. The tree in front of us lit up brilliant electric white. But only I felt the shock of the electricity spreading through the ground. My son later said that he had only felt the concussive wave.

I have often wondered about this event in our lives. First, I try to honestly tell my son one of the most difficult truths in my life. And then I get jolted by lightning. That made about as much sense to me as some of the following stories. But I don't know that I can – or need to – make sense out of them. If these stories are raw and unapologetic, so be it.

So, *I was out of my mind --- drug crazy.* I look back and shake my head at what a risk-taker -- what a fool -- I was at times. There was a period of my life that was at the same time exciting, dangerous, magical, and full-speed-ahead; where any month of my life might have been like a year of someone else's. I did anything first, and then maybe thought about it later, if at all. But most likely, I just went on to the next thing --- and the next thing --- and the next thing. Living free and wild, I recall rapt feelings of awe and joy and excitement, of terror and fear, and everything in between. In the end, I would lose it all. But I could not have seen it coming, and I would have denied it until the bitter end—which did come.

A number of people had suggested that I put these stories to paper before I... well... died. I had written some of these stories well over thirty years ago. Then they languished in my desk. There must be at least another fifty more. I did not want to publish these stories while my parents were alive, as I had already put them through enough grief. But with their passings, I am now free of the direct guilt that they could bring upon me. Yet their ghosts still perch on my shoulder, constantly giving me their unasked-for opinions. Maybe they should, as I cannot silence them. Perhaps we all have to live with that.

I AM GRATEFUL for the help, support, and advice of the following people: Susan Burk, Kenn Crook, Sharon Dorr, Louise Hillery, Mike Kelsey, David Stewart, Douglas Trenfield, and Allen Tucker.

# 1

# Wounded Hawk

Smashing a leg-hold trap

In the distance I saw my sixteen-year-old brother Kenny walking through the snow toward the back porch. Winter was setting in early this year in northern Indiana. Kenny held his shotgun over one shoulder and something large under his arm.

"Pudgie, you won't believe what I found." He held a big bird up with his glove. It stretched one wing out and flapped it violently. Kenny grabbed the wing and folded it back. I ran up to him. It was a young red tail hawk.

"You shot a hawk!"

"No. I found it in the woods, Four-eyes. It was already wounded."

He walked over to the chicken coops, opened an empty cage, and squeezed the hawk into it. "You feed it for me. I'll pay you to do it. Okay?"

"Then what you gonna do with it?"

"Umm – maybe train it to catch rabbits. I don't know. Just you feed it when I'm gone, okay?" The hawk turned away from us and hid in the corner of the cage. Then my brother left.

The hawk beat its one good wing. The blood on the other wing was fresh. The cage was too small for it to stretch out both its wings at once. I went inside and thawed out some rabbit meat in hot water. I put the bowl of meat and fresh water in the front of the coop. The hawk stayed in the corner. I watched it and it watched me, but it showed no interest in the food or water. I left it for the night.

Next morning before school I checked out Hawk. As I opened the door, he turned away from me. The water and meat were both frozen. I went inside and thawed the meat out again then returned with it and fresh water.

After school I ran over to the cage. The meat had frozen again, and it looked untouched. But the water was lower. While I was putting in fresh meat, Kenny and his hunting buddy Gibby came over to the cage.

"Man, that thing looks wicked. So how'd you catch it?" Gibby asked. He stuck his gloved hand in the cage and waved it at the hawk. Hawk jumped back from him.

"It was flying along the edge of a cornfield. I was hunting pheasant when I saw it. Got it with number 4 shot in my twelve-gauge."

"What? You said you found it already shot," I shouted.

Kenny shoved me. "So what? What you gonna do now? Tell Mom? It's just a chicken hawk."

"They don't kill our chickens. We've never lost one to a hawk."

"Hey Gibby, you won't believe Four-Eyes here. I took him rabbit hunting for the first time and Four-Eyes kicks one up and actually shoots it. Not a bad shot. The rabbit's wounded and is squealing. I tell him to grab its rear legs, step on its head, and pull it off. And Four-Eyes here, he couldn't even do it. He looked like he was gonna cry himself. He hasn't gone hunting with us since."

Gibby looked at me funny. "Well, I don't know if you can train hawks. But if you can't, he'd sure make a great wall mount."

*A wall mount?* The walls of Kenny's bedroom were covered with mounted birds already. He was always hunting for something new to add to it.

I pushed the warmed rabbit meat for Hawk, but he ignored it. I told him he'd have to start eating soon.

That night got really cold. First thing in the morning, I ran out to the cage. I was afraid I was going to find Hawk frozen stiff. But he was all fluffed up in the corner. He looked at me with his sharp yellow eyes. The water and rabbit meat had frozen solid again. But this time most of the the rabbit meat was gone. *He's finally eating!* I switched some warm meat and water with the frozen food. I told Hawk to keep on eating.

At school that day, I got a book in the library on hawks and falcons. I read through the whole thing at lunch and during library period. The book said that you could train young red-tail hawks to hunt and retrieve, but you had to start early and practice about every day. It also said that the females were much larger than the males. I went to my biology teacher and described Hawk to him. "Sounds like you've got a female," he said. It was hard for me to think of Hawk now as a *she*.

When school let out, I rushed home straight to the cage again. The rabbit meat was all gone. "Good boy" I said. Then I said, "Good girl".

I ran inside to get more thawed meat. As I was coming up the basement stairs, Mom stopped me.

"Where are you going?"

"To feed the hawk. You know she's started eating."

"I know. It's been eating hamburger for two days."

"You've been feeding her too!" I hugged Mom. She smiled.

"Don't tell Kenny I said this, Mom. But he shot that hawk."

Mom shook her head. "I thought so. Just like your Dad. They'll shoot anything. Now take this hamburger out to him. And don't tell your Dad we're feeding it this."

"Mom, it's a 'her'. I was wondering---it's been real cold outside---I'm afraid Hawk might freeze to death. Can I keep her in the basement--at night?"

Mom looked around. "If you can make a good cage for her, I guess so. Just don't let her get out while I'm washing clothes."

I ran out to the tool shed and got some old two-by-fours and chicken screen. By dinner, I'd built a hawk cage about four feet high. I broke a big branch off a dead elm tree and propped it in the middle of the cage. Then I went out to Hawk. I put on a thick coat, goggles, my football helmet, and heavy leather gloves. I opened the door slowly and held meat up to her. She turned away. I leaned halfway into the cage and reached for her. She fought. I put one arm under her leg and moved my other arm around her chest. She stepped up on my arm. When I closed my arm around her, she opened her beak slowly, but did not make a sound. She didn't fight when I lifted her out of the coop. I carried her into the basement and put her in the cage. She immediately climbed onto the elm branch. She sat there turning her head around in quick jerks. I sat in the corner and watched. Then she climbed down the branch and began pulling apart the rabbit meat. This was the first time I had seen her eat.

That night I asked Kenny if I could buy Hawk from him.

"No."

"Why not?"

"Because I'm gonna train him."

"You haven't begun doing anything. The book says you got to train them almost every day."

"Beat it."

It snowed heavily that night. Kenny got up early to check his traps before he went to school. He had a line of them set for rabbits, muskrats, and anything else he could catch. Dad said Kenny had to check his traps twice a day. But sometimes Kenny skipped doing it for a day or two. Kenny promised to pay me twenty-five cents a day to check the traps for him. He owed me two dollars already.

I rushed home from school that day and followed Kenny's tracks in the snow. I made sure to step right in the middle of Kenny's footprints. When I found the first trap, I sprang it with a stick. I did the same to the next two traps. I left the fourth one alone and knocked the bait off the next few traps. Then I sprang a few more. When I came up to the next trap, it had a cat in it. It hissed at me like it was wild and dragged the trap all around. Its leg was broken and bloody. I wanted to let it go – do something -- but I would make so many footprints that I'd give myself away. Besides, that cat would have torn my hands off. So I left it be. I followed Kenny's trail down to the stream. There were some traps set for muskrats. I sprang one of them and pulled the stake out of the ground. Then I tossed the trap into the middle of the stream. I jumped from rock to rock across the stream to the other side. Then I went back home a different way. *Ha ha, Kenny.*

Next day Kenny didn't check his traps until after school. When Kenny came back, he was carrying a rabbit.

"Dad, half my traps were sprung. There was a dead cat in one of them too. Good. They're just out there killing all the game. And one of my traps is missing. I looked all over for it but it's gone. What could have been strong enough to pull out the stake?"

"Could have been a coon," Dad said. "They're smart enough to dig stakes out. You should have been able to track him easy though, cause he's bound to snag that trap onto something while he was getting away."

"That's what I thought too. I looked all around, but the only tracks I found was someone else's footprints on the other side of the stream."

"You better hide your traps better then," Dad said. "Someone out there hunting and finds your traps, he's gonna take 'em every time. That's just the way it goes."

"Maybe the raccoon went into the water and drowned with the trap on. You might find it next spring," I said. They ignored me.

Next day I went out after Kenny left. I sprung some more traps and pulled up another one. I brought that trap home and buried it in the field behind our home. Now I could say "Yes Kenny this," and "Yes Kenny that," and it didn't hurt so bad. I felt powerful with my secret. I wasn't done with his traps yet.

Kenny moved some of the traps, sure enough. But I didn't have any problem tracking them down. It now became fun finding and springing his traps. Kenny would come back and tell Dad about how much game there must be out there because all his traps were getting sprung. If he could only catch them. *Ha ha Kenny.*

Every day when I got home from school, first thing I did was feed Hawk. If no one was around, I would take her out of the cage and set her up on Dad's work bench. Hawk would sit there and stretch both her wings out all the way. Now the wounded wing was moving just like the other one. She looked so big and noble with her wings spread. She never took her eyes off me, and I kept looking at her too. I *knew* that she recognized me from everyone else in our family.

One day when Hawk was on the workbench, I took off my glove and reached over to pet her. I'd always wanted to, but was afraid. She watched my fingers come to her. When I touched her chest feathers, in a flash she wrapped her talon around my wrist and held it hard. I froze, suddenly afraid she was going to tear my hand apart. I waited. I felt her grip loosen. Then she lifted her talon and put it back on the bench. I slowly pulled my hand back. I never tried to pet her again.

I watched her and she watched me. She stretched her wings out and beat them again. Then she jumped off the bench and tried to fly. She flapped twice before she crashed into a blanket that Mom had hung to dry. I gathered her up and put her back onto the bench. She jumped off and did the same thing. She was just too big for our basement. When I went up to her, she hopped around on the floor and ran away from me. Now she was acting different.

That night I asked Kenny again if I could buy her. "No. And it's a 'him,' not a 'her.' Go wound one yourself, tattletale."

That same night I dreamed of Hawk flying high and free. I was below her and she was soaring. She looked down at me with her golden eyes and dove right over my head.

I was jumpy all day at school, but I knew it was time. When I got home, I put on Dad's leather gloves and went straight to Hawk's cage. I slowly lifted her out. She didn't resist. I climbed the stairs and went outside with her. Then I started running with her to the railroad tracks. When I got to the tracks, I held her in front of me. She stared into my face. I watched her. She was so beautiful. I put both my arms under her, bent down, and flung her as high as I could into the air.

She went up in a ball and opened up her wings. As she was coming down at me, she began beating her wings. She started flying slowly--about three feet off the ground to my side. I ran along side of her. She lifted up over my head, but still flew low. She went straight for a big cottonwood tree next to the railroad tracks and landed on the lowest branch. I ran to the tree. She had her wings straight out on both sides, stretching them. I stared up at her. We were both breathing hard. She let out a shrill cry. It was the first time I had ever heard her make a sound. Then she leaped off the branch and began flying. She still flew low, but higher than before. I watched her fly to a bigger tree a few hundred yards away. I ran to that tree. When I came up this time, she took off flying into the woods nearby.

I never saw her again.

I went home and did my chores. I told Mom what I did, and she approved. Later that afternoon, Kenny came home from school with some friends. They quickly left. Kenny didn't even notice that Hawk was gone. It took Kenny two days to discover it. Kenny came up to me.

"Hey! Where's my hawk?"

I breathed deep. I had been waiting for this for days.

"I let her go."

"You WHAT? He couldn't fly."

"Yes she could. We'd been working on it."

"What do you mean? I was paying you to take care of him."

"You never paid me anything."

"*I was going to.*" He punched me hard on the shoulder. "Goddamn you. You're paying me."

Mom heard the commotion and came running. "You get your hands off him. Next time you shoot any more birds for no reason, I'll take your gun away. Now leave your brother alone."

Kenny and I left the basement. As soon as we were outside, Kenny said, "I'll get you for this."

I thought of all the excuses and lies I had been saying to him just to protect myself. All the times he scared me. Just like now.

Then it just happened. "I been springing your traps!" I yelled. I hadn't planned on saying it at all.

"WHAT?"

"You never check 'em anyhow! Yeah, I been springing 'em."

Kenny slapped me. My glasses went flying. I swung back, but it wasn't much use. He was four years older. I didn't have any chance to win. Never did.

"You damn little brat crybaby!" Kenny was holding me so I couldn't swing at him anymore.

"I'll keep springing your traps too!" I shouted at him. I managed to pull away and run across the yard from him.

"If you stole that trap, you're paying for it!" Kenny shouted.

"Never! You can't make me!"

"I'll take your money!"

"I'll sell the rest of your traps!"

"I'm telling Dad!" Kenny shouted.

"Squealer! Tattletale! You said we could never squeal on each other!"

"This is different!"

"Different when you're the squealer!" Then I did it. I gave Kenny the finger. That was the first time I ever did that to him.

There was a sudden silence. Then Kenny came charging at me. I took off full speed. He wasn't much faster than me and I had a good lead. I ran down the path into the woods. But I slipped on the ice and fell hard. "HAAA!" I heard Kenny coming up on me. I jumped up and ran to the edge of the stream. Then I slowly stepped out onto the thick ice. I kneeled down and crawled. I heard Kenny coming up behind me. As soon as I got to the other side, I scrambled up the bank. I turned around to see Kenny run out onto the ice. He crashed right through it and shrieked. He was standing in the ice water almost up to his waist. He was cussing up a storm.

"HA HA, Kenny!" I shouted.

"GODDAMN YOU! I'LL GET YOU!"

"I'll keep springing your traps! You can't stop me." I gave him the finger again.

"Not after I beat the shit outta you! Just you wait."

I climbed up the other bank and ran from Kenny. When I got away from him, I began walking home. In the west I saw a 'V' formation of Canada geese flying against the cold, gray winter clouds of sunset. I knew I was in *big* trouble when I got home. Kenny would squeal to Dad. It was one thing to let the hawk go. But to mess up Kenny's trap line? Dad would really get me on that one. So I stayed outside, afraid to go in. But finally it was night and I was cold. When I opened the back door, Dad, Mom, and Kenny were standing there, like an Indian gauntlet. Dad looked scary mad to me, and Mom looked like she had been crying. I started taking off my boots.

"You leave him alone," Mom commanded. "Kenny wasn't doing a thing with that hawk, and he wasn't checking his traps hardly at all."

Dad stared at me, but he didn't say a thing. As I stepped by him, I turned my head away, to avoid the slap. But it never came. Then I walked by Kenny. He looked me in the eye. I knew that look. There would be punches later. I looked back at him.

"Squealer," I whispered.

I thought this was the end of the story. But thirty years later, after my Dad died, my mother asked me to clean out the garage. My eight-year-old son Jesse helped me. My Dad had never thrown anything away. Later in the day, in a far corner of the garage, I dragged out a disintegrating burlap bag filled with rusting metal. I tore it open, and there lay before me all of the leg hold traps of our family. We had not used or even seen these traps for 25 years. I showed them to my mother and asked her what I should do with them. I said we could give them to Kenny, or take them to metal recycling.

My Mom looked the traps over. "Looks like someone could still use them. Let's give Jesse a job first."

My mother went into our tool storage, found a sledge hammer, and handed it to my son. Then, one at a time, Jesse proceeded to smash all the traps while my mother smiled.

# 2

## Ten Mothahfuckin' Dollars

In all-white Highland, Indiana in 1960, my brothers and I used to caddy for wealthy colored folk. They drove down from the south side of Chicago to golf at Wicker Park. They were doctors, lawyers, retired sports stars, and professionals of all sorts. My oldest brother Kenny caddied a lot for the former world heavy-weight boxing champ, Joe Louis. I regularly caddied for the Olympic track star Jesse Owens. Jesse religiously played golf three days a week, rain or shine. He arrived at 9 a.m., and by 2 p.m. we were finished with 18 holes. He paid five bucks. That was good money for a 13 year old in 1960. Back then, I had no idea that these men drove 30 miles to Wicker Park because they could not get tee-off times at any of the public golf courses in Chicago. This was just before the big storm.

One day that summer, Jesse told me that he would be going to Rome, Italy for a few weeks for the 1960 Olympics. In the meantime I'd just have to find somebody else to caddy for. Kenny told me this would be no problem; I'd start caddying for the gamblers just like he did. These gamblers were also colored men who came down from Chicago to golf at Wicker Park.

Kenny caddied for Fat Long and I started caddying for Duke Cumberland. Both these guys had played on the original Harlem Globetrotters basketball team. Duke had been a long, tall forward, and Fat Long a stocky guard.

Duke wore a thin gray mustache with his graying hair plastered back on his head with this sweet-smelling Dixie Pomade oil. He wore slick clothes that always looked like they were brand new. There was sort of a twinkle in his eyes that made it easy for me to approach and talk to him. He'd smile with a gold tooth showing, and talk about whatever. Unlike the other golfers, he seemed to take an interest in the caddies.

On that first day, I shagged balls for Duke out on the driving range. I was cleaning his clubs at the first tee when another caddy looked up at Duke and said, "How's the weather up there, mister?"

Duke looked puzzled at first. Then he looked down and said, "Fine. Now how's the weather down by my ass?" Everybody laughed except for that caddy. Then Duke hit a long drive. The others teed off and we picked up our bags and took off down the fairway. Kenny, myself, and two other caddies,

# The Wild Years

along with Fat Long, Duke Cumberland, and two other Chicago men, Seville Williams and Grant Lane.

As soon as we got down to our balls, Fat Long shouted to Duke, "Hey Duke, I gotcha fifty dollah a hole, with presses, Okay?"

"Hold off on the presses for now."

"Whatsamattah Duke, you aint got no money?" Fat Long's voice sounded deep as a barrel. Then he shouted "Duke aint got no money! I took it all last week. Duke is mothahfuckin' *broke*!" Now Fat's voice was all high-pitched and screechy, like someone dropped a brick on his foot.

"Y'all tryin' to psych my ass, an' ya ain't."

I walked over to my brother. "Are they serious? *Fifty dollars a hole?*" I asked.

"They're just getting started," Kenny said. "Just you wait when they get the presses going. All Fat and Duke does for a living is gamble."

The first hole was a 520 yard par 5. As a caddy, you carried the golf bag up to your golfer's ball. Then you put your bag to the side, or wherever your golfer told you to, and you made sure to never move when anyone was swinging. Kenny beat that point into me. My man Duke hit the longest drive, so he was last to hit his second shot. He put a 3 wood close to the green. When we got around the green, everything got quiet and serious, They walked up on the green and examined it like it had land mines.

"Green's still wet, so it's slow right now," I heard Kenny whisper to Fat. I repeated what I heard to Duke.

"Good, You just keep spying. And keep an eye on Fat too. Make sure he don't cheat."

Everyone chipped onto the green in three shots. These guys were playing *good*. Duke was getting ready to putt first.

"Duke, you gonna putt it so hard it gonna go in the muthahfuckin' sand trap!" Fat Long shouted.

Fat's face was all lit up. He had the biggest head I ever seen on anybody. It was like a rhinoceros, with flappy ears sticking out and a wide nose you could look up into. A thick gray mustache hung over his big lips. His cheeks drooped down so far they looked like they was melted. They pulled down the corners of his mouth. There were big crater marks all over his cheeks from an old pimple battle he had lost. Across Fat's jaw was an ugly scar. He looked like he was always mad about something. And Fat said the F-word every other word. They never talked like that in Jesse Owens' group. I never heard my dad or any of his friends ever say that word either. But now I was hearing grown men say it all the time. My dad ever heard me

# Ten Motherfuckin' Dollars

say that word and he'd whup me up side my head *good.*

Duke shook his head, then backed off and realigned his putt. When he stroked it, the spinning ball actually threw water into the air, the green was so wet. Duke's ball took the slope and curved right at the hole. But it stopped three feet short.

"HAAAA!" Fat Long waved his putter over his head. He and Kenny stood in back of the ball and talked about his putt. Then Fat stepped up and hit a curving 12 foot putt that dropped right into the hole for a birdie.

"MUTHAHFUCKAH! FAT LONG, MUTHAHFUCKA!" Fat waved his putter over his head as he did this goofy dance across the green. "You gonna miss that putt again, Duke."

Duke looked up. "My putter sure won't miss your ugly head." Duke putted. The ball lipped the cup and stopped on the edge. Bogey. Seville and Grant each parred. I got out my scorecard and asked everyone what they got, even though I knew.

"Caddy, don't keep no mothahfuckin' score here," Fat yelled at me. "Put that away. We know what the score is. You just carry your bag an' do as you're told."

I stuffed the scorecard into Duke's bag and carried it to the next tee off. Then I washed his ball and took a tee and cleaned the grooves on the clubs he had used.

"You down two already, Duke MuthahFucka. You ready for a press already, on the second hole?" Fat grunted.

Duke told Fat to go fuck himself and the press too. While we were waiting to tee off, I took out an extra scorecard and asked Duke if I could have his autograph.

"Sure, sonny." He signed it and handed it to me. "Been a long time since I done that." Then I went up to Fat Long and asked for his. I called him Mr. Long for safe.

"*My autograph*? Why you want *my* autograph, caddy?"

"Oh, you see, I seen the Harlem Globetrotters on TV. You know, that movie about the Globetrotters—it was called *The Harlem Globetrotters*, or maybe *The Abe Saperstein Story*. But you and Duke was in it."

"THE ABE SAPERSTEIN STORY, HUH?" Fat shouted. "Well who the hell you think Abe Saperstein was? Did he go out there and play basketball every night? HELLLLLLLLLLLL NO! He just got his name on the movie and a lot of our money, That's the real *Abe Saperstein Story*, goddamnit!" Fat Long just stood there, glaring at me. I didn't know what to do or say.

Duke came up to Fat. "Oh shut up Fat and *sign* the boy's card. Ain't the

# The Wild Years

boy's fault what Abe did. The boy's treatin' you with respect. And don't go signing it FAT MOTHERFUCKER LONG."

Fat laughed. "Gimmee that scorecard, boy." He signed it. "Duke, I never signed no autograph 'Fat Motherfucker Long' in my life."

"You sure as hell did once."

"I may of wanted to, but I'd a been too scared then. But now I ain't. I don't give a fuck no more." Fat handed me back the scorecard, There was a big scrawl in pencil on it that said *Fat Long.*

They teed off and we went down the fairway. They went on playing, gambling, and cussing. It was a sunny, windy day, just great to be outside. Each hole was like the other, loud before teeing off and dead quiet on the greens. I kept a mental score anyhow. Fat Long was winning. He wasn't a long knocker when it came to driving, but man could he play around the green. The bets stacked up and the golfers got more serious. I was rooting for Duke to beat Fat like I rooted for the Chicago Cubs to beat the Milwaukee Braves. Fat had Duke down two holes after the 5th hole, so Duke called a press. Kenny told me that a press was a new bet from this point on for the same amount as the original bet. If Duke did better than Fat on the next four holes, then he would win the press. That would cancel out his losing the first bet. It was sort of a double-or-nothing from this point on. Duke and Fat were beating Seville and Grant badly enough not to worry about them.

It seemed like nothing you did for Fat – pull a pin, wash a ball, replace a divot, got any attention from him. All of our names were just "caddy" to him, even though he knew my brother Kenny was Kenny. Whenever Fat hit the ball into the rough, he made Kenny walk in front of him to make sure "there wasn't no snakes". Then Fat walked into the rough by himself for a while. He got behind a tree, but it wasn't to pee. He fooled around with some snuff or something. Then he came back from the woods with a big smile on his face. He covered up one side of his nose and blew a *monster* glob of snot onto the ground. The ol' farmers' handkerchief.

"Duke, I'm gonna kill yo' muthahfuckin' ass now. I got my mojo on and you caint stop it." Fat sort of bellowed and barked at the same time. It was hard for me to understand what he was saying. His voice would go low, and then real high. He'd rumble something, then shout so loud like he wanted to fight. I didn't know people could make such sounds, since there were no colored folks living in Highland, Indiana. I hadn't learned how they talked yet.

Across the road from the sixth hole on the other side of the fence was a

## Ten Motherfuckin' Dollars

private golf course, *Thee Woodmar Country Club*. Kenny said they were all rich people there. They all had caddies because the country club included it with anyone who golfed. *Thee Woodmar* caddies had to dress up in these cute little uniforms. Kenny said they were stuck up about caddying at a private course. Not like us delinquents. Kenny said they just got paid a dollar eighty-five a day, plus little ole piss-ant tips.

The Woodmar caddies watched from the other side of the fence as our guys were teeing off. One of them made a face at us. Just as Fat was hitting the ball, the Woodmar caddy shouted. Fat turned to the Woodmar caddies. His drive was good, but Fat looked to kill. Kenny dropped his bag and ran up to the fence. "What you think you doin'?" Kenny shouted. The Woodmar caddies didn't say anything back. "Don't do it again." Then we finished teeing off and started down the fairway.

From behind us, one of the Woodmar caddies yelled, *"Nigger lovers!"* We all heard it. Kenny dropped his bag, ran up to the cyclone fence that separated the courses and in one motion grabbed it, jumped, and swung his body over it like it was a gymnastics bar. He landed on all fours, then ran full speed straight for the four Woodmar caddies. All of them started running from Kenny, up ahead to the green where their golfers were putting. The golfers looked up.

"What the hell?" one of them shouted. "You get out of here right now – or we're calling the police."

"Your caddies was calling our golfers bad names," Kenny shouted. He pointed to the caddies. "DO IT AGAIN AN' WE'LL BEAT YOUR ASSES! LOOK AT YOU CHICKEN SHITS RUNNING!"

Seville and Duke and Fat were all shouting for Kenny to get back over here *right now*. Kenny swung himself back over the fence and came trotting back. He picked up Fat's bag and caught up with our group.

"We don't wanna start no war here," Duke said as he put his arm on Kenny's shoulder.

"I'll git the sonsabitches!"

"Maybe so. But not on our time, sonny," Duke said.

Fat Long was grinning. "You see them little bastuds run? Ha! Four ginst one and the little shits run. We shoulda let 'em fight it out. Hell, we had to in our time. Our caddies woulda whupped they asses good."

"Bullshit Fat. You'd just be taking bets on who was gonna win," Duke said.

Fat rubbed Kenny on his head. Kenny sort of grinned. Then Fat Long handed Kenny a five-dollar bill. "Go up to the food stand there an git all the caddies 'freshments. Good 'freshments."

Kenny ran over to the refreshment stand and got all the caddies Dr. Peppers and hot dogs. When he came back, Fat told Kenny to keep the change. *Keep the change?* I bet that had never happened in the history of the Wicker Park Public Golf Course.

The ninth hole was a par three. Duke hit a seven iron within three feet of the pin. Fat cussed. He needed a four iron. "Don't make no difference what club I use goddammit as long as I get there," Fat mumbled. Duke birdied the hole, and Fat missed his birdie putt for a par.

"MUTHAHFUCK!" Fat waved his putter, then he swung it down and smacked it *deep* into the green. As soon as he pulled it out, Kenny fixed the divot. You don't normally fix divots on greens. Only then Fat started laughing at what he had done. Duke had won the press and evened out with Fat for the first nine. Fat had beaten the other two guys. But no matter to Fat, cause he wanted to beat Duke so bad.

At the 10th tee, Duke unzipped his bag and got out bottles of whiskey. *So that's why my bag was so heavy.* They all took swigs together and made more bets. Seventy-five bucks a hole. *Wow.* My dad did good to make $25 a day at the refinery. They drank some more. Fat yelled that they all had to drink the same amount, so that their drunk handicap was all the muthahfuckin' same. They all laughed hard together at that one and drank.

Another caddy in the group, Mick, said that when the golfers weren't looking, he was going to steal him a swig too. Kenny said that would be easy. Just walk ahead to the next tee off when they were putting, take a quick blast, and put it back. And sure enough, on the next green, Kenny and Mick unzipped Seville's bag and had a swig of his whiskey. *Whoowwee* Kenny was grinning. Kenny lit up a cigarette, he said to cover up his breath. Kenny said no whiskey for me. I was too young.

After the 13th hole, they upped their bets to $100 a hole. You didn't dare move when they were playing for that much. They were taking whiskey snorts every few holes, but it didn't seem to affect their game much. They sure got louder though. Other foursomes could now hear our group cussing from a hole away, and our guys didn't care at all. Some of the whites looked at us funny. "Fuck em," Fat Long grunted. "They been lookin' at me funny my whole mothahfuckin' life, ever since I come outta my mother's pussy. I was ugly then, an I'm ugly now. So why should I care what *thee* fuck they think of me now?"

By the 15th hole, everything they said was muthah-fuckah this and muthah-fuckah that, muthah-fuckah putt, muthah-fuckah green, muthah-

## Ten Motherfuckin' Dollars

fuckah club, muthah-fuckah wind, muthah-fuckah trap, muthah-fuckah course, muthah-fuckah wife, muthah-fuckah girlfriend, muthah-fuckah thief, muthah-fuckah lucky, muthah-fuckah Duke-Grant-Seville-Fat. The whole world had become one big *muthahfuckah* to them. On this day I heard more cuss words than I'd heard in my whole life. If my daddy *ever* heard me say any of those words once, he'd of whupped me upside my head good.

Kenny snuck ahead and took a swig of Fat Long's whiskey. Kenny spit it out. "Tastes like goddamned tea water! That's not whiskey." Kenny put the bottle back.

Duke and Fat were even on the 18th hole. Duke hooked his drive to the left. It rolled as far as the other drives, but we were in the rough. When I found the ball, I said to Duke, "You know, my brother says that Fat don't smell like he's been drinking whiskey."

Duke looked up at me with a serous face. "Your brother sure didn't find that out by gittin' close to Fat. Cause Fat's breath'll kill a skunk. You know how your brother found that out?" I wasn't saying anything. "Oh I seen 'em sneaking ahead for those sips. I know Fat don't drink when he's betting. But Seville and Grant don't know that. Fat, he's got two bottles. One for the enemy, and the other for him. And you don't say a word about this, caddy--- never---or no tip and it's the last time you ever caddy in this group."

I promised Duke that I would *never ever* tell anyone ever about this, ever, for the rest of my life. Then Duke looks up and says, "And what make you think I'm drinking?" He smiled a bit to himself.

Duke and Fat played it out to the end, and they both tied again. Fat was pissed. We walked up to the clubhouse. While I was cleaning Duke's clubs, I watched Grant and Seville pay up Duke and Fat. Hundreds and hundreds of dollars passed hands, the most money I'd ever seen in my life. A real wad.

Duke and I walked back to his Cadillac. I put the golf bag in the trunk. "You did well, caddy. You kept up with us and helped my game. We won us some money." We shook. My hand got lost inside of his. "You be here next Sunday at nine, cause next time we gonna beat Fat Long's ass."

"Yes sir." Duke handed me some money. I took it and walked to the caddy bench. Then I counted the money.

Ten dollars. *I'll be rich!*

I turned to Kenny and shouted, "TEN MUTHAHFUCKIN' DOLLARS!"

## The Wild Years

Our golfers, three other caddies, and myself,
with a stolen beer, at age 13

# 3

## Caddy Raid

Us caddies had an emergency meeting at the caddy fort. Our fort was perfectly hidden in the middle of a thick clump of thorny blackberry bushes. No one could walk through those blackberries without getting their clothes torn away and their skin cut up. My brother Kenny had discovered this spot while looking for mushrooms. Close to our fort was the creek that ran along the west side of both Wicker and Woodmar golf courses.

On the backside of the fort, we had hacked a winding tunnel through the thorns. To get to it, you had to crawl on your belly. If you lifted up, you got snagged bad. Once inside our fort, no one from the outside could see you. Whenever we caddies had no work, we'd go down to the fort and fix it up, smoke, throw knives, play cards, just do stuff. We built up the inside walls with dead branches and old wood. For seats we had some rocks and logs in a circle around a fire pit.

We had rules that we had all pledged to:

-1 Only caddies could know about this. No one else, ever.

-2 Anything we ever did here was secret for life.

Three other caddies, Roy, Micky, and Sonny, showed up with Kenny and me. We sat in the circle while Kenny built a little fire. Then he mixed some corn silk, tobacco, and dried cattail together. Kenny reached inside a hollow log and pulled out the clay pipe. He lit it, puffed, then passed it around. When I puffed, I coughed. I always did.

When we were finished smoking, Kenny started the meeting. "A while back, the Woodmar caddies called us 'nigger lovers' again. Fat Long heard it too. Even if we was nigger lovers, we can't let them call us that and get away with it. I know the faces of the caddies who shouted it. I been checking Woodmar out, and here's the plan."

Kenny got a stick out and drew into the dirt. He went over everything each of us was supposed to do. He said he needed one volunteer for the riskiest part. I raised my hand and so did Roy. But Kenny choose me. Then we all stood up and put all our right hands into the circle. HEE---YEAH! we all shouted at once.

We rode our bikes fast down the path along the creek. When we got to the Woodmar fence, we hid our bikes in the weeds. Like always, I locked up my bike. Then we went under the fence onto Woodmar. Enemy territory. Kenny shouted for everyone to get down from here on. Not a sound. Just like they always did against the Japs on TV. We weaved along the stream bank, through stinging nettles, thorns, poison ivy, and the smell of sewage

# The Wild Years

until we came to a bridge. Kenny crept ahead to the next tee-off, then came running back. "This is it. It's between the sixth and seventh holes. They should be coming by soon."

Kenny waved everyone to the edge of the creek. He took a stick and poked it around the mud. Smelly bubbles came out of the black gook. Little black catfish came to the surface to breathe. Kenny grabbed some mud and rolled it up. He mixed some grass in with it, then wrapped it in leaves. We all started making mud balls.

We heard someone walking on the path to the bridge. We all dove into the weeds, then watched four golfers walk across the bridge, followed by their caddies. We waited until they left before we went back to the creek. I found a big pile of cut fairway grass. It was rotten and gushy and stunk real bad. I waved everyone over and we all used this grass for our mud balls.

Kenny went over the plan again. "And this is where Pudgie comes in. Pudgie, here's what you do." Kenny gave me my orders. Then we waited.

We saw another group on the sixth hole green. The caddies were silent while the golfers lined up their putts. They took the pin as the men putted.

"It's him!" Kenny whispered. "That's one of the caddies who called us *nigger lover.* Look at them, wearing Woodmar caddy shirts and shorts. Shorts! Just like girls. Pudgie, take your position. You won't be able to see who's coming, so you just have to watch me. Never take your eyes off me. And be quick. Remember, no one does nothing until after Pudgie does his job. Got it?"

Once again we put our hands into a circle. Then I scurried under the bridge while the rest of them hid in the weeds. Soon after, I heard some people approaching from above. I felt like I'd just drunk three bottles of Dr. Pepper. I was staring at Kenny when he gave me the thumbs down signal. Then I heard some people walking over the the bridge above me. Men's voices talking and the cleats of their shoes. Golfers. I leaned back and waited against a bridge post.

A minute later I heard another group coming. Sounds of boys talking and laughing. Kenny was looking at me, slowly nodding his head. The walking and the voices got louder and louder until they were on top of the bridge. Kenny flipped his thumb up.

I banged on the side of the bridge hard with a stick.

"GROOOWWWWWLLLL! I'M THE TROLL!" I roared as loud as I could.

I jumped out from under the bridge and saw two Woodmar caddies leaning over the edge of the bridge looking down. I flung a mud ball hard

# Caddy Raid

as I could right into the chest of one of them. It splattered good. The mud balls came in flying. SPLAT SPLAT SPLAT! I flung the rest of my mud balls point blank. POW POW POW! Direct hits.

Then we were all out of mud balls. There was a funny silence. The Woodmar caddies were shouting to the golfers. Kenny and the others took off running. I ran full speed along the stream after them trying to catch up, but they were way ahead of me. I heard the Woodmar caddies shouting behind me. They were chasing me. I fell once and skinned up my knee. I was up and going in a second. I got to the fence and slid under it. I snagged my shirt on it, yanked hard, and ripped it loose. I sprinted as fast as I could to the weeds where we had hidden our bikes. I looked behind and one caddy, the big one, was still chasing me. I found my bike and started fumbling around for the key. *Where is it?* The faster I tried to find my key, the worse it went. My hands were shaking too bad to hold steady. Just as I opened the lock, the Woodmar caddy jumped into the clearing in front of my bike. His cheeks were red and he had mud on his shirt and neck. We didn't make any plans for this. I let go of my bike and charged him swinging. Kenny said never give them give them no warning. Just do it. The caddy just stood there as I hit him. He didn't even swing back. *He was crying.*

"THAT'S WHAT YOU GIT FOR CALLIN' US NIGGERLOVERS!"

I jumped onto my bike and took off as fast as I could. I never looked back. Then I remembered I had left my lock and key behind. That caddy probably found it. So at the fort I hid my bike in the weeds and crawled through the thorns. When I got close, I tried to make the bird whistle call. Only my throat was so dry it barely came out. I heard someone whistle back. Then I crawled into the fort. Everyone was waiting for me.

"Yeeeaaaahhhh! We got them! Let's hear it for the TROLL!" They cheered and slapped my back. I told them about the fight. They cheered me again. They saw my bleeding knee. I said it wasn't nothing. Kenny held my arm up. "Way to go, little bro!" I felt like I'd just hit the winning grand-slam home-run--run in the winning touchdown--dunked the ball to win the Indiana State High School Basketball Tournament – all at once.

"We sure as fuck aint no nigger lovers!" Roy shouted.

Then Kenny built another fire. A small one, Kenny said, not a white man's fire where you burnum balls and freezum ass. Kenny got out the pipe and we smoked it again. Then he pulled out a bag from under the bench. It had some other bags with different colors of clays inside. Kenny began mixing them with water. They turned into bright colors of yellow, red,

## The Wild Years

orange, and black. Then he called for each of us to stand in front of him while he painted wild lines all over our faces and bodies.

"This is what the Arapaho did after they won battles."

I was last. Kenny really smeared it on my face, chest, arms, and back. Then Kenny jumped up and started beating on things and drumming and dancing around the fire. We all followed, wild and goofy, whooping it up, jumping up in the air, elbowing and kneeing each other, knocking each other down. Then we were acting like we were attacking the Woodmar caddies and throwing mud balls and fighting. I went running around the fire fist-fighting a ghost, knocking that ghost on its invisible butt good.

Woooweee --- wooooweeee --- we shouted as we jumped over the fire.

Some of the caddies, in 1959, before the storm of the real war. Some came back scarred. A few did not make it.

# 4

## The Great Ball Buzz

## A water hazard, just filled with golf balls

The Wicker Park Public Golf Course bordered the private Woodmar Country Club in Highland, Indiana. They were separated only by a service road and a seven-foot-high cyclone fence. But they were worlds apart. On one side were the factory workers, and on the other were the wealthy.

Directly across from us in Woodmar was a tee-off that had a water hazard pond in front of it. Every day from the sixth hole in Wicker Park, we watched their golfers hit balls into that pond. My brother Wayne and I cheered and clapped our hands when their golf balls splashed into it. They gave us dirty looks. Wayne said that pond must just be filled with golf balls from all those Woodmar hackers. We paused for a moment, and then nodded our heads silently. We both saw the *big* business opportunity: *Ball buzzing.* There had to be some way to get out all those golf balls and sell them. So we came up with a plan.

The next day Wayne and I worked extra hard getting our yard and garden chores done. We knew Dad would check our work out anyhow. Then we waited for him to get home from work. He pulled into the driveway, exhausted again from having worked another double shift for the overtime. For over twenty years, Dad had worked sixty-plus-hour weeks to support us. He truly lived up to our last name of "Worker." His face was tired and covered with stubble. He checked out our chores. His silence meant that he approved. Then we began working him.

"Dad, there's gotta be hundreds---thousands of golf balls in those ponds. We could sell them for lots of money. Hundreds of dollars. We'd be careful. Please let us go, Dad. Please. *Please.*"

Dad didn't say "No" immediately, and that was a good sign. We knew Dad liked the idea of us being industrious and making money. My brothers and I had a local work mafia in our neighborhood for any and all odd jobs: weeding gardens, pedaling ice cream carts, cutting grass, painting. You name it, my brothers and I got the work. When one of us got too old for that job, the next younger brother inherited it. There was no choice in this matter. My brothers and I fought with neighbor kids for local jobs, and Dad encouraged this.

The big events in our parents' lives were the Depression and World War II. It showed in everything they did for their whole lives. They drummed frugality, hard work, and savings into us daily. Our parents continued their own Victory Garden until 1970. Our kitchen in August was truly sweltering with all the food-canning going on. Four-houndred quarts of tomatoes, green beans, peaches, pears, and corn relish was standard for our Dad and Mom to can. You would have thought that World War II was still going on. "You never know," our Mom would say.

Our Dad found work for us in the neighborhood too, whether we wanted it or not. He absolutely made sure that we did a good job at whatever we were paid to do. If we ever did unacceptable work, he would grab my brothers or me firmly and shout in our faces *"What's your last name, boy?"* Then he would march us back to finish to *his* standards whatever we had been doing. There was no debating here. With Dad enforcing our work, the neighbors came to him whenever they needed help. They knew that we would get the job done, or else.

"You be careful gettin' them golf balls!" Dad barked.

"Sure, Dad, sure. Don't worry. After dark, no one is on the golf course. We can walk the railroad tracks practically all the way there. The tracks just cross two streets, and we'll make sure the coast is clear before we cross them."

"You be damned careful then," Dad ordered. "I gotta rest up now. I'm working another double tomorrow." Then he paused. "Why, it sounds like it might even be fun." Dad rubbed my head.

We both gave him a hug. We asked if we could borrow his new

# The Great Ball Buzz

flashlight. He told us that we could, but only if we replaced the batteries with all that money we were going to make.

Wayne and I packed up a duffel sack and burlap bags with the gear we would need. As soon as it was dark enough, we started hiking up the Monon railroad tracks northward. Far behind us, we heard a train coming. It slowly got louder and louder, coming straight at us – just like an army tank – just like a dinosaur. Just before we were in its lights, we hid in the bushes to the side of the track. We could feel the ground shaking as it came slowly upon us, its diesel motors roaring under the load. We laid on the ground as low as we could. I don't know why though, because we weren't breaking any laws – yet. As the train came by, Wayne grabbed my shoulder and pointed. Right behind the five diesel engines, we saw the outline of one – two -- THREE steam engines. There was no fire coming from them. Behind the steam engines was a long line of hoppers filled with coal. Their wheels thumped hard on the tracks. We could feel a bad railroad tie go up and down with each wheel truck that passed. We saw fire coming from a glowing wheel box. "Hotbox!" Wayne shouted. "They better catch that one soon, or it'll stop the whole train! Even derail it." We felt the heat glowing from it while it passed us. They were taking those steam engines up to Inland Steel for scrap. We hadn't see steam engines pulling trains here on the Monon for years. Finally the caboose came, with its red light at the rear. Now that would be a great job, I thought, working on a train. We climbed back up on the tracks.

Wayne balanced himself perfectly on the rails when he walked. He could walk the rails for an hour, day or night, without falling off once. Me, I couldn't no matter how I tried. When we came to the first road crossing, we checked both ways, then ran across it without anyone seeing us. It wasn't curfew yet, but it was more exciting running across the roads than walking. We were practicing for curfew. Or acting like it was World War II and we were escaping from the Nazis. We came to the trestle where the Monon line met the Grand Trunk. We switched left onto the Grand Trunk and picked up our pace. We were getting close to Woodmar Golf Course. The moon was now up, so we could see the tracks from its reflection.

When we got up to where Woodmar bordered the railroad tracks, we dropped down into the ditch. We used the flashlight to find a loose spot on the fence. Then we slipped under it and climbed up. We passed through some brush and found ourselves on a fairway. It was misty and cool and silent. A fog drifted around us. We looked around in the darkness. We had the whole golf course to ourselves.

We started trotting down the fairway. Then we started running, faster and faster. Our feet seemed to carry us flying on this smooth, soft, wet grass. I was keeping up with Wayne and I wasn't tired at all. We went down another fairway and got to a green. Wayne laid down on it, and I did the same. Wow, a golf course is completely different at night than at day. Everything was magic. We rolled over and over on the green. Even at night we could see that Woodmar was a much better golf course than Wicker Park.

Then we crept up to the edge of the water hazard. I started stripping naked but Wayne said No. "We got to *re-con-a-cents* it first."

I wasn't too sure what *re-con-a-cents* was, but it sounded like a good idea. He said we should each go and scout in different directions---look for late golfers, greens keepers, security guards – all that stuff. That's the way they'd do it in the army -- that's the way Dad would have done it.

"Be back in ten minutes," Wayne said and ran off.

I stood there for a Moment, and then went in the opposite direction. I searched around and did not find anything unusual or dangerous. I guess that was re-con-a-centing.

Wayne came running back a little bit later. "Coast is clear!" he whispered.

I took my clothes off.

"You bring your bathing suit?" Wayne asked.

"Naw. You never told me to. I'm going in naked."

"I shouldn't hafta tell you to. You can't go in naked, 'cause a snapping turtle could bite your peter off. Then you'd be a queer."

"What's a queer?"

"A guy who runs around kissing other guys."

"That happens if you don't got a peter?"

"Yep."

"How you know that?"

"Look. Girls don't have peters and they kiss guys. There's lots a stuff you don't know."

So I pulled my underwear back on. Then we slid into the water. It was cold and the bottom was real slippery muddy. As soon as I stood, bubbles came up from the bottom, tickling me on my legs and butt and down there.

"I got one!" Wayne whispered.

I felt one with my foot. "Me too!" I went underwater and grabbed it. Then I threw it on the shore. Got another! Me too! Another one! Another! Got two! Me too. This time I got three. The bottom was just *covered* with golf balls. Every time we moved, we touched golf balls. We could hardly see each others' faces, but we sure could feel. We walked around the edge of the pond together, bumping into golf balls with every step. *Did you feel that?* No. Something just nibbled on my leg. Oh yeah, I did too. I think it was a little fish. Hope it's not a snapping turtle. If it is, *pleeeeeeease,* Mr. snapping turtle, don't bite my peter! I put one hand between my legs.

"Next time I'm bringing a bathing suit."

"Next time I'm bringing a catcher's cup!"

"Ha! Me too."

We walked around the edge of the pond and must have gotten 75 golf balls. When we got to where we had started, I started to get out.

*"Where you going?"* Wayne yelled at me. "We can dive into the center of the pond and feel them with our hands."

I was scared to do that. Wayne went under first. I stood in the water and waited. About 15 seconds later he came up with a splash.

"I got four! They're all over!" He tossed them on the shore. Then I breathed deep three or four times and dove under. I kicked to the bottom toward the center of the pond, sweeping my arms in and out along the cool soft mud on the bottom. Immediately I hit balls with my hands. Some I grabbed, some bounced away from me. I soon had two in each hand. I went to the top.

"I GOT FOUR TOO!"

"I JUST GOT THREE MORE!"

We dove again and again and again. On every dive we got at least two balls. Wayne set the record with five on one dive. We kept going and going until we thought we had pretty much covered the whole pond. I was shivering. I asked Wayne how were we going to carry all these home. He said it wasn't going to be easy. Maybe we should call it a night. Wayne agreed.

We climbed out and pulled our clothes over our wet bodies. Then we went around the pond throwing all the balls into our burlap bags. We must have had 200. Wayne said we couldn't leave *one* golf ball laying around, because if the greens keepers saw them tomorrow, they'd know that we had been here. And that would mess it up for next time. So Wayne quickly turned on the flashlight. We searched all around until we were convinced we had gotten all the golf balls. Then Wayne broke off a branch from a shrub. He started sweeping over all our tracks in the mud. Just as he was finishing up, we heard a car motor running. On the next fairway we saw headlights.

"QUICK! Hide the balls and get back into the pond!" Wayne yelled.

We grabbed the two bags of balls and hid them in some bushes at the edge of the pond. We saw the headlights of the truck now. It was coming right at us. Wayne slid into the water with all his clothes on, and I followed him.

"When the truck's lights come by, stay under water as long as you can." I heard the whine of the engine getting louder and louder, and the lights getting brighter and brighter. Just when I thought the truck lights were going to be on me, I slid underwater. Five, ten, fifteen, twenty, thirty, forty seconds. Then I bobbed up slowly. The truck was gone. "Wow, you really stayed under a long time," Wayne said. My brothers and I always had breath-holding contests, and I always won. I could hold my breathe under water for three minutes. No one could beat me.

We climbed up the shore, grabbed the bags, and started running. We couldn't go very fast because the bags were heavy and they bounced against our legs and made us wobble. We ended up walking rapidly in the roughs alongside the fairways. If the truck came again, we'd lay flat on our stomachs behind the trees and not look up. We moved as fast as we could until we got to the fence line. We slid the bags under the fence, slid ourselves under, then carried the bags through the ditch up to the tracks. Now we felt safe. Wayne and I slapped each other on the backs.

"I bet we got forty, maybe fifty dollars worth of balls. Maybe a hundred!"

"Wow. We'll be rich. Thanks to the Woodmar hackers. Lets come back and clean this pond completely out."

"Let's hide the balls in the ditch and go exploring," Wayne said. "I want to show you something."

I was ready to walk home, but Wayne was the boss here. He sure rubbed it in, being two years older than I. So we went back through the fence and started running again down the fairway. We went a good ways before we we came to a big building with bright lights coming from it. Wayne pointed to it. "This is the Woodmar Country Clubhouse Center."

"How you know?"

"I been here before, watching them."

"Watching them what? You never told me."

"Like I told you, there's lots of stuff you don't know---about me either," Wayne said mysteriously. Then Wayne grabbed me. "Look. We're gonna run real fast to those bushes next to the window and hide. Let's see what's going on."

"We could get caught getting that close."

"Chicken?"

We ran across some trimmed grass and crawled under some pine bushes next to the big building. The dirt and needles stuck to us. We heard some music. Through the big front windows we saw a dance going on. Everyone was all dressed up in suits and fancy dresses. With mud and dirt all over us, we stared at all those people. I guess they didn't go ball-buzzing on Friday nights.

"Look. There's Barbara Etherton in the pink dress. See her?" He was pointing. "She's in your class – a cheerleader."

I saw her there, sure enough, looking all so pretty. She wouldn't ever talk to me at school, no matter that I got good grades or was good at sports or anything.

"So why don't you go in there and ask her to dance?" Wayne said. "I'm sure she'll say yes. Just scrape some of the mud and dirt and stink off ya. If she don't wanna dance, you can always give her a few Podo golf balls. Then she'll dance with ya for sure."

We lay there for a while in the dirt, watching them all dance and run around and talk. We might as well of been on the moon. Wayne yanked on my arm. "Come here with me. I wanna show you something else." Wayne went running away from the clubhouse, and I followed. We crossed a ridge just out of sight from the buildings. Below us there was what looked to be a par 3 hole. In front of the green was a big water hazard. It completely surrounded the front half of the green. If your tee-off fell ten yards short, you were in the water.

"I betcha that pond is half full of golf balls, 'cause all those Woodmar hackers gonna dub their shots. And they're too rich and lazy to try to get their balls. They just'll open another pack. We gotta come back next time and hit this pond. I bet we'll get 500."

"How we carry them all back?"

"Make a few trips. Bring some extra burlap bags. Just stash the bags of balls off to the side of the railroad tracks and keep carrying 'em until we get them all home. We can figure that out when we get there."

We ran back across the golf course to the fence where we'd left our stuff. Wayne and I each walked a rail home. Wayne bet me a quarter he could stay balanced on the track all the way home without falling off once. I took the bet. Wayne stayed balanced on the rail for about a mile while carrying a heavy bag of golf balls. But me, I fell off regularly. Then he shouted in the darkness.

"What the hell!"

Wayne turned on the light and there was a big fat opossum standing on the railroad track. It didn't get off the track or run away at all.

"You fell off. You owe me a quarter!" I shouted.

"That don't count, stumbling over a possum. I'm not paying."

"You're breaking your bet."

"Yep. And I'm never going to pay you either."

When we got to the street crossings, we crept up in the ditch to its edge. We waited for cars to pass and checked and checked for anyone watching. Then we ran across the intersection. We finally hit the tracks again for the final section back home. It must have been past midnight by now. Dad and Mom would never let us stay out this late, unless we were fishing at the ponds. The summer night was so exciting. The air was cool, you had everything to yourself, and no one could see you.

We got home and left the bags of golf balls in the garage. We went quietly to the basement and took cold showers. Then we ran upstairs and pulled up the covers. Even though I was dead tired, I couldn't fall straight to sleep. My head was dancing down the fairway.

"Hey!" I shouted in bed. My face was all wet. My Dad standing there with an empty glass. If we were late getting up, Dad would throw a glass of water in our face. He was just like that.

"I called for you to get up and you didn't." Dad was laughing. He was dressed in his work clothes and  ready to go to the refinery. "Let's see all these thousands of dollars of golf balls you got last night."

I rubbed the sleep out of my eyes and shook Wayne awake. We knew not to complain to Dad about getting up. We pulled on clothes and ran out to the garage. Then I grabbed a washtub and poured all the golf balls into it. There were more than even we remembered. Wayne got a hose and we filled it with water and washed them off.

Dad came out carrying his black lunch box and looked at them.  He nodded silently.

I looked up. "We'll sell them for lots of money today."

"Heard that before," Dad puffed on his cigarette. "Til you got that money in your pocket, you don't got it in your pocket. Show me the money first." Dad walked over to his car and backed out of the driveway.

Wayne and I sorted out the golf balls. Some had turned gray from being in the water too long. Others had big gashes in them from the Woodmar hackers. But what could you expect from them? We threw those away. The bulk of the others would make good shag balls. But within this pile were at least fifty new-looking Titleist and Spaldings. We put them in separate bags.

After breakfast, we rode our bikes to Wicker Park and went straight to the shag field. In five minutes, we had a bunch of golfers around us. They bought them all. Gone, just like that. We were right.

We counted the money. Sixty-one dollars. *Sixty-one dollars!* We'll show you the money, Dad.

We remembered to buy a set of batteries for the flashlight. Then, for safety's sake, we bought another set. We couldn't wait for Dad to get home from work. When he pulled in, tired as always, we walked confidently up to his car. He looked at us puzzled.

"Don't got anymore golf balls, Dad," Wayne said.

Dad didn't answer. Then Wayne got out the money and counted out fifty-eight dollars. I handed Dad two sets of batteries for his flashlight. When Dad saw them, he paused for a second. Then he smiled. "You didn't waste any time, did you?"

"Told you we could do it." We had to control ourselves from jumping up and down. "There's gotta be a thousand more balls in those ponds, Dad," I said.

"And we're gonna get em all!" Wayne added.

Dad put his arms around each of us and we walked back to our home, and to the waiting dinner that Mom always made, and that we always took for granted.

Wayne and I continued to ball buzz throughout the summer. We had nights where we made a hundred dollars from our golf balls. Every time we went, Dad told us to be careful. But we could see he was proud of how much money we were raking in. One day he even joked about going along with us *to watch.* He sensed our adventure in doing it. Maybe he was remembering when he was a kid himself. Wayne and I were embarrassed that he even suggested it. *What if we all got caught? What would people think?* Dad saw our reactions. It must have hurt his feelings, because he never mentioned it again.

Wayne and I worked the pond until we couldn't get more than 50 balls a night. Wayne said we had fished them all out. Twice we had gone to the big pond near the Woodmar Country Clubhouse, but both times we saw men working and walking around. So we chickened out.

One day we took our golf balls to Wicker Park to sell. But we couldn't sell them all. And the golfers who wanted some offered us half the price of what we had sold them before. Wayne and I had to make a decision. We said no, and took the rest of the golf balls back home with us. We would stockpile them until people ran out. We figured 500 or a thousand golf balls would eventually be money in the bank. We were learning our first lessons about supply and demand in the marketplace, although we had no idea what that was.

We figured other golf courses had to have water hazards too. So at night we scouted out the Sherwood Country Club and Turkey Creek golf courses nearby. We rode our bikes out at sunset and waited until dark. We felt like spies on a mission. Me, when I rode my bike at night, I was on a night-bombing raid over Germany, hitting them good, just like the US bombers in World War II.

Wayne decided that we would attack Sherwood next. It was close by, and it was a private country club, so it deserved it. It took us two trips to find where the golf balls were. This time it was more difficult. We had to dive deeper and stay longer to get the balls. It took us until midnight to get over a hundred balls.

Our problem now was how to get home without being stopped by cops. We had no railroad tracks to walk home on. The 10:30 p.m. curfew was the problem. We would have to ride our bikes back while carrying bags of golf balls. We knew that if the cops caught us, that would end our ball-buzzing for good. We were making too much money to let that happen. We rode our bikes as fast as we could on the side streets. Whenever we saw any approaching headlights from a car, we quickly ran our bikes off the road and laid down. After it passed, we were pedaling full blast to home again.

One night, as we came around a corner, we saw a car driving slowly toward us. From it the beam of a spotlight was moving around a warehouse. "Cop car!" Wayne shouted. I slammed on my brakes. "Quick! In the ditch." Wayne yelled. We pushed our bikes straight into the ditch. It was filled with cattails and about a foot of water. We laid our bikes down and laid in the water and froze still. Slowly, the headlights on the road got brighter. We heard the car engine as it came up to us. The  spotlight from the car flickered around, and then over us. Wayne squeezed my hand hard. The light moved on, then the cop car continued down the road.

"They didn't see us," Wayne whispered. "Don't tell Dad any of this."

In a minute we were on our bikes and we quickly finished riding home.

Wayne and I had over a thousand golf balls in storage. In the future, if any golfers wanted cheap shag balls or discounted new golf balls, they would have to come to us, for we had no competition. We had cornered the market, although we didn't know what that meant either. Each week we sold some balls at the golf course, at our prices.

There was only one water hazard that we had left untouched. It was the big pond near the Woodmar Clubhouse. Every time we had scouted it out, we had seen too much going on to try it. But this time, we had a different plan. We wouldn't go there until after midnight. Everything would be closed by then and no one should be around. We would sneak out of our house and get back before dawn. We wouldn't actually lie to Dad and Mom; we just wouldn't tell them what we were doing.

We opened our bedroom window and slid out to the front porch. Then we ran to the railroad tracks with our new flashlights and four burlap bags. We walked as fast as we could on the ties. Most of the houses that we passed now had all their lights off. We saw no cars on the streets either. When we came to the  cross roads, we still sprinted across them. But there wasn't a car in sight. By the time we got to Woodmar, a crescent moon rose like a hammock in the East. It was so low I could have swung myself up and slept in it.

We ran across the fairways to the clubhouse. We surveyed it from a sand trap. Except for one big parking lot light, all the other lights were off. We saw no one. Then we ran to some shrubs and watched the garage and work shop. From the inside we saw fluorescent lights, but nothing else. Wayne motioned for me to lay still. He ran up to the window and looked inside. Then he ran back.

"No one's inside. Let's hit the pond."

We ran over the ridge past the tee off to the green. The front of the green quickly sloped down to the edge of the pond. Wayne said that he figured that most of the golf balls that went in would be hit short and roll back from the green. We dropped our burlap bags there and stripped down. On with our bathing suits and we waded into the water. No sooner had we stepped in and we were standing on golf balls. At first we shouted to each other about how many golf balls we were stepping on and finding, but soon we were just too busy reaching down under the water and putting them in our burlap bags. The bottom was just covered with golf balls. In some places they were so thick that they were laying on top of other golf balls. It looked like no one ever had gone ball-buzzing here. Every now and then Wayne and I passed each other, saying that we couldn't believe it. This might be a 300 dollar night!

By the time we had finished wading up to our shoulders on the green side of the pond, we had two burlap sacks filled with balls. I asked Wayne if that was good enough. "Hell no! Let's get them all." We got out and stashed those bags deep in the rough, next to the fence line. Then we began diving along the bottom, feeling with our arms. We would come up whispering "Two! four! three! I just got five!" That was how fast we were getting the golf balls. You could hardly hold any more golf balls in your hands than five. We never came up with just one ball.

We tossed the golf balls to one side of the pond and kept on diving. I was shivering now with each dive. It was getting so late now that soon it would be getting early. I told Wayne that we should be leaving. But he insisted on more dives. He said we hadn't covered the whole pond yet. We dove more and more until, finally, Wayne figured we had enough.

We got dressed and began gathering up all the golf balls. There were hundreds laying alongside the pond. We needed our flashlights to find them all. We got between the golf balls and the work shop and pointed our flash lights across the grass. Then we filled our bags.

We had just about picked them all up when we heard a sound from the shop. A garage door was opening! I grabbed a bag and ran to the rough. Wayne went the opposite way and got behind some shrubs. We heard a motor start. A truck pulled out of the maintenance shop with its headlights cutting through the mist. I buried myself down behind the trees as the truck came along the fairway in front of me. Then, in the headlight beams of the truck, I distinctly saw *golf balls laying in the fairway.* The truck stopped. I heard the door open. A man stepped in front of the headlights of the truck. He was long and skinny and had a green workman's overalls on. He picked up a few golf balls, then he went back to the truck. He couldn't have been more than 20 feet from me. I heard him fumbling around for something in the truck. Then he came out of the truck with a flashlight and shined it around the pond.

"Hey. I see you. Stop right there. You're under arrest for trespassing."

He kept shining the light around. He was pointing it to the bushes where I had last seen Wayne.

"HEY! Stop right there!"

On the edge of the beam I saw Wayne take off running. The guy pointed the flashlight toward him and started chasing Wayne. But there was no way he would ever catch Wayne. Then I saw and heard it at the same time. A yellow fireball from the blast of a pistol shot straight up into the air."

"STOP!"

Wayne kept running. Then there was another blast. This one more horizontal. The truck driver went running down the fairway after Wayne. I laid down as low as I could and froze. Then I went to the bathroom in my pants.

I got up, grabbed the bag of golf balls, and started running in the opposite direction from them. *Oh no. did he shoot Wayne? What would I say to Dad?* I got to the cyclone fence but couldn't find enough space under it to scoot through. So I flung the bag over and climbed the fence. When I was coming down, my pants caught on the wire on top. I heard my pants tear. I felt a big hole in the butt of my pants. I ran with the bag of balls banging on my legs until I got to the railroad tracks. When I came to the road crossings, I ran across them as fast as I could. Then I ran on the railroad ties. But that was awkward. My stride wasn't right. One step wood, the next step rocks. I twisted my ankle, so I switched to walking as fast as I could. I was crying all the way. Finally I turned onto our country road that crossed the railroad tracks. I could see the beginning of light in the east. I was running up to garage when I heard a voice.

"What took you so long?" It was Wayne. "Hurry up. Just strip down and wash off with the hose. If we take a shower, we'll wake Mom and Dad."

I did as Wayne told me and he sprayed me off with water. I lathered up to get the dirt off me. I was wet and butt-naked when we snuck back in through the window. We got under covers in our bunk beds and acted like we were asleep.

Wayne finally whispered, "We got to go back tomorrow and get those other two bags of balls before they find them."

"Are you crazy? The second time he shot was *at* you."

"You sure?"

"I don't want to go back."

"You afraid? This'll be easy. We just walk there at night, grab the bags and come back. We won't be on the course for more than ten minutes."

I was even afraid to tell Wayne that I was afraid again. I didn't want him to think I was chicken.

So the next night we went back to Woodmar. Wayne acted like he was so brave. But I could tell that Wayne was worried that they had found the bags of golf balls. But me, I was more worried that they had found the golf balls *and* were just waiting for us to come back and get them. We went deep into the rough to where we had hidden the balls. But we couldn't find them! Had the greens keepers found them? What seems to be a good hiding place at night is easy to find in the daylight. Just about when we were ready to go home empty handed, Wayne shouted "HERE!"

I ran over to him, and sure enough, there were our two bags of golf balls. We each grabbed one and began hightailing it out of Woodmar fast. We didn't feel safe until we got to the railroad tracks.

Wayne balanced himself on the rail and began wailing. "I bet we got 700 balls total," he said. "A lot of them are gonna be good ones too. We might make 300 dollars. But don't ever tell Dad what happened."

Wayne stopped and we shook hands.

"That's right," I said. "*We're gonna be rich.*"

# 5

## Queen of Tits

"Not on school property!" Bailey shouted. "We'll have to walk over the bridge. Then I'll show them to you."

We hiked to the other side of the bridge. Then Bailey stepped off into the weeds and opened the deck of cards. And there, before me, was a playing card of a beautiful naked woman in color. I can't remember for sure what card it was, ace or a deuce. All I can recall now was that it was the *Queen of tits*. The card didn't show anything else but tits. I mean, it showed her smiling face and arms and legs. But it didn't show anything *down there*. But what it did show looked just great. I reached for the card. Bailey pulled the deck back.

"No way. I'll show you a few more. But if you want to see them all, you'll have to buy them."

There was just so much you could imagine from the Sears catalog. I had seen breasts before in *National Geographic*. But those pictures just lasted a day or so in the library before someone tore them out. Next time it would be me. But in the meantime...

"How much for the deck?"

# The Wild Years

"Four dollars."

"FOUR DOLLARS!" I shouted back, just like my Dad did whenever someone quoted their price. But I would have shouted back, "ONE DOLLAR!" or, "TEN DOLLARS!," whatever price Bailey had said. It was just our family's method of negotiating. "That's toooooooooo much."

Bailey put the cards away.

"Will you sell them one at a time?"

"No. Altogether only."

"Are there fifty-two?"

He looked at me, irritated. "What the hell you gonna do with them? Play cards?"

"Let me see them again."

Bailey held out a different queen of tits this time.

"Don't sell them to anyone yet. I'll get the money."

I found my brother Wayne and told him about the cards. I asked him if he wanted to go halfsies with me. "Only if they're pretty. If I don't like them, you'll have to give me my two dollars back."

We agreed and I ran back to Bailey. I forked over the four dollars and he quickly handed me the deck. I stuck them in my pocket and went back to school. I'd have to hide them good. Because if the school caught me with them, they'd expel me for sure.

But first, I wanted to see what I got. Where could I look at them? I went to the boy's room, locked myself in a toilet, and sat down. Sure enough, there they were. Tits, tits, and more tits. The most beautiful tits in the world. But I couldn't see one vagina. Not one. The way all of the women were sitting, it was blocked out. I never got around to counting the cards. This deck was complete enough for me.

I heard the warning bell ring. Five minutes until class. I went to my locker and hid them at the bottom of all the junk. It would be safe as long as we didn't have a locker search. What if my locker mate found them? I didn't think he would turn me in. But he might steal them, just because he couldn't help it. With stuff like this, you never know.

I took the cards home and hid them in the wood shed. When Wayne got home, he inspected them for a long time. His verdict: They were worth it. Now the only question was where to hide them. Not in the wood shed because they could get wet, a mouse could chew them, *or Dad could find them.* That would be the worst. Anyone but Dad. Wayne suggested hiding them in the back of *my* clothes drawer. It would be dry, and no mice. I told him so would his clothes drawer. He didn't answer. We could hide them in our oldest brother Kenny's drawer. At first we liked that idea. But then, we thought about it. If Dad found the cards in Kenny's drawer, Kenny would tell Dad the truth. Of course Dad wouldn't believe Kenny. But then, Kenny would punch the truth out of Wayne and me. Then we would have to deal doubly with Dad and Kenny. And if Kenny found the cards in his drawer before Dad, he would punch us around and keep the cards for himself. Then he'd probably sell them for cigarette money.

So we had to hide them someplace. Wayne and I went downstairs. We searched and searched, until we finally decided on the top of a heating duct. There were just a few inches of space between it and the ceiling. From where we stood, we couldn't see it. To put them there, we had to stand on a small stool and reach over the top. We would then have to feel around to find them.

Next day, I came home from school and went to check the cards. They were gone! Oh no. Did Dad find them that quick? But when Dad pulled in from work, he didn't act funny. Neither did Mom. When Wayne finally got home, I told him the bad news. Wayne shook his head.

"I was showing them to my friends. Don't worry."

"No fair. You should have told me."

Wayne said it was no big deal. "And halfsies is halfsies." Then Wayne said that his friend Richie offered ten dollars for the whole deck.

"Ten dollars? That's quick money, man." Then I thought about it. "You didn't sell them, did you? 'Cause if you did, that's not halfsies either."

"No I wouldn't sell them. Not yet, and not without your agreeing. That's halfsies. But good to know we can make money on them whenever we want."

So in the coming month, Wayne and I each took the deck of cards down and looked at them. We never looked at them together. Whenever I went to get the cards and they were not there, it was always late at night. And we never asked each other what we did with the cards.

One day Wayne and I decided to let our oldest brother Kenny in on our secret. So when Dad and Mom were out shopping, we showed Kenny the cards. He shuffled them, then looked through them. "This is nothing," was his verdict. "All they show is tits. This is for kids. Now if you want to see real pictures, I can get those for you on Washington Street in Gary. But it will cost you some money."

"How much?"

"At least ten dollars. Maybe fifteen."

Wayne and I looked at each other, shaking our heads. These cards would have to do for now. Then Kenny asked if he could borrow them from us. No way. At first he refused to give them back. But Wayne grabbed them back and took off.

So we had our cards. Wayne and I returned them to the same place every day. We borrowed them for, well, whatever. No longer did we have to search for where Mom had left the Sears catalog.

One day at school Wayne gave me a dollar. "I sold four cards for fifty cents each. This is your share."

No one had to tell me how good that profit was. Now I would try to buy another deck from Bailey. It never occurred to us that we had just made money from selling pornography. We didn't know, because back then, we didn't know what that word meant. It just had too many syllables for us.

"But which ones did you sell?" I asked Wayne.

He looked at me weird. "They were girls -- with tits. You know. Why you ask?"

"Well, there's a few that are my favorites. Just don't sell those."

"Okay then. Just mark what ones." He shook his head and walked out.

Then one day it happened. Wayne and I came home from school and Dad was standing there. He looked at us even more serious. Wayne and I knew that look. We didn't know what it was for, but we knew it was bad. He took us by the arms into the garage and shut the door. Then he held up the deck of cards.

"Where'd you get them?"

"School," we answered together.

"Whose are they?"

Wayne and I both answered each other's name at the same time.

Dad shook his head.

"Please don't tell Mom," Wayne pleaded.

Dad didn't answer. He just stared at us. He had kindling already built up in the wood stove. He struck a match and started a fire. When it was flaring up, Dad threw the deck of cards in.

The cards scattered over the flames. Wayne and I watched the corners of the cards turn black and then start to curl over. Their feet and legs began to burn. Their hair caught afire. Their lovely smiles disappeared. And lastly, their beautiful, inviting breasts, and our fantasies of them, all went up in smoke.

We never recovered.

# 6
# River Maple Ford and the Pitchfork

I returned from college to my parent's home in Indiana to find them arguing again. They were so locked into it that they hardly greeted me. Nothing unusual so far, except this time, the topic was different.

"I AM *NOT* GOING TO GO TO CLUB IN A CAR THAT LOOKS LIKE THAT!" my Mom screamed.

"Well you better walk then, cause that sign stays on it 'til they give me a new car," Dad barked back.

"You've been parked out front of that dealership for a month and all it's got you is a lawsuit. What are all the neighbors thinking with that thing parked out in front? Just look at it."

Mom led me to the garage for me to see for myself Dad's new Ford Fairlane. The front end was all chrome and shiny new. It was two-tone brown, with one of those plastic, fake-leather roofs. But looking at it from the side, everything suddenly changed. The entire rear end of the car was crushed forward and upward. The wrinkled sheet metal was almost rubbing the rear wheels. The trunk stood up like a dog taking a dump. It was a wonder that this car could drive at all. Along the sides and rear end hung a bunch of yellow plastic lemons. Painted onto the doors of the car was a large, rough yellow lemon with the words --

DONT BUY LEMONS FROM RIVER MAPLES FORD
THERE THIEFS AND LYERS

Someone had mounted a large, professionally made sign on the roof of the car. It said --

I BOUGHT THIS LEMON AT RIVER MAPLES FORD
DON'T BUY ANYTHING FROM THEM

Mom took one good last look at it. "What will the neighbors think?" Then Mom started crying and ran into the next room. That was how most of Mom and Dad's fights ended.

"What are you going to do with it now, Dad?"

"Gonna keep parking it right in front of those sons-a-bitches and hand out these pamphlets." He handed me one. "You wanna come with me?"

"No, Dad."

"You come. They started giving me trouble yesterday, so I need help. We'll stop at White Castle on the way back."

I got in. I saw a pitchfork in the backseat. Huh? Dad pulled the car out of the garage. Out in front of our home, our neighbor Katzy was looking at the new sign on our car. "Nice new car you got there, Fred," Katzy yelled.

"And you can kiss my ass too, big nose," Dad answered.

We took off in the car down the highway. We got a lot of stares as we went along. Sometimes a guy would give us a thumbs up or a honk. But most of them just stared at us. I turned my head away and stared straight forward. Dad parked right in front of the dealership. No sooner had we parked than a man in a suit and tie came walking up to our car.

"You can't park that car here. You'll have to move it."

My Dad got out of his car as quick as he could and stuck his face into this man's space. "HELLLLLLLL NO I WON'T! This is public parking here. You can't stop me."

"I'm calling the cops," the sales manager threatened.

"Go right ahead. I ain't breaking any laws."

A few minutes later a cop car pulled up. The sales manager walked up to the cop and started talking to him. They walked over to my Dad. I stayed in the car.

"I want this guy off my property right now. His car looks like hell."

"Can I see your driver's license?" Dad got it out. "This is a public road," my Dad stated. "And I got a right to park here. Ain't that right, officer?"

The cop looked at the street and didn't say anything.

"Look, we're members of the Kiwana's club, the Better Business Bureau, the Chamber of Commerce."

"-- and I worked for Ford at the River Rouge plant for years, and Ford never treated me like yous," Dad shouted.

"-- we can't have this sonnobabitch driving our customers away. It'll cost jobs."

"You cost me my car. So I'm staying til you replace my car."

The cop looked at the sales manager. "Look, I don't know what laws he's breaking. If he was, then I'd make him move. If he was parked in your lot, then it would be trespassing. But this *is* a public road he's on."

Dad waved his fist at the sales manager and put his other arm on my shoulder. "Let's go, son." Dad stood on the roadside with his pamphlets and I stood awkwardly next to him. The cop drove off.

"You put one foot on my property and we'll bust your ass!" the sales manager yelled.

Dad flipped him the bird. My Dad was in his sixties and he still flipped people the bird. He still shouted at people when he thought he had been wronged, and it hadn't been all that long ago since he had been in a fist

# River Maple Ford and the Pitchfork

fight. Home sweet home.

Dad saw an older couple looking at his car. He walked over to them and handed them a pamphlet. "You don't wanna buy a car from River Maple. No way. They don't honor their warranties. They got lousy service too."

The woman went up to the smashed rear end. She touched one of the plastic lemons. "Why, they wouldn't sell you a car like this, would they?"

"They sold me a bad one that caused the accident." Then Dad launched into *the speech*. He had told it so many times that he knew it word for word. I was quickly learning it, whether I wanted to or not.

"I bought me a new car here, a brand new car. When we went to drive it off, it wouldn't start. Well, the salesman brings out a mechanic and he says there must just be ice on the solenoid. So he turns the key on, takes a screwdriver out, jumps the wires, and starts it. So I drive off. On the way home I stop at White Castle to eat. When I come out, my car still won't start. I call River Maple Ford and tell them. I have to wait hours for a mechanic to come out. Now I'm getting hot under the collar."

"So would I," the man agrees.

"And you know what?" My Dad waits until whoever is listening says "What?" "They do the same damned thing. Jump start it with a screwdriver and say the solenoid's just got ice on it. So I drive it home and park it in the garage. When I go out to start it again, the damned thing still won't start! I call 'em up an' tell 'em to get a mechanic out here *right now* an' fix it. And River Maples Ford doesn't send out a mechanic all day Friday or Saturday. I got a brand new car I'm paying for and I can't even drive it."

"Yeah, but what does that have to do with the accident?"

"I'm getting there. Well I decide that I'm going to an auction on Sunday, solenoid or no. So I turn the key on just like the guy did and take out my screwdriver and jump it like he did. And the car starts, all right. But damned if I hadn't left it in reverse. It takes off right out of my garage going down the driveway. Just misses my daughter Lanette. I go chasing after it but it hits a telephone pole before I could get to it. It bounces off the pole, goes through a parking lot, across a street with traffic, and crashes into a barber shop."

"You don't say. Lucky someone wasn't hurt. Won't your insurance pay?"

"Sure they would, but I ain't gonna let 'em. Wasn't my fault, or theirs. If River Maple had a sold me a good car or come out and fixed it like they should, then it never would have happened. But they finally come out *after* the accident and put a solenoid in without saying anything was wrong with the other one. Then they just told me that was it, there was nothing wrong with the car. They wasn't doing a thing more, and I'd just have to go to my insurance. So that's why I'm here."

"What have they been doing to you?"

"Ohh, calling the police on me, threatening me. Here. Read the pamphlet, and then go tell River Maple what you think of them."

They shook hands with my Dad then the couple walked into the dealership. I could see the man talking to the sales manager. Then the couple walked out to their car. As they drove by us, the man honked. Dad waved. The woman rolled down her window. "We told them."

"Thank you, ma'am," my Dad said in his southern way. Dad turned to me with a big smile. "That'll get 'em *real* mad now. Just you watch."

Unfortunately, Dad was right. I saw the men huddling together inside the dealership. Whenever they looked over at Dad, Dad would wave at them with a big smile. He gave me some money and told me to bring back some cheeseburgers. I happily ran off from my Dad's one-man picket line.

When I came back there were two new cars parked in front and in back of my Dad's car, right up against his bumpers. They did not leave him any room whatsoever to pull out. Dad was shouting at the two men. One of them was pretty big.

"Remember. It's a public road, Fred. And we can park anyplace on it we want to, too," one of them shouted. They laughed.

"If those cars are still there when I get ready to leave, why I'm just gonna put my car in reverse, floor it, and push that piece a shit outta the way. I don't have to worry about damaging my rear end any more."

"Your ass you will."

"YOU DON'T BELIEVE ME! LIKE HELL I WON'T."

*Oh no.* They were calling my Dad's bluff. My brothers and I had learned *never* to do that. Dad walked over to his car, got in, started up the motor, and revved it real loud. Then he grabbed the gearshift. The big guy ran over in a panic after Dad, reached into the car, and turned the engine off. He tried to pull the keys out, but Dad grabbed his arm. Dad and him wrestled around over the keys. Dad opened the door and jumped out of his car with a screwdriver in his hand. The guy jumped back. Then Dad reached in the backseat and *grabbed the pitchfork. Oh no, Dad.*

"THAT SONNOBABITCH IS CRAZY. CALL THE POLICE RIGHT NOW. CALL THE POLICE!" One of the men shouted. So two burly men in their thirties jumped back from an old man in his sixties and ran back into the dealership. Dad was standing there with a pitchfork, puffing real hard. His glasses were bent and he had a little cut on his nose. He came up to me with the pitchfork.

"That'll teach 'em, goddamnit. Now where's my cheeseburger? You got it with extra ketchup, right?"

Dad brought home the papers from the River Maple Ford's attorney for me to read. I asked him if he had shown them to his attorney.

"My attorney? Hell no. I don't have one and I don't need one. I settle my own disputes. That saves me paying lawyers."

I read it. It said that Fred Worker agrees to never return to River Maples Ford or set foot on the premises again, to never distribute pamphlets, leaflets, or photographs of said Ford Fairlane, to never do any radio or television interviews concerning anything related to his purchase or alleged problems with said Ford mentioned previously. Violation of said agreement will be considered breach of contract and Fred Worker will be held accountable for legal liabilities. In return, River Maples Ford agrees to exchange his Ford Fairlane for a new Ford LTD. The Ford LTD will have these features: I read a list of extras that would be on the new car. It was loaded with a number of things the Fairlane one did not have.

A week later a young guy pulled into our driveway with the new Ford LTD. He handed Dad the keys and books. He said that River Maple had arranged that all the service and warranty work to be done at another Ford dealership nearby. Then the guy walked back to the car that had followed him here and they drove off.

"Git in," Dad ordered me. I hopped in. Dad's new LTD had plush seats. Dad started the engine. He had never had a car with air conditioning before. He turned it on and smiled. We pulled out. But first, Dad stopped in front of Katzy's home and kept honking the horn. Katzy finally came out and looked at Dad and the car. Dad pressed the button that rolled down the windows automatically. He smiled at that.

"Hey Katzy. They gave me a *brand new LTD*. A lot better than that piece a crap you're driving. *Brand new.*"

Dad hit the horn and pulled out. He looked at me with a big smile. "Let's go get some White Castles now." Dad sped up.

As we were rolling along, I asked my Dad if he had saved any of the photos of the wrecked Fairlane.

"No, son. I agreed to return them. So I did."

What I would give now for a picture of that wrecked Fairlane, with the signs, the hand paintings, the dangling lemons, and my dad's grit, all over it.

# 7

## The Day I Did Not Throw the Brick

My Dad helped get me a summer roustabout job at the Shell Oil refinery in East Chicago, Indiana, in 1966. These were do-anything type jobs that paid about $3.25 an hour, back when the minimum wage was around $1.25 an hour. We considered this good work and good pay. If I worked as much overtime as I could and saved my money, I could almost pay for a year's college. Long gone are those days.

Dad had worked at Shell Oil for 29 years. He started on a pipeline from New Mexico and worked with it as it moved cross country all the way to East Chicago, Indiana. There he met my mother and settled down.

Many of the older workers at Shell Oil had never finished high school. They had gone straight from their parents' homes during the depression into World War II. After the war, they got jobs at the refinery. These workers let us college kids know on day one how easy we had it. To them, we were spoiled shits. These guys had risked life and limb for our country and had never had the opportunity to go to college themselves. And here we were, getting all of the benefits of their sacrifice. So no matter how hard I or the other summer help worked, they were on our asses. At the time, I just didn't get the class resentment going on here.

At first I took it personally. So I worked harder than ever to prove them wrong. One day they gave me the job of weeding and cutting all the grass around the front office building. I got started early and worked hard without taking breaks. I finished the job by 1:30. I eagerly reported back to the foreman that I was ready for another assignment.

He looked at me darkly. "What the fuck you doing, little Worker? Killing work? That's an all-day job. The union'll really get pissed at you if the superintendent here finds out you can do that job in a half day. Now go hide someplace the rest of the day, and DON'T let the superintendent or me find you."

"What should I do with all the grass clippings?"

"Stick em up your ass." He walked off.

My Dad had taught me to ask the men of his generation if they were

# The Day I Did Not Throw the Brick

veterans. If they answered yes, my Dad told me to shake their hands and thank them for my freedom. By the time I started working at Shell, this had become second nature to me. So I found myself shaking hands with most of the older men. For a moment, they stopped their insults.

"So your Dad really taught you to do that?" One veteran asked.

"Yes, he did."

He paused for a moment. "Well, it's the only good thing he ever did." Then he walked off.

I recall that Shell Oil mentioned in its monthly employee magazine that it had about 30,000 employees in the U.S. But I heard at work that Shell now had a problem with their employees. Not one was African American. The new Title Seven of the 1964 Civil Rights Act expressly prohibited racial discrimination in hiring, and Shell had to do something about it.

I was working summer help at the refinery the first day Austin Grange came to work. I saw him standing by himself in the locker room. I introduced myself. He was a friendly enough guy, well-spoken and shy. Word had it that he was the Salutatorian at an almost all black high school in Gary, Indiana. He had just turned 18 and was going to Indiana University in Bloomington, Indiana, just like me.

All of us summer help newbies got the abuse from the regulars. We took it mostly in good humor. But Austin Grange got something more. Some of the older men refused to work with him, or even let him ride in the company trucks with them. After the work shift was over, they banned Austin from the shower room until they were done showering. By company rules, everyone had to take a shower and leave their dirty company coveralls in the laundry before they left. Refineries were dirty enough places with all the lead contamination so that no one had to tell you to shower at the end of the day. The rest of us summer help could shower when they did, but not Austin.

Austin looked dazed as he waited on a bench in front of the shower room. After the older guys finished showering, Austin showered as fast as he could and left. After that run in, Austin either waited until they were done before showering, or drove home without bathing.

It got worse for Austin. There were race riots in the U.S. in the summer of 1966. The older guys talked non-stop about them. Austin never said a word about it. In straight World War II fashion, some of the men told Austin that if they were the cops, they would shoot all the rioters dead on the spot. Then they waited for Austin to answer them. Austin said nothing. They treated Austin as if he were personally leading all the riots and protests. I

# The Wild Years

watched Austin withdraw more and more.

Many of the WWII veterans at Shell Oil were decent to Austin. They kidded with him like they did the rest of us summer help, and Austin could take that. But every day, Austin got some racist baiting from somebody. I could see from Austin's face that this was taking a toll.

I was conflicted in a major way. My father had taught me to honor all World War II vets, and that had always worked fine for me. I knew a few of these guys at Shell Oil had more than one purple heart. I saw their war wounds in the shower. Two of them limped as they worked. You didn't ask them about their war wounds and they didn't tell. But now, some of these very same men were being vicious to a young man who was just trying to make a living. I wondered how my Dad would have treated Austin if Dad were still working here. I didn't feel any better about it. At times I was embarrassed as a white man, as if I had some choice in the matter.

Whenever I saw Austin take some crap, I made sure to talk with him afterward. He was distant from me too, but I think he appreciated the friendship. The rest of the young white summer help all took to Austin too. I think he felt safe at least among us. But Austin never knew where or when the next comment or attack or slur would be coming from.

At the end of the summer I asked Austin if he would be back at Shell Oil next year. He said his Dad had arranged for him to work in US Steel next summer.

"But this job pays more, and it's way cleaner than the steel mills. This is a better job," I said.

"For you, maybe," was his only reply.

Back at college, I was living off-campus, working in a restaurant, trying to make every cent last until my next summer's job. I called Austin up one day. He was surprised to hear from me, but he was friendly enough. He said he was taking pre-med and was very busy with the chemistry and biology classes. I told Austin I was active with voter registration with SNCC, The Student Non-Violent Coordinating Committee. Did he know who they were? Austin laughed "Well *of course* I do. Drop on by."

We met at Austin's dorm and ate dorm food. We both agreed that the food was terrible. Austin said he really missed his mother's biscuits and gravy. I told him I knew just the place. We could get an immense plate of them for forty-five cents.

"LET'S GO!"

"Tomorrow morning then."

## The Day I Did Not Throw the Brick

Austin came over to my boarding house. Mike Sparrow came out of his room and greeted Austin with a smile and a businessman's handshake. Mike too was pre-med. Mike told Austin that although he was a member of Sigma Chi fraternity, he simply could not live in the Frat house anymore. He said there was too much drinking and partying at the frat to study.

Austin and I started hiking over to Countryman's Cafe. On the way, we passed Sigma Chi Fraternity on Seventh Street. From the top balcony of the front of the frat a large confederate flag was hanging. Austin and I both stared at it.

"Sigma Chi," Austin said. "That's the fraternity your roommate is in, right?"

"He's not my roommate. I didn't choose him. He just rented a room in the same building as me." Austin just sort of smiled. "No problem. I pledged to Alpha Phi Alpha. It's an all black fraternity. But I pledged for different reasons."

"What you mean?"

"I pledged for *safety.*" Austin looked back at the Sigma Chi building. "How far south is Bloomington anyhow?"

I had been eating breakfast at Countryman's, a local cafe, a few times a week. It was a good distance from campus, a place where the locals ate. I rarely saw any other students or IU faculty there. We walked in and took a window seat. Several people glanced in our direction. A blond, middle-aged waitress walked rapidly past our booth. I recognized her as the one who had waited on me before. She gave me a dark look. There was no smile or greeting.

"I'll take my regular," I said to her. "Two of them."

She passed by again without a word. We waited some more. No glasses of water, no silverware, no menus. I got up and got two menus. More people came into the restaurant and sat down. She went to their tables and gave them menus and a waitress smile. As she passed me again, I told her that we are ready to order. She ignored me. She passed me again, with the same irritated look, and went to another table of newcomers.

Austin said nothing. Then he got up to leave. As he walked out, I followed him. He started walking away from me. I grabbed his elbow. He turned and yanked his arm from me.

"Austin, I had no idea---"

He looked me straight in the eyes. "You white folks all alike." He had tears in his eyes. Then he walked off.

I stood still in front of the restaurant. *I had no idea.* But then, how

## The Wild Years

would I? I figured it wasn't the restaurant's policy, but just the individual waitress. But it didn't matter. After all, they *did* hire her. I resolved on the spot to return to the Countryman's Cafe late at night with a brick for some night work.

The next day I went to a SNCC meeting. In the coming year, we did benefits, voter registration drives and community organizing. On campus, I ran into Austin a number of times. He refused to acknowledge my hellos. He had grown his Afro out and hung out only among African American students, Black Nationalist style. At the beginning of the second semester, I was helping run the SNCC table when Austin approached. I said hello to him. He studiously ignored me. He never spoke to me, and I never saw him again.

The sixties were not all sex, drugs, and rock-and-roll.

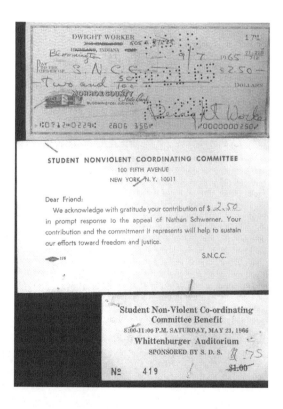

# 8

## First Demonstration

Dwight J. Worker, a senior at Indiana University and one of 35 persons arrested during Monday's melee at the School of Business building, lies limp as he hauled away by two Bloomington police officers. Worker and the others arrested were protesting the appearance of job interviewers for Dow Chemical Co., which makes napalm used in the Vietnam war. Worker was one of two students treated at the Student Health Center for cuts.
(H-T Photo by Bryan Moss)

"To be right too early, that is to be wrong"
Emperor Hadrian

The professor finally said it. "If it is *my* private property, the laws should NOT require me to offer my services to everyone. It should be a matter of freedom for me to decide with whom I do business. I feel strongly that Title 2 of the Civil Rights Act grossly violates the rights of private property owners. Remember, *You cannot legislate morality.*"

All of the other students sat there quietly. Agnes nudged me. We were sitting in the back of the lecture hall with over a hundred other students. One of our African American friends, Robert, was taking this class and had told Agnes and me about this guy. We saw Robert sitting to the side of the lecture hall. Here we were, in the Spring of 1965, and a professor was saying this.

"Forget morality then," I interrupted. "Let's just legislate to control their behavior." My voice carried across the hall.

He stopped and stared at me. "You did not raise your hand."

"I'm sorry."

"-- but I will answer your point anyway. Now, I personally would not refuse service to someone of a different religion, or race, or whatever, in my own business. But I would NOT want anyone to take from me that right to do this, no matter how reprehensible that behavior might be. I think allowing the federal government to intrude into the private affairs of a business is a very bad precedent."

"-- but doesn't this kind of discrimination cause riots and violence? Is that what you want?"

"You did NOT raise your hand. You are out of order," the professor stopped me. "And are you a student in any of my classes? I don't recall seeing you. Are you a student at all? Or are you trespassing?"

All of the students were staring back at me. There were some mumbles of "shut up" and "get out". I felt Agnes tugging on my elbow. I had this tight feeling in my gut. I saw Robert looking back at me. Something inside me was saying *don't back down.*

"I am a student here, but not in the business school. Excuse me for being out-of-order, but you are out-of-date---"

"Leave this room right now, or I am calling campus security." His voice rose.

"---then we students should discriminate too against bigoted professors like you!"

Agnes yanked on my arm. We stood up and walked to the door. While we were exiting, other students yelled "BEAT IT, BEATNIK --- HIPPIE --- GREENBAGGER--"

Agnes opened the door and took off walking fast to the stairway. I followed her. We flew down the stairs, dodging students until we got out of the street. Only then did we stop.

Agnes hugged me. "That was great!" she shouted. "Now he's going to have to explain for the rest of the class that he isn't a racist, and all the while Robert will be smiling at him. That emperor has NO clothes. *You fucked up that class.*"

We laughed. I tugged her hand while checking behind me to see if campus security was coming. I saw no one following us but I still dragged her fast through the campus park. Only when we were completely out of sight of the business school did I pause.

"All those little sheep just nodding their obedient heads. I just couldn't take it," I said. "Someone had to call him on it. If I have to go to the dean's office, at least that prof will have to be there too. Then I can confront him in front of the dean. And the dean will know what that professor is saying in class. Then I'll dare the dean to defend him."

"I can't wait to hear from Robert what happened after that," Agnes said. "Oh, I wish I had had my 8 millimeter camera with me to film it." And then Agnes, this beautiful, petite, left-wing, red-diaper baby violinist, New Jersey Jewish goddess puts her arm around my neck, pulls me to her and kisses me. Now my heart was truly going.

What had started this venture anyhow? Agnes had come up to me earlier, eyes aglow with mischief, and said, "Hey, Dwight. I heard about this asshole professor over at the B-school. Let's go give him hell." But many years later, about the only thing I recalled from this confrontation was Agnes' first kiss. Just what had been my true motivations?

Once a month, I drove to my parents' home near Chicago. Then my Dad and I drove to the Hines Veterans Hospital in West Chicago to visit my quadriplegic brother, Wayne. He had been paralyzed for seven months now from an accident while he had been serving in the US Navy. Wayne had been unconscious for the first six months. But now he was slowly coming out of the coma. To our collective family horror, what was emerging was no longer Wayne. I stood there with my Dad at the edge of Wayne's bed, holding my Dad's hand. We did not normally hold hands. But now my Dad would not let my hand go.

We talked to Wayne. He nodded to us to tell us he understood. But when Wayne tried to speak, we could not understand what he was saying. He kept repeating '*Waaaa aaapuhhhhh --- Waaaa aaapuhhhhh --- Waaaa aaapuhhhhh*'. I would guess what he was trying to say and he would respond by slowly shaking his head. My Dad stood there crying, unable to speak himself. I had only seen my father cry when my baby brother Dale had died at six months old. Wayne kept repeating and I kept guessing. Finally I guessed "What happened?" and Wayne nodded.

"Wayne. You were in a bad accident seven months ago and had a fractured skull. You are just now coming out of it."

"*Ahh dunnnn ummemmmuh --- Ahh dunnnn ummemmmuh*"

"You don't remember?" I repeated. Wayne nodded. I told Wayne today's date and where he now was. He clearly had no idea. And I had no idea how

Our father, with our paralyzed brother

Wayne was seeing the world. What would it be like to wake up from a seven month dream to discover that you could not move? He even seemed to have trouble remembering who he was. Wayne looked over his body.

Then Wayne began repeating *"Ahhhhh wwwaaa diiiiiiii --- Ahhhh wwwaaa diiiii."* I sat there and quickly got the meaning. But I dared not translate in front of my Dad what Wayne was now saying.

So my father and I sat next to Wayne and talked with him all day. We struggled to understand what he was saying to us. My Dad ended up just sitting there, crying. He had not brought up his sons to be paralyzed for life.

Dad and I drove back to Hines Hospital the next day and visited Wayne. He looked surprised to see us. I asked Wayne how he liked our visit yesterday. Wayne looked confused. *He could not remember anything about our visit.* I had to tell him again what had happened and why he was in the

# First Demonstration

hospital. Again he was amazed that it was seven months later. Now my Dad was really crying. Before we left, we talked with the doctor. He explained to us that Wayne had anterograde amnesia from organic brain damage. Wayne was having difficulty remembering anything that had happened since the accident.

"How long will this take to heal?" I asked.

The doctor shook his head. "Wayne has lost memory sections of his brain. Usually these injuries do not recover." Dad had to sit back down. But Wayne's memory of events *before* the accident was near perfect. He and I could talk about anything we did in childhood or in high school and Wayne would recall it and enjoy talking about it. But his new memories had ended forever at November 15, 1964.

On both sides of Wayne's bed at Hines Veterans Hospital were a growing number of young, freshly-minted disabled veterans from the Vietnam war. Limbs missing, faces completely bandaged, in comas or pain, surrounded by medical personnel and grieving relatives. Fathers and mothers, siblings, stammering and crying, trying to get some response from from their broken child. Wails of pain and grief. They did any busy-work they could tending to their child, anything to get their mind off of how profoundly and forever their lives were changed. They looked shocked, broken, and devastated beyond repair. *Why --- they looked just like us.*

My Dad was going into the army just as World War II was ending. He had an 80-hour a week job at the refinery which had been considered war-essential. My Mom said there were times when he worked three months straight of 12 hour days. When Dad was called up, he said he was ready to do whatever the government told him to do, and that was that.

If anyone had said anything negative about the United States to my Dad, that person would be as likely to get a fist as a rebuttal. But now, as my Dad and I visited Wayne throughout the summer, we witnessed more and more basket cases coming back from Vietnam. My Dad looked at the other grieving parents and sat there shaking his head crying, saying, "It just don't make sense. It don't make no sense at all."

The following fall I moved into an off-campus rooming house. I had one of four rooms upstairs with a shared bathroom and no kitchen. I would be cooking all year on a hot plate. A guy came up the stairs carrying a box. I introduced myself and shook hands with him. Mike Sparrow was his name. I went downstairs and helped him carry boxes from his car.

When we got back upstairs he said "Haven't I seen you before?" I looked him over. Short blond hair, madras shirt, off-white levis. I couldn't recognize him from a thousand others. "I *know* I have seen you before." I helped him with a few more boxes. "Then he said "I *know* where I saw you. You were in the back of that business law seminar yelling out stuff to our professor. That's it."

I suddenly felt uncomfortable. "Yeah. That was me." I would not be able to keep my politics separate from my home this year. Well, this is what you get. He stood there smiling at me. I would learn later that it was not a smile at all.

I went back to school in the fall angry. Angry at the war drums going on in the U.S., angry at what I had seen at Hines Veteran's Hospital, angry about the terrible waste, angry at the big lie. We had studied the Nuremberg Trials in high school. We had even read William Shirer's *The Rise and Fall of the Third Reich.* They had taught us that Adolf Eichmann's excuse that he was 'just obeying orders' could never apply when there are crimes against humanity at stake. Our civics teachers taught us that this applied worldwide. No one had been able to explain to me that what we were doing in Vietnam was strategic, or honest, or justifiable. So I helped organize one of the first anti-Vietnam War demonstrations at Indiana University.

Indiana University was the southernmost of the Big Ten schools, and this showed in many ways. It showed by all the large Stars and Bars flags that hung from so many of the fraternities and apartment complexes. It showed by how the campus Negroes – soon to be African-Americans – kept to themselves, hardly ever venturing off-campus into the hostile land of rural white America. It showed on my dormitory application form on my first year when the form asked me what would be my preferred ethnic background of my roommate. There was a list of about six ethnic groups, including, of course, Negro. All I had to do was check what type I preferred. The form assured me that they would try to match me with my preference. This dorm application form might as well have printed on it DO YOU WANT A NIGGER FOR A ROOMMATE OR NOT?

So we had our first demonstration at Showalter Fountain at IU in November of 1965. We were a pretty harmless bunch, perhaps twenty of us in total. A few Quakers, Christians, a Canadian, some Jewish students, one Vietnam war veteran, Agnes, myself, and a few others. We gathered up on the fountain surrounded by perhaps ten campus cops and over a thousand jeering, shouting, counter-demonstrating students. Many of them were in madras shirts.

"COMMUNISTS! COWARDS! TRAITORS! Send them to Vietnam

instead!" they were shouting. It got worse. I held up my sign that said "Negotiate, Don't Bomb". I quickly felt it jolt in my hand. Something had hit the sign. They were throwing things at us. I looked to a nearby policeman and told him about it. He said nothing. I repeated myself to him. He finally answered, "I would be throwing things at you too."

I stepped between Agnes and the counter-demonstrators. I found myself holding my protest sign at face level as a barrier between me and them. I felt things bouncing off the sign. Two guys that I had gone to high school with walked up to me. One was wearing his green fraternity pledge cap. He looked me straight in the eye. "You're a communist, Dwight." The other one said, "Only a communist would do this." Then they drifted into the crowd of counter-demonstrators.

In the distance I saw a number of fraternity boys standing on the steps of the Fine Arts building. They had a box and were reaching into it. Then I saw Mike Sparrow, my floor mate at the rooming house. He was grinning as he flung something. Eggs! They splattered around us.

"Where are we?" Agnes shouted to me. "In Mississippi? What kind of state do you live in, Dwight?" Suddenly, I felt ashamed that my home state of Indiana could be so sorry-assed ignorant and hostile. The cops did nothing to stop the counter-demonstrators from throwing things.

We continued around the circle like voluntary targets, being pelted with whatever. When they ran out of eggs, they began tossing rocks, gravel, dirt, anything they could grab. Dixieland would have been so proud of them. Then I heard Agnes yell. She buried her face into my chest. She had her hand on the back of her head. When she pulled her hand back, there was a spot of blood on it. She was sobbing.

"WHAT KIND OF PEOPLE ARE THESE?" she implored.

I told her that we should go to an emergency ward to see if she needed stitches. She said she was afraid and wanted to leave the demonstration. We quickly stepped down the fountain stairs, passed between the cops and into the counter-demonstrators. We dropped our signs and I pushed through while holding Agnes' hand. Fifty feet later, we were anonymous.

We walked fast. Agnes was still sobbing. She said that they might have beaten us to a bloody mess if allowed to. I knew what kind of people they were. I had grown up with them. But I now found myself embarrassed that Agnes saw it. I walked Agnes back to her dorm. She said she would put ice on her cut and if she thought it was any worse, she would go to the emergency ward. I left her at the dorm.

Next day, I called Agnes. She said that she had a headache, but she was otherwise okay. The cut on her head had quickly stopped bleeding. She said she had called her mother last night and had a long conversation with her. Agnes said that her mother had told her to thank me in her family's behalf for being with Agnes last night. Agnes said she had something to tell me that might be better said face-to-face.

I rode my bike to her dormitory and we sat in the lounge together. Then Agnes said that she would be transferring to another college.

"Where to?"

"Back east, maybe Julliard. They have an excellent violin program there too."

"Did that demonstration change your mind?"

She said it was a lot of things, but in the end, she did not really feel comfortable here. We talked for a while more, until I had to get to work. She kissed me and told me she would miss me. She suggested that maybe I could come out east and visit her. Her family would like to meet me. I told her I would like to do that. But in the end, for whatever good or bad reasons, I never did visit her.

When I returned to my rooming house, I saw Mike Sparrow. With his perpetual smirk he said, "Oh how'd you like the demonstration, ehhh? Who won this time?"' This went on for months. Yet for the most part, I did not answer back. I wanted to blind side punch him out good. In a fight with him, I might not win, but I knew I could do good damage to him. But it never happened.

Thirty-two years later, I finally received my FOIA (Freedom Of Information and Privacy Act) from the FBI. I had waited over four years for it. Three times the FBI had sent me letters asking if I still wanted my FOIA. They stated that if I did not respond affirmatively, they would cancel my FOIA request. Each time I responded in writing with a loud, YES I STILL WANT IT.

It finally arrived in a large cardboard box. When I opened it up, I found that they had redacted almost half of it in black pen. I read with morbid fascination the FBI's documentation of my youth. *My God, had the FBI been watching me.* They knew all of my movements, where I lived, who were my friends, what I was doing. They even quoted my comments and speeches verbatim. Clearly they had been taping me at meetings and on phone conversations. Sometimes I found myself amused at the absolute confidence and self-righteousness of some of my statements. *I had ALL the answers.* But in the end, I was not ashamed of them. I felt there were villains in civil rights movement and Vietnam War. And *yes there were.*

My FOIA abruptly ended in 1989. The implication was that my file was still active. I now completely assume that the FBI and/or other intelligence agencies are still watching me.

The FBI clearly had informants at every open anti-war meeting that we had. From my FOIA, I figured out who three of the informants were. One was a Cuban refugee. In retrospect, that should have been obvious. Another was a dim loudmouth who always showed up for meetings urging us to 'fight back' and 'get the pigs'. Our very own *agent provocateur.* The FBI had agents demonstrating with us at every anti-war march. They wrote statements with us and even helped us 'plan' demonstrations. I discovered that three days after my first anti-war demonstration, the FBI had gone to my high school and gotten a copy of my high school records.

From my FOIA, I gathered that they had also been watching Agnes. Some comment in the FOIA indicated that they believed that 'my female associate' might be a 'Communist'. I knew that Agnes' parents had been active in the labor movement in the nineteen-thirties. Agnes had never been anything close to an informant.

So thank you Agnes, wherever you are, for being yourself. And Agnes, may life have been good to you.

# 9

## Does This Always Happen?

"And why did God create friends?"
"To make up for relatives."

A coed I knew stopped me on campus during final exams week in the spring of 1967. Could I keep a secret? Sure. Then she said she wanted to try marijuana for the first time. She said she figured that I smoked it, even though I had never mentioned it to her.

I picked her up on my Honda Dream motorcycle. I suggested we go out to Griffy Reservoir for the sunset. We would be alone, away from prying eyes and urban disruptions. She hopped on the back and we took off.

She complained about being cold, so I stopped and gave her my jacket. When we got there, I rode the motorcycle over the top of the dam. Half way across, we passed two men who were sitting on the dam and drinking. I had to slow down to miss all their empty beer bottles. Then I parked the cycle at the far end of the dam. We sat down on a trail near the spillway and I rolled a joint. I lit up, toked, handed her the joint, and told her to hold the smoke in her lungs. She did like I said, and then started coughing.

"It sure burns your throat," she complained.

We smoked the rest of the joint. It was good marijuana. It did not have any of the sugar or tobacco mixed with it that you often found in cheap Mexican marijuana in those days. We sat there and watched the sun drop into the treetops on the other side of the reservoir. I watched a water snake swim along in front of us, and then quickly grab a tadpole. Wow.

She turned to me. "What did you say?"

"I didn't say anything."

"Yes you did. I heard you." She looked at me funny. "You know, I don't feel a thing. I think this is all bunk. And what did you say?" she repeated.

"I didn't say anything."

We sat in silence, watching the light change across the reservoir as the sun set. Then I did hear something, the sound of children splashing and

# Does This Always Happen?

screaming. I looked down the dam spillway and saw a small child about a hundred yards away struggling in the water. A young girl reached to pull the child out. But she slipped and fell in too. Now two kids were struggling in the water. The girl also began to scream.

"I think--I think they're drowning."

We got up and ran along the trail at the edge of the reservoir to the spillway and sprinted along its top. As we passed the two drunks, they looked up at us. When we got to the kids, I could see a little boy under water, with an older girl splashing next to him. She was going under too.

I scooted down the steep, angled cement to the waterline. It was a dirt fill dam surfaced with concrete slabs. There was a rim of wet moss on the concrete, well above the waterline. The moment I put my foot on moss, I lost all traction and slid into the water. I swam to the kids and reached for the boy. I grabbed his arm and pulled him up. He came to the surface coughing and crying. The girl grabbed at me from behind and climbed onto my back, pushing me under water. I tried to push her off me and get both the kids' heads out of the water. But they were scratching and clawing at me, climbing on top of me, pushing me under again and again. I paddled them over to the edge of the dam and tried to push them up the slope. But the concrete embankment was too steep and slippery. The kids were both too panicked to control themselves.

"I'M COMING!" my smoking companion edged down the side of the dam toward me.

"STOP! Don't step on that moss or you'll slide in too. It's too slippery! Find something to pull us out with."

She climbed back up the slope of the dam as the kids continued pushing me under. I was struggling just to keep myself up. She came back down the slope, this time holding my jacket. She held one sleeve and swung the other to me. Then she leaned back against the cement to keep her balance. I had to reach for the sleeve several times before I got a hold on it. All the while the two children were clawing at me and gasping for air. I grabbed the little boy and shouted for him to hold onto the sleeve. He grabbed it but wouldn't let go of me. I pushed him up the concrete embankment. She pulled him up the mossy cement. The boy then scrambled to the top of the dam. We did the same thing with the girl. At the top of the dam, the kids coughed and spit up some water. Then they took off running toward a nearby subdivision.

We walked back to my motorcycle, past the drunks. They looked at us and didn't say a word. They had watched the whole thing and had never

# The Wild Years

offered to help at all. Goddamn drunks anyhow.

I reached into my pocket for the motorcycle key. I found it, but my wallet was gone. I had lost it in the water! We went back to the dam, but couldn't see a thing. Damnit. There went my driver's license. I was planning on driving home tomorrow for a summer job.

We decided to go to the police station to report my lost driver's license. I figured that the police could give me some kind of temporary driving receipt until I got home. We also decided to report how unsafe the dam was. No signs or safety fences of any kind. Any kid could fall in and drown.

My smoking partner continued wearing my jacket on the motorcycle ride. I shivered on the ride back, riding at 40 miles per hour in the cool evening air while soaked. We walked into the police station in Bloomington, Indiana, wet and disheveled. The cop at the desk looked us over suspiciously. When we told him and the police chief what had happened, they warmed up to us. The police chief thanked us and said that they would look into putting up signs and a fence. Then he told us to wait while he made a few phone calls. He had a clerk type up a note for me explaining what had happened to my driver's license.

While we were waiting, my smoking partner nudged me. She had a look of panic. She gestured down to the pocket of my jacket that she was wearing. I could clearly see the bag of marijuana.

"You think he knows?" she asked.

"Shhhhhhh."

The police chief came back into the room. He said someone from the newspaper would be coming shortly. After they took a few pictures, we were out the door. Outside the police station, she handed me my jacket. Her face was grim.

"Dwight, does this always happen when you smoke marijuana?"

I am quite convinced that was the first, last, and only time she ever smoked marijuana. Shortly afterward, she decided that her lifelong drug of choice would be cigarettes. Afterward, she chain-smoked cigarettes for over forty years. But she never complained once about them burning her throat, or her emphysema.

Does This Always Happen?

DWIGHT WORKER

# Student Saves Toddler

BLOOMINGTON — The price of bravery is $20 and considerable inconvenience, an Indiana University student learned Tuesday.

But the parents of the recipient of the heroism of Dwight Worker, a third-year psychology student, have compensated him for his cash and inconvenience.

Worker, resting after completing final exams, by walking along the bank of Griffy Lake with his sister Lola, also an I.U. student, saw three-year-old Kent Manuel slide into water and go under.

The youngster, son of Mr. and Mrs. Jack Manuel, who live by the lake, was chasing his dog when he slipped on the moss-covered cement incline and slid into the water.

His two sisters, Michelle, 15, and Lindy, 13, attempted to go to his aid, but Worker spotting their difficulty, throwed off his jacket and jumped into the water. Worker, the two girls and their brother were helped up the slippery incline by Lola with the aid of her brother's jacket.

In the process Worker's billfold, containing $20, his driver's license and other identification, was lost in the water.

ater Tuesday, Worker con-
Bloomington police to get
on to drive to his home
n Page o. Col. 1 1

## Student Saves...

FROM PAGE 1

in Highland, Ind., today without a driver's license to start his summer vacation.

Mrs. Manuel said afterward, "We'll certainly see that the loss is covered. It's the least we can do for the way he helped the children." Worker got his $20 today.

Mrs. Manuel and other residents of the area say children often play around the reservoir, but explained that it is dangerous territory.

No fences protect the children from the steep incline and water. Swimming is prohibited, but neighborhood children often go to the area for recreation.

"I know one family at least that is going to stay away from now on," Mrs. Manuel declared today.

# 10

## You Guys are All Such Assholes!

Hitchhiking across Europe, drunk, in 1965

"Get out of the car!" I heard the driver yell. I felt the car braking to a stop.

From the back seat I opened my eyes and looked around. We were on the side of Highway 80 in southern Wyoming, in the middle of no place. I shined my flashlight on my watch. Three a.m. The warning lights of the car were blinking yellow into the darkness. I saw no traffic on the highway. We were not at a highway exit. There was nothing around.

I elbowed Paul in the back seat to get up.

"Where are we?" Paul mumbled.

"Fuck if I know."

# You Guys are All Such Assholes!

Linda had gotten out of the front seat of the car and was standing at the trunk.

"Guys, don't get out of the car until we're sure we've got all of our gear out."

"That's right," Paul yelled. "Don't let him try any of that ripoff shit."

"I wouldn't do that to you," Bill said. Bill was the driver. He had picked us up hitchhiking 600 miles ago. "Don't worry. You'll get all of your stuff." His voice was high pitched and wobbly.

I got out of the car and looked around. A cool Wyoming summer night, full of stars.

"Why are we stopping here?" I shouted. "The cars will be going 80 miles an hour when they pass. We'll never get a ride here at 3 a.m. We'll have to walk to the next exit."

"Yeah," Paul yelled. "And that might be twenty miles. What's up, Bill, with this here middle of the night eviction shit?"

"It's her," Bill pointed to Linda.

*What the fuck?*

Bill had picked us up hitchhiking in western Utah. We were headed back east, coming back from the 'Summer of Love' in San Francisco in 1967. For us, it had been many things, but it had not been a summer of love. But I did see some of the best rock and roll concerts ever.

In San Francisco, Paul, Linda, and I quickly ran out of money. So Linda got a job as a go-go dancer. She made great tips. Some people might have called her a stripper, but we called her our sugar momma. Paul and I didn't ask her much about it. After all, she was sharing her strippings with us.

Paul, Linda, and myself had been stuck hitchhiking on an expressway ramp entrance in Western Utah for four hours. We all had big back packs, and that did not look inviting to any driver. But it wasn't enough that they did not pick us up here in Utah. They also waved fists and threw pop cans at us. No beer cans though, not in Mormon country. Twice, cops stopped and threatened to arrest us. We told them that we would get out of their state as fast as we could.

Then Bill pulled up in this monstrous new red car. It was a Oldsmobile Toronado. Bill was almost middle-aged, short, balding, and chubby. His face was red. He looked us over and asked questions. He said he was driving back to Nebraska from a sales conference in Las Vegas. There were empty beer cans laying all over the floor of his car. He was obviously drunk.

# The Wild Years

"Hey, you better be careful driving drunk in this state," Linda said. "Or them Mormons here will *nail your ass.*"

Bill sort of nodded.

"Look. We need to get out of this god-forsaken state," I said. "I'll buy you a tank of gas and drive this baby to Wyoming. You can rest and sober up."

Bill slowly nodded. "You drive safe?"

"Sure. It's our lives too." I handed him a ten dollar bill. He got out and we piled our back packs into the trunk. Linda threw out all the empty beer cans and put the remaining beer in the trunk. I took the wheel, Bill rode shotgun, and Paul and Linda collapsed in the back seat.

This was a *big-assed* car. I could have slept on its hood. I hit the gas and this car squealed. But the squeal came from the front.

"Careful!" Bill yelled. "This car is front-wheel-drive. Can you believe that? It's got the biggest engine going. A 455. My wife --- now my EX-wife --- she said I couldn't buy this. Not even with my own money. *Can you believe that?* So I showed her."

"No I can't believe that Bill. And I'm not used to so much power," I said. Or air conditioning. Or space. Or reliability.

Three months earlier, we had driven our VW bug until it gave up its ghost with a loud engine explosion just outside of Bakersfield, California. We got out and watched the remaining oil drain from the engine in the 100 degree heat. By the next morning, we had sold that blown-up VW for $75 to a Bakersfield grease monkey. After we signed the title over to him, he shortchanged us $25. We stood there arguing with him until he gave us $15 more and then threw us off his premises. He said he needed the ten bucks to register the dead VW, and if we stepped on his property again, he'd call the cops. "*And if you don't like that, call a hippie!*" he sneered. So we had been car-less ever since.

Riding shotgun, Bill quickly passed out and was snoring up a drunk storm. I flipped on the AC full blast and scanned the radio stations. Radio then just meant AM. There was no rock and roll to be found, so I had to settle for country music. We would be listening to done-me-wrong and drinking songs for the next 500 miles.

We were well past Salt Lake City before Bill woke up. He wanted food and water, so we pulled over at a truck stop. Over sandwiches, Bill gave us his abbreviated life story. Every driver did. They wanted to talk and stay awake. Maybe they were just lonely. Bill's wife had left him for his best friend. They had no kids. Bill was working his ass off on the road selling farm implements, and doing very well at it.

Bill wanted to know all about this here 'free love' stuff he heard was going on with the young people. Is it true that everyone just *did it* with everyone else all the time, that you didn't have to promise the girl that you'd marry her, and that you did it on the *first date*?

Linda looked over to Paul and me with a big smirk. This wasn't the first time we had heard this line of questioning from our rides either. All the drivers wanted to know *the details*. And this wasn't the first time that Linda did the answering. She knew the gig.

"Yeah Bill, there's free lovin' going on all over the place out there," Linda said. "Why, everywhere you look, they're doing it. Take me for example. I get it all the time --- and I don't have to pay a cent for it," Linda exclaimed. "Why just the other day, I was done loving up these two fellows here and I still wasn't satisfied. So I had to get me another---"

This was all news to me, and Bill was all ears now.

"---So I just went out on Haight Street, waited for the first handsome hippie boy to pass, and dragged him in. And let me tell you Bill, *I test drove* that piece of talent *good*."

"Wowwww," Bill nodded. "I was just born too late. You think I could go out there and well, have some fun too?"

"Sure," Linda said. "Just stop shaving and getting haircuts and put on some love beads and the mini-skirts'll bang you good."

"I'M GOING!" Bill was all awake and laughing now.

"You gotta be careful though, or you'll do it so much you'll get skinny."

"What a diet program!"

So Linda and Bill talked on and on. The more excited Bill got, the crazier Linda's stories got. Bill appeared to believe everything. Every now and then, when Bill wasn't looking, Linda would make eye contact with us and we'd break up. We laughed especially when Linda said she always slept between Paul and me, and that we'd flip coins for her. Then Bill said that maybe the three of us guys could play rocks-paper-scissors for Linda. He really laughed at that one. Well, from this point on, Bill insisted on paying for all the food and refused to take any more gas money from us.

When we hit western Wyoming, I felt a big relief. So much so that Paul and I started drinking the case of Bill's beer that Linda had put in the trunk. I tell you, those Utah people were in the nineteen-fifties and marching backward.

Bill and I had been taking turns barreling that Toronado down Interstate 80 at up to 100 miles per hour. Twice as fast as our old VW bug used to go.

## The Wild Years

But with all the beer we were drinking, it seemed every time we got to a 100 mph, we'd have to stop and piss again. Paul and I toyed with the idea of all of us pissing out the window while driving. But when Linda heard that, she shouted, "No fair!" We figured that at 100 mph, we'd get a lot of blow back anyhow. So it was either quit drinking beer, or keep stopping to piss along the expressway. We chose the latter. Finally, the case disappeared, and Paul and I passed out in the back seat. Bill took the wheel.

I thought we were having a great time. But now Bill was *throwing us out of the car in the middle of the night.*

"Bill, how can you do this to us?"

Bill stood there in the dark shaking his head. "You shouldn't have said that," he was saying to Linda.

"I'm sorry, Bill. I'm truly sorry. I didn't mean it. I mean, I was asleep, and I was just trying to be funny."

We stood there for a while, waiting. Then Bill says "Okay. I guess I just can't leave you out here all alone."

Linda got back into the front seat and Paul and I stayed in the back. I was too jarred awake to pass out quickly. But many miles of the humming engine finally got to me and I faded into limbo land.

Just before dawn, I heard Linda say up front, "OH MY GOD! LOOK AT THE SIZE OF THAT THING! THAT'S THE BIGGEST ONE I'VE EVER SEEN!" I looked up and from the back seat. I saw Bill's right shoulder going up and down. I heard his heavy breathing, and then a high-pitched grunt. Bill was panting. The car swerved. Linda reached over and steadied the steering wheel. *What the fuck?*

Well, we sped along in the daylight into Omaha. Bill made sure to feed us well and to find us the best on-ramp for catching another ride. He wrote down all of our addresses too.

When we got out of the car and on the entrance ramp, Bill shook hands with us and said, "Don't be surprised if you see me out in California next time. Course you might not recognize me with my long hair!" We laughed and waved as he pulled away.

Once he was out of sight, Paul said to Linda, "So why did he try to throw us out back in Wyoming?"

"You really wanna hear?"

"Of course."

"Well, when you guys were passed out drunk in the back seat, ole Bill

## You Guys are All Such Assholes!

whipped out his pecker and began jerking off in front of me. We'd been talking about sex all day, so maybe he got worked up. So I'm watching him, and it's sort of funny. I didn't feel threatened at all. But really, I'm just hoping he don't crash the car. And then he says to me in this real tough voice 'So *what do you think of this hard cock, hippie girl?*'"

"And?"

"Guys, I didn't know what to say. I mean it was such a surprise and all. It was all so ridiculous."

"AND???"

"Well, I said to him, '*Well Bill, Actually, I think that's the smallest cock I've ever seen in my life.*'"

On the edge of Interstate 80, in the mid afternoon sun, in Omaha, Nebraska, in the late summer of 1967, we all gut-laughed until we couldn't breathe.

"And?" Paul asked Linda.

"And what?"

"Was it really the smallest cock you'd ever seen?"

"Yeah. Are our cocks that much bigger than his?" I asked.

Linda paused from hitchhiking and looked at both of us gravely. Then she shook her head.

"YOU GUYS ARE ALL SUCH ASSHOLES!"

# 11
# Rolling in Pussy

Picking buddies with a pile of freshly harvested
1960's ditch weed

"Let's go pick us a bunch of that wild marijuana then," Terrell yelled with a puff of smoke. "We can get hundreds of pounds of it in just one night." He handed the joint to Jerry.

"Thousands," Jerry affirmed. "We'll be millionaires. You know where the pot grows, right, Dwight?"

"Yeah. I saw it when my dad took me hunting to Willow Slough years ago. They used to grow it there for rope in World War II. Now it just grows wild—for free."

"Wow. Free marijuana." Jerry puffed. "We'll be rolling in money."

"Can I go?" Rita asked. "I can pick, too."

"I don't know," Terrell said. "It's hard work, and maybe a little bit risky."

We had just rented this little farmhouse  north of Bloomington, Indiana. Each of us guys was paying $33 a month. It was an isolated, four-room place that had recently had running water added to it. It now had a basic working kitchen and a tiny bathroom. An outhouse still stood in the back. We affectionately called our home *the ole Henderson place*. Then Rita just sort of moved in. It wasn't decided on or anything like that. We just weren't that organized. Terrell sleeps with Rita one day, and she doesn't go home the next. Rita didn't cook, unless you counted opening cans, or packages of macaroni. She didn't clean up either, just like us, so our country home was always a mess. She was almost as bad as us guys.

It did seem to me that all Rita and Terrell did was eat, sleep, smoke, and fuck. And not necessarily in that order either. Oh, Terrell played a pretty good lead guitar too. He sat around in a cloud of smoke doing that a lot. On the weekends we had parties there. I would end up crashing on the living room couch. Late at night I would hear Rita bellowing like a cow in labor with Terrell as they boom-boomed away in the next room.

"Wait a minute," I said. "We could use Rita as the driver. The way cops bust people picking marijuana up there is they see their cars parked along side the country roads where the weed grows. The cops never go into the fields and wait for people. They just find the cars parked out there and wait until the pickers come back. Now, if Rita would drop us off, and then come back before sunrise to pick up us and the pot, it would be way safer. We'd just drive home on the back roads until we got out of Newton County.

"Yeah. I can drive the car and pick you up," Rita nodded to herself.

Terrell and Jerry didn't argue. "So we'll take your van," Terrell said to me.

"No way. It doesn't have the room for how much we want to pick."

"Then my car's too small. We'd fill the trunk up in five minutes."

"I got it!" Jerry yelled. "My buddy Ray --- his dad has a pickup truck and a horse trailer. We'll just borrow it from him – tell him we have to move stuff--"

"Like horses? Who's got any fucking horses?" I asked.

"Your uncle--maybe. I don't know. We'll just tell him we have to move something. It don't hafta be fuckin' horses!"

"There's no way Ray's ever gonna loan you his dad's truck," I said. "He'd be a fool to."

We pulled out at about sunset with the borrowed truck and horse trailer. We had a pile of burlap bags, flashlights, gloves, bottles of water, and tarps in the back. The truck was a Ford F-100 with a big ass V-8 and a four speed off the floor. I filled up the dual tanks and we headed north to the promised pot fields of plenty. Rita and Terrell were big-assed, wide-bodies themselves, so even though Jerry and I were skinny, we were all squeezed together on the front seat. First thing Terrell does is light up a joint. Then he hands it to me. I tell them no, I got to find the fields first.

Terrell pushes the joint at me. "Smoke this and it will tell you where the marijuana is. It will *draw* you to those pot fields."

"Not me."

"It would me," Jerry says.

# The Wild Years

It didn't matter that I didn't smoke any, because soon the cab is so full of smoke that I got high just breathing.

"The way I see it," Terrell blows out a mouthful of smoke, "if God didn't want us to pick it and smoke it, he wouldn't have grown it in the first place." I guess it made as much sense as anything else we were saying, and more sense than the Vietnam war. That was where Terrell first started smoking too.

I drove two hours on the main highway until I turned off at Willow Slough, the duck hunters' paradise in northwest Indiana. It was dark now. I weaved down gravel roads onto a muddy farm trail until we were just a few hundred yards from where I remembered seeing a big field of wild marijuana. I recalled a farm house somewhat up the road too. We didn't want to go past it, even though a truck pulling a horse trailer would not look suspicious around here. I stopped the truck. We unloaded all our gear into a deep ditch next to the road. I gave Rita directions to a truck stop a few miles away. She should fill up the truck with gas first. Then she could park there, go in and eat, and sleep in the front seat, do whatever she wanted. At exactly four-thirty am she should drive slowly down this road, right here, with her right blinker on. We would stop her, quickly load up, and be on our way home. We synchronized our watches. Rita nodded and slid over into the driver's seat. She fooled around with the steering wheel.

"Where's the 'D'?"

"It's a stick shift."

"I've never driven stick before. Only automatics. What do you do?"

!!!

"Now you tell me! What you think I been doing the whole time I was driving here?" I was shouting.

"Hey, take it easy. I'll teach her," Terrell stepped in.

"Oh, she's going to learn stick shift on a big truck with no power steering while pulling a trailer—in the middle of the night?"

Terrell slid into the front seat. "We'll be back in a little bit." Terrell drove off.

"What the fuck?"

Jerry and I stood on the muddy road. Suddenly it was completely dark on this cool October night. Stars were out all over. Jerry handed me the rest of the joint. Then we each grabbed the duffel sacks and headed out, walking around a corn field. The corn was dry and ready to harvest. A heavy dew was already covering everything. We stepped across a drainage ditch, and then, suddenly, we were standing in a forest of large marijuana plants. They stood like grand Christmas trees. I turned on my flashlight and showed Jerry how to identify the female plants. They were loaded with full buds of old flowers and seeds. Jerry ohhhed and ahhhhed. The male plants were skinny and dying back. They had served their purpose already and were no longer useful. Sort of like some of my buddies already. "Only pick the females," I told Jerry.

"*I can't believe it,*" Jerry said softly. "I been smoking this all my life, but this ---" he held his arms out. "This is magic." He danced around in a circle. "I can't believe it!" he shouted. "Tons of marijuana. We'll be rich!"

"Let's get to work. Watch me." I hung the duffel sack strap over my neck. With the flash lights off, I took my plant clippers and cut the full female bud off and dropped it into the sack. Jerry did the same. Then we were off the races, cutting away at the full female plants as fast as we could. In a half hour, we had each stuffed large army duffel sacks full. We stashed them at the ditch and grabbed two more empty bags. We saw a truck coming down the road. It had its right blinker on. When it got close, I saw that it was our truck. I jumped out and ran over to the driver's side. Terrell rolled down the window.

"Hey guys, Rita's not gonna be able to learn stick shift tonight. What should we do?"

We stood there in the dark, with the engine idling and the lights on.

"You can't believe all the pot out there!" Jerry shouted. "How about Rita picks with us, then. You wait at the truck stop, then you drive back and get us."

"It's cold out there," Rita said.

"I'm hot. Once you get started, it's not cold at all," Jerry said. Rita got out.

"I'll be back at four-thirty," Terrell said. He drove off.

Jerry and I showed Rita what to do. At first she was slow about it, but in time, she got into the rhythm. The half-moon rose in the east. The plants were now covered in a heavy cool dew. As we picked them, we got soaked up to our shoulders and our pants up to our knees.

After midnight it got cold. If we stopped picking, we would be shivering in a minute. So it was work or else. Now Rita got trucking, working harder than I'd ever seen her do. She was a big, friendly girl,who knew what made her feel good. Together we carried three more duffel sacks to the ditch.

All we had left now were burlap bags. They were harder to work with because they didn't have a strap to hang over our necks. But we managed to fill them them. Jerry lit up another joint. We all smoked.

"What could be more magic than to be in a marijuana field at night?" Rita sighed. Jerry agreed. We went on picking and picking, until we got down to our last burlap bags. Before we left Bloomington, we never dreamed we would fill up all fifteen bags. I checked my watch with the flashlight. Three forty-five am. I grabbed the last full bag.

"What we gonna put the rest of the marijuana in now?" Rita asked.

"You could spread out the tarpaulin and cover it with grass and then roll it up. Then we could toss that into the trailer," I said.

Jerry grabbed the tarp and he and Rita walked off together. I carried the bag

# The Wild Years

to the ditch next to the road.

When I returned to the field, I looked all around for Jerry and Rita. I couldn't find them. But in the distance I heard something -- repeating itself again and again. It was not so faint either. It was the sound of Rita humping. I would recognize that sound anyplace. So she and Jerry were--- I didn't want to interrupt them, but we had to get going. Terrell would be driving by soon to pick us up. So I called their names out into the darkness. Sudden silence.

"We're over here," Jerry yelled after a pause. I followed his voice to the tarp.

"Did you hear us?" Jerry asked me. He was pulling up his pants.

"Hear what?" I said. There was another pause. Then I burst out laughing. "I'm more worried that the farmer down the road heard you."

"Don't tell Terrell," Rita pleaded. "He has his groupies too when he's playing his music, you know."

"Not a word from me," I said.

They pulled up their clothes. I checked my watch. Quarter after four. Terrell would be coming soon. We cut some whole plants and covered the tarp. Then we rolled it up and carried it to the side of the road. In front of us was by far the most massive amount of marijuana I had ever seen. We all admired it.

We waited. Four-thirty, four-forty-five, four-fifty-five. *Where the fuck was Terrell?* We heard a motor. Then we saw lights coming down the dirt road. But it had too many lights to be our truck, and no blinker was flashing. We stepped back and hid. The sound of the vehicle became a roar as we watched a massive combine come upon us, bright lights all over. Some farmer was most likely going to get the rest of the corn or beans in some far patch. As it passed, its lights lit up the the roadside. When it came directly in front of us, we saw clearly in its lights our stuffed bags of marijuana piled in the ditch.

The combine stopped. We heard its door open. Then an old man stepped the front of its bright lights and walked to the edge of the ditch. He was wearing blue bibs and a brown jacket. He shined a flashlight down on our bags. In the darkness, Jerry, Rita and I squeezed each others' hands. The farmer stood around for a moment and then he climbed back into the combine and continued driving.

"He's found us!" Jerry said. "What we going to do now?"

No sooner than he was out of sight and we see another pair of lights coming down the road.

"You think he called the cops that soon?" Jerry asked, panicked.

"Couldn't have. There's no houses nearby enough."

Then we saw the right blinker of the oncoming vehicle blinking. It could only be Terrell. As soon as he came up to us, we jumped out and we ran over to his window.

# Rolling in Pussy

"A farmer saw us! He's calling the cops!" Jerry said. "Let's get out of here!"
I quickly told Terrell what had happened.

"But he ain't seen you --- or our truck. Just the pot."

"Yeah."

"We ain't leavin' all that marijuana. Not all that work for nothin'."

Terrell got out, opened up the horse trailer, and began loading up the duffel sacks. Jerry and I followed suit while Rita got into the cab. We quickly loaded all the bags into the trailer. I took the wheel and we took off. I turned the heater up full blast. Three of us were soaked and cold. I took a right turn on the next country road to get off this road and out of here as fast as we could. Get The Fuck Out! We had five miles of back roads before we got to the main highway. I could not speed with this heavy trailer behind me. The trailer brakes were not working, and all we needed was to jackknife it and get stuck in a ditch.

Everybody was talking non-stop. Finally I pulled onto the main highway and accelerated to fifty miles an hour. Now we all felt safer. The heat was pouring out and it felt good. Terrell was sitting next to me. I smelled booze on his breath.

"How come you so late?"

"Sorry, man," Terrell laughed. "There was this great country bar next to that truck stop. A band was playing and the place was rocking. Filled up with hillbillies. My people. I tell you, I had a *good* time."

"While we was all working our asses off," Rita whined.

"Next time, drive stick shift," Terrell grumbled.

The cab was getting warm and we were drying out. Moisture was coming from our wet clothes and steaming up the windows. I turned the defroster fan on full-blast and cracked a window to dry out. Then I glanced at the gas gauge. We were almost empty.

"Terrell, you didn't fill up the tank!" I yelled.

"Oh shit! I forgot. You can fill up at the next station."

"Yeah. With a ton of wet smelly marijuana in the trailer. Goddamnit."

We rode in silence. But I had no choice. I pulled into the next station. It was a small one with just two pumps. There were farm trucks at both of them. We waited to the side until one of them opened up. I tried to back up the truck, but I quickly jackknifed the trailer. Back then, I didn't know how to backup vehicles while towing a trailer. I finally just had to pull forward and out of the station again and come back around. By the time I got back, another truck had pulled into the open pump. So we had to wait again. It was starting to get light in the east. Finally we pulled up. I began filling up both tanks. A farmer came out of the gas station and looked us over.

"You from around these parts?" he asked.

"Uh yes," "No," we both answered. "Sort of," we compromised.

# The Wild Years

The farmer looked over the trailer. "Hauling livestock today? Market's down you know."

I looked at the pump. It just wouldn't fill any faster. Jerry was standing in front of me. In the back of his long hair I saw a distinct five-petaled marijuana leaf. I slowly picked it out of his hair. Jerry jumped when I touched his hair.

Ding. The pump finally went off. The farmer was looking at the trailer. I ran in and paid the bill. Then we hopped in that truck and took off. I couldn't wait to be out on the road again.

"That guy knows!" Jerry was shouting. He woke Rita up. "I bet he's calling the cops right now."

"Naw. He's just another farmer, kicking the shit," Terrell said. "You're paranoid."

I kept cruising just below the speed limit. Ten, twenty, thirty, fifty miles down the road. I didn't feel safe until we were south of Indianapolis. The full sun was up now, and anyone could see inside the trailer. As soon as I could, I took a back road to the *ole Henderson place*. I was so relieved when we finally pulled in. Rita ran into the house ahead of everyone else, shouting she really had to go pee. Before Jerry and I could get out, Terrell grabbed us.

"Guys, I'm really sorry I was late and didn't fill up the truck. But I got a reason. Now don't tell Rita this, but a guy in the band last night let me grab an ax and jam with him for a while. Next thing I know there's this cute country girl buying me drinks. Oh, she's a chubby alright, but so am I." Terrell laughs at that. "Before you know it, we're drinking. Then she comes out to this truck with me, and we *do it right here on this front seat! Why If it wasn't for all that marijuana, you could still smell it!*" We all laughed. "Now you guys woulda done the same thing. Don't tell me any different. Just don't tell Rita."

Ha ha ha. "Don't worry, Terrell. We won't say a word. Never." Jerry and I both promised.

The three of them all wanted to go straight to sleep. But I told them we had to spread all the marijuana out right now in the living room so that it didn't ferment and burn up in those bags. I can sometimes be Mr. Responsible. We carried all the bags in and emptied them on the living room floor. When we were done, it was covered with three feet of marijuana. Jerry dove into it. He just couldn't resist. I put a window fan on it. Then I went outside and walked around the home. I swore I could smell it from fifty feet away. I went back inside and built a good fire in the wood stove. I put the fan behind the stove to blow the heat on the marijuana. Get this stuff drying.

We spent days drying and cleaning that marijuana. Then we burned an immense pile of stalks and stems in the sweetest smelling bonfire ever. I paid a guy to weld a marijuana press, only I didn't call it that to him. With a hydraulic jack, we took the dried, cleaned marijuana tops and pressed them into the

# Rolling in Pussy

cleanest, prettiest looking kilos you ever seen. Just filled with tops and seed, and none of that damn sugar weed the Mexicans were sending up back then with coca-cola poured on it to stick it together.

Then we all smoked it. We stood there admiring all our home-brew kilos. Made in the good ole US of A. We had done it ourselves, we were proudly thinking. Jerry breathed out another puff of smoke, still waiting for a high. "Man," he said to no one in particular, "After we sell all of this, we'll just be *rolling in pussy.*"

I soon had my first real lesson in life about quality control and the marketplace. Terrell, Jerry and I tried selling our ditch weed to everyone we knew. Our friends examined it and said it looked beautiful and smelled great. But when they smoked it, there was just one minor problem. They didn't get high at all. So our friends returned it to us and we gave them their money back. We tried mixing it with good marijuana. But that just ruined the real smoke. In the end, we literally couldn't even give it away. Terrell observed that we had the worst of two worlds; we could get arrested with this marijuana, but we sure as hell couldn't get high with it.

In the meantime, Rita and Terrell had another one of their screaming fights. These could be even louder and more public than their humping sessions. But this time, Rita packed her bags and announced that she was leaving once and for all. I didn't see Terrell crying, or trying to stop her. But before she left, she said she needed *MONEY.* That's just how she said. *MONEY.* She held her hand out and did not put it down. Then she and Terrell started fighting about the money. Finally, they agreed that she got everything in his wallet. Now, with some money in her purse, Rita demanded that I give her a ride to town. When I dropped her off, the last thing she said to me was, "That son of a bitch was always broke anyhow."

So Terrell had the idea of the burning party. We invited friends over one night and started a bonfire. This time we smoked *real* marijuana first, along with our beer. Then we began throwing our ditch-weed kilos into the fire. When the flames rose, we began drumming and dancing around the bonfire. I stood downwind and smelled the smoke. It still *smelled* like real marijuana. It was a great all-night party as we watched our dreams of easy money all go up in smoke. In the middle of the blaze, Terrell grabbed Jerry and shouted, "So you'll be rolling in pussy, huh? Just let me tell you this; free marijuana is just like free pussy. There ain't no such thing."

# 12

# A Nigger Lover and a
# Goddamn Com-man-ist

In early 1990's, I applied to the FBI for a copy of my Freedom of Information Act (FOIA) report. This document basically told the applicant the information the US Government had on him. It did not include any currently active case information, or any information that would reveal the identities of informants. At that time, all US citizens had the right to see their FOIA. This is no longer the case.

I received my FOIA in 1998, fully fifty months after I had applied for it. In those intervening years, I had received a few letters from the FBI explaining that I would have to pay for the printing expenses. The letters also stated that if I did not reply affirmatively, they would terminate my FOIA request. I thought the FBI would use my non-reply as an excuse for them not to send my FOIA. So I returned registered letters each time to the FBI repeating that Yes, I STILL wanted my FOIA.

The box that finally arrived weighed several pounds. Inside I found well over a thousand pages of FBI records about me. I looked at photos of me, fingerprints, school records, transcripts of speeches I had given, and detailed logs of where I was on certain dates.

A large amount of my FOIA was redacted. Black lines covered much of the pages. There were numerous pages where the only thing readable was my name. Apparently the FBI was protecting the identities of the numerous informants around me. There were many filler pages stating that this page replaced an entire page that they had redacted. It appeared that the FBI had even redacted their redactions.

I read my FOIA with morbid fascination. I was amazed at just how closely the FBI had monitored me. I saw my name listed each time I attended an anti-Vietnam-war planning meeting. My former teachers could not have kept better attendance sheets. I found that my high school guidance counselor gave the FBI my school records a few days after my first anti-war demonstration. I had never thought of myself as that important, but apparently the FBI had. They had followed me and documented a decade of my life far better than I ever could

# A Nigger Lover and a Godamn Com-man-ist

have done.

When I moved to New Mexico in 1968, I deliberately lived entirely off the grid. No phones, electricity, water, gas, rent, or traceable bills of any sort. I had left Indiana in fear of arrest because of my refusal to cooperate with the Selective Service Board after they drafted me. I wanted no one to know where I was. But in my FOIA, I found that the FBI knew my whereabouts within six weeks. My FOIA disclosed that they had tapped my parents' phone and sent at least one 'hippie-looking' agent to my parents' home to ask questions.

In my FOIA, I read about my having sold a small amount of marijuana to an informant. But they choose not to arrest me because it would reveal the informant and because they hoped I would lead them to more wanted suspects. I was clearly not nearly as smart as I imagined myself, and not hidden at all.

The end of my FOIA report documented my decline into drug addiction. This was painful reading for me. I relived my descent from my political ideals to living for drugs and the money to buy them. I sat there thinking, "How could I have gone so wrong?"

I left my parents' home early on Sunday, July 10, 1966, for Chicago by train. Martin Luther King was speaking at Soldier Field and I wanted to hear him. It was a hot day and I was wearing shorts. When I got off the train, I passed several black teenagers of about my age. They saw my shorts and began to catcall me. These were serious, vulgar insults. Apparently to them, only women were supposed to wear shorts. Then they began shouting insults about my white skin. I told them that I was their friend, but they wouldn't have any of it. One of them aggressively stepped forward toward me, as if to fight. Suddenly, I was frightened. I quickly turned and hiked to Soldiers Field.

When I got there, it was mostly full. I rendezvoused with my friend Spence and we went in. I was happy to see that there were also a lot of white people there. All the black folks I met there were friendly to me. After that hostile street encounter, I was relieved.

In the distance, Martin Luther King spoke about the need to continue non-violently. He talked about organizing workers for peace and not wasting money on wars. I recalled him saying that there would be a demonstration afterward. I told Spence that I wanted to shake MLK's hand, and have my photo taken with him. Spence said that I wouldn't be able to get close to him, so good luck.

At the end of the speeches, I followed the crowd out. Eventually I got within handshake distance of MLK. He was smaller than I expected. He looked preoccupied and maybe tired as he talked with many people around him. I raised my voice a bit and said something like, "We're with you, Mr. King". I reached out my hand to his. He nodded and reached back. And then he was whisked away.

# The Wild Years

When I returned home late that afternoon, my Dad asked me where I had been. I told him. That stopped my Dad cold.

"Goddamn it, let them solve their own problems. Don't you go agitating with them. Ever since you started caddying for Jesse Owens and Joe Louis and all them other coloreds, you become a nigger-lover."

I started to shout back, but suddenly I couldn't. I walked into the back yard. I wasn't going to cry in front of my Dad again -- ever again -- if I could help it. But he came charging out and saw me crying.

"Oh Jesus Christ! What the hell's wrong now?" he barked.

"I'm not crying for me, Dad. I'm crying for you." I quickly got away from him.

Later that evening, my Dad's good friend, Mr. Howard, came over. He was always kind and reasonable to me. Mr. Howard asked me what I had been doing today. So in front of my Dad I said, "I went up to Soldier's Field and saw Martin Luther King speak. So I've been a nigger-lover today."

I saw my father's discomfort, and I enjoyed it. My Dad started complaining to Mr. Howard about how I should stay away from all of that. But surprisingly to me, Mr. Howard said that maybe I would learn something. As I walked away, I heard Mr. Howard telling my father that what had happened in the past just wasn't right...

That was the last time my father ever called me a nigger-lover. But he wasn't done yet.

In November of 1967, I came home from college to visit my parents. Much had happened in the last year. My brother Wayne had been permanently paralyzed while serving in the U.S. Navy as the war in Vietnam was escalating. My high school friend, Steven Stofko, had recently been killed in the Vietnam war. And I had just been arrested in an anti-Vietnam War demonstration.

I had no moral problems with getting arrested in the demonstration. But now I had legal problems, and I decided not to tell my parents. I did not want them worrying about me, or arguing with me. I had come home only to visit my family, and to see how my paralyzed brother was doing.

When I opened the door of my parents' home, Mom quickly came up to me. Her face was serious as she turned behind her and said, "He's here."

I hugged Mom, but she was clearly distracted.

My Dad came striding up to me, his face hard. I knew that look and walk. When I was a kid it terrorized me. He stood in my face, his lower lip twitching.

"NOW YOU A GODDAMN COM-MAN-IST!"

He swung at me. I deflected his arm.

"NOW STOP THAT!" my mother jumped between us. She was already crying.

# A Nigger Lover and a Goddamn Com-man-ist

"We know!" my Dad shouted. "We know what you been doing down there in Bloomington. Get out of here and don't ever come back!" He lifted his right arm ominously again. I would never swing back at my Dad, but I would block his punches.

I hugged my crying mother and left. That was the last time I saw or spoke with them for years.

For me, the worst part in my FOIA was the FBI contact with my family. They tapped my parents' phone when I was not wanted for any crime. They sent agents to my parents' home and called my parents under the pretext of being old friends of mine. My parents once mentioned this annoying person who continued calling up, asking about me.

When my mother passed away, I helped clean out all of her old records. In them, I found a large folder with my name handwritten on it in my mother's handwriting. Inside of it, among other things, were many letters addressed by hand to my parents. Only one letter had a return address. But the postage cancellations showed that all of them were mailed from Bloomington, Indiana, in 1966 and 1967. These letters were filled with newspaper clippings about me. They concerned speeches I gave on civil rights, anti-war activity, and photos of me in demonstrations. One had a picture of me being arrested.

A few of the newspaper clippings had comments written along the margins. Next to a newspaper article and photo of me someone had written, "Do you know this is what your son is doing?" Another newspaper article mentioned that I had helped organize a fund raiser for the Student Non-violent Co-ordinating Committee (SNCC). Someone had crudely written along the side, "your son helping the nigitators." I had never heard that word before.

So, my parents had been reading all this stuff about me while I was at college. They never told me they had received any of it. I now understood better my father's rage at me when he threw me out of his home.

I went back to that one letter that actually did have a return address. I looked at that address. *I knew that house.* It was in the middle of the off-campus student ghetto. I had been to parties at that home at the very time this letter had been sent. The student who lived there was a Cuban refugee. He regularly showed up at anti-war demonstrations, but he never said a thing. Now I wondered why would the child of anti-communist, anti-Castro Cubans actively oppose US military policy? He most likely did not even have citizenship yet. It seemed questionable to me. Later, I spoke with other activist friends of mine from that time who had also gotten their FOIAs. By the process of elimination we determined whose names had been redacted. Others told me that this man was in fact working as an informant for the FBI. Now I had evidence of the kind of work he was doing.

## The Wild Years

So, this was my tax dollars at work. Paid FBI informants writing nigitator on the side of newspaper articles and sending them to my parents. This was trivial compared to what the FBI did to the Black Panthers and the American Indian Movement. In those instances, the FBI had flat-out helped others to commit murder. What the FBI did with me worked. It made a split in my family that never healed.

So what do I have to say to the FBI about these specific acts? I guess I could write a long discourse on what a lie the Vietnam war was, and how the FBI under Hoover was used to repress human rights. I could say all of that, but others have already written eloquently about this.

A university professor contacted me and asked if he could review a copy of my FOIA. He had studied the FOIAs of many other activists from the 60's. When he finished, he told me that it was clear that my file was still active and that I was a 'priority one'. I asked him what that meant. He said that, in case of any declared national emergency, I would be within the first group to be detained. What I want only to say to the FBI/NSA/CIA/Homeland Security and whoever else is that I am not, and will not be, intimidated by you, whatever you might do.

# 13

# The War is Over

The front and back of
my original draft card

On March 1, 1966, Allen Ginsberg and Peter Orlovsky read poetry to to
an overflow audience in Ballantine Hall at Indiana University. Ginsberg and
Orlovsky shocked most of the people in the audience that day, myself
included. After this poetry reading, I no longer thought I was so weird. At
the end, Ginsberg read his new poem "Wichita Vortex Sutra". In the poem,

# The Wild Years

he declared the the Vietnam War to be *over.* Done with; no more.

*The war is OVER,* he said. I liked the sound of that. What a relief to my ears from the steady escalation in this war. So, inspired by Ginsberg, I mailed my draft card back to my Selective Service Board. I altered it first, as you can see above. But I did not burn it up. I enclosed a note telling them I was returning my membership card. I declared myself free to associate, or not, with whatever groups I wanted. With this action, I had given the government evidence that I had committed a federal felony. Now my problems with the U.S. government would begin in earnest.

In our high school government class, we had read William Shirer's *The Rise and Fall of the Third Reich.* We got through all 1500 pages of it. We studied the Nuremberg trials. Our teacher stressed that humans had a higher calling than only to patriotism. "Our country, right or wrong," could no longer be the final justification for our actions. They actually taught this in high school back then.

President Lyndon Baines Johnson used the 'Gulf of Tonkin' incident to justify US escalation of the war in Vietnam. Even to my seventeen-year-old ears back then, it sounded contrived --- a manufactured excuse that our government was using to justify the escalation that they were going to do anyhow.

Forty-one years later, the National Security Administration admitted that the Gulf of Tonkin incident never happened. Instead, they called it the USS Maddox incident. This final report was entirely different from what the U.S. Government first reported. In it, we admitted that we were the first to fire on and attack the Vietnamese patrol boats. Up to that point, the U.S. had always claimed that the Vietnamese had fired first. Thus, the pretext for the War in Vietnam was a falsehood to start with. But in the 1960's, this did not matter. They had started a war, and now it would be easy to rally an angry and patriotic public around the flag.

The week I turned 18 years old, I picked up a form from my Selective Service Board and applied to be a conscientious objector (CO). In it I stated that I had no objections to working in medical service of the U.S. military. I just did not want to kill anyone if I could avoid it. Then I came to the 'God' question. The form asked me if my motivation to apply for CO status sprang from a belief in "God or a higher being," or something like that. I paused.

Well, I hadn't believed in God since I was about 13 years old. And

# The War is Over

previous to that, I just didn't care about the question at all. I had spoken with a pacifist Quaker professor at Indiana University about this. He had warned me that if I answered no to this question, there was a very good chance that the Selective Service Board would reject my CO application. What were they really saying here? That only approved religious people had the moral right not to kill? Do I lie and take the easy way out? If I lie to them, do I then have to show that I am a member of an approved pacifist religion? Does my answering yes give them the right to inspect my mind and thoughts? To me at age 18, this seemed like bullshit. I was willing to do years of free community service, Conscientious Objector work, you name it. I believed in and I still believe in a national service corps. My idea was that everyone would have to perform some form of service to our country when they reach an approved age. No exemptions, no excuses, and only minimal pay. Upon successful completion of the program, participants would have access to educational loans and such. Like in Switzerland and Israel. I would do that. I looked at the form. Then I wrote NO to the 'God or higher being' question. I mailed the form back to the Selective Service Board. A few weeks later, I received their response. They had rejected my application. They had determined that I was morally unfit not to kill.

I appealed the Selective Service ruling on my Conscientious Objector Status. On January 19, 1965, I went to their board meeting in Hammond, Indiana. Now I saw them face-to-face. They were ordinary folks, like the people I grew up with. I sat down in front of the three of them and told them that I would be happy to perform years of community service or medical service in the military, but that I simply was not planning on taking up arms against anyone. At the time, I truly believed that I was a pacifist.

All the board members were concerned with was my belief in a God and my religion. I tried to explain to them what I felt, but it wasn't easy. What eighteen-year-old is so articulate about such beliefs? They told me I could not change my answer on the form about my belief in God. I told them I wouldn't anyhow. Then they quickly concluded that because I had answered no, I had disqualified myself from being classified conscientious objector. They had concluded that I was morally fit to kill.

I asked them how they were chosen to serve on this board. They said they applied. What were the qualifications? You had to be a U.S. Citizen with no serious criminal record. That was me. I asked for an application form. They were shocked. I repeated myself. The lady finally handed me a copy. I took it and said my goodbyes.

But I had a different plan. When I got back to Bloomington, Indiana, I got a brick. On it I painted, "IF DRAFTED, I WILL NOT GO AND KILL PEOPLE." I signed my name on it. Then I boxed it up and shipped it parcel post to my draft board, with a registered receipt. I think it cost me around four dollars back then. That was a lot of money for me, considering that the minimum wage was just over a dollar an hour back then.

Later that year, the Selective Service Board summoned me to review my application for membership to their board. They did not want to, but they had to. An older man asked me why I thought I would be qualified to be a good member of the board. I told them that they could be assured that I would not discriminate against any man.

"What do you mean by that?"

"Well currently, according the the U.S. Army, over 25% of all combat-related deaths are to African-Americans, and they just represent only 11% of the U.S. population."

"And just how would you fix that?" the questioner looked irritated at me.

"Well, I would end all deferments. Draft everyone, regardless of how rich or poor they are."

"The draft laws have exemptions for good reasons," the older man intoned. "So just who should we draft, under your new *system*?"

"I think we should draft all senators' and congressman's, and government officials' sons too, just like everyone else. I think we should eliminate the 2-S student deferments, which protects the children of rich people --"

"-- like yourself."

"-- like myself. Yes sir," I answered. "Although I never knew I was rich."

The board members looked at each other. A few shook their heads. The older began to speak. "It is not this board's responsibility to determine what proportion of which group gets drafted. Our government passes laws for that---not the members of this board, or you. It is our job only to execute these laws."

"I paused for a bit. "Well, I would not discriminate against anyone, regardless of race, religion, or color, because *I would not draft anybody.*"

We sat there silently for a moment.

"If you could step out of the room now, we would like to confer by ourselves about your application."

I left the room. A minute later, they opened the door. "Please come in." I entered. "The man looked at me and stated "We have reviewed your application and we have decided to reject it."

"Why?"

"We feel you are clearly not qualified to execute the laws of our land."

"What makes someone qualified to decide who kills -- and who doesn't?"

They didn't answer. There was a long pause.

"Well then," I said, "While I am here, I would like to look at my draft file."

They looked puzzled.

"By Selective Service rules, it is the legal right of anyone registered with the Selective Service to see and review his files," I said.

"We didn't come here for that."

"Are you going to deny me my legal right? It'll just take a minute."

The man looked irritated. Then the lady volunteered, "I'll go get it."

A minute later she came back with my file. I went through the file and found everything that should have been there. Everything except one thing.

"Where is the message I sent you stating, 'IF DRAFTED, I WILL NOT GO AND KILL PEOPLE'?"

The lady looked at me. "You mean that brick you painted on? We threw that out."

"You mean you *tampered with my draft file*? That is illegal, you know."

Looks of rage shot from across the table. "You may leave now," the man finally said. I got up.

"I think they should draft the sons of Selective Service Board members first!" I shouted as I left.

I did not know what to expect after I returned my draft card. I had not heard of anyone doing it before, so I was in new territory. So what happened next? Surprisingly, nothing. I remained in school and did not hear from my draft board.

Then I got a rare phone call from my mother. Telephone calls back then could cost up to a dollar a minute, so we only called long distance for emergencies. My mother was crying on the phone. She told me that my high school friend Steve Stofko had just been killed in Vietnam. I had known Steve most of my life. My brothers were friends with Steve's brothers, and our parents knew each other. What a waste. More gasoline on the fire of my anger.

Finally, I received a letter from the Selective Service in the fall of 1967. I was still a student at Indiana University, and the Vietnam war was in full escalation. At the time I received the letter, I was with my girlfriend, and we just happened to be stoned on marijuana. I opened the letter. Out fell my old draft card. They had returned it to me. But inside was my new draft card with my new classification. The Selective Service had classified me 1A-Deliquent. They informed me that I could be inducted at any time. Even as stoned as I was at the moment, that got my attention.

"And just what are you going to do now?" my girlfriend asked.

"They have classified me fit to kill. I offered to serve in some non-military way, but they refused. Just who are these people?"

On the floor of my apartment was a newspaper. In it I found a picture of the head of the Selective Service, General Hershey, giving a speech. I cut out the picture of Hershey's head from the article and pasted it onto a 3" by 5" card. Beneath it I wrote

WC-3

I explained in a note to General Hershey that I had *reclassified him* to War Criminal to the 3rd degree. I ordered him to report to my apartment *immediately* to join the Peace Revolution. His first assignment would be to shut down all induction centers.

I showed it to my girlfriend. We giggled. "But you are not really going to send that, are you?"

Did she think this was a joke? *Did I think this was a joke?* They had already reclassified me. I no longer recognized their authority. What difference would it make if I sent this or not? I would later discover that this would make a major difference in my life, but not as I expected. I stuck the 3" by 5" card into an envelop, addressed it to the national Selective Service Bureau, and we walked to a mailbox. After I dropped the letter in, my girlfriend was no longer smiling.

Weeks passed. The war got worse. You could feel the tension on campus. I got arrested in an anti-Dow Chemical anti-Vietnam war demonstration. Dow Chemical made the napalm used in Vietnam. I got hit solidly on the head with a billy club and was out cold when they dragged me out. I was facing some stiff charges of disorderly conduct, resisting arrest, and assault and battery.

My girlfriend and I saw the movie *How I Won the War*. It was an anti-war flick. Afterward she commented that my draft board should see that movie. I thought that was a good idea. So I mailed my draft board five two-dollar checks and told them to use the money to buy tickets to see this movie. A few weeks later, my draft board returned my checks. I said to my girlfriend that I thought they were ungrateful. So I sat down and wrote out five, one-million dollar checks on my personal checking account made out

# The War is Over

▓▓▓▓▓▓▓▓▓ a national officer of the SDS at Chicago, is coming to the teach-in at IU, 12/1 - 3/67 to give a speech. The FCPV is not connected with the IU-CEWV and appears to be formed for this teach-in only. Members of the FCPV were the faculty group which organized a demonstration outside of the auditorium on 10/31/67 at the convocation speech of Secretary RISK on the IU campus.

After this teach-in, no other activity is planned until the end of the first semester.

The Anti-Draft Union (ADU) is not active any longer at IU. This was started by ▓▓▓▓▓▓ or the IU-DCA so that they could have an organization to run their anti-draft activities. The IU-DCA and ADU will have no activity until they find a good issue or cause. Their lack of activity is blamed on ▓▓▓▓▓▓ a good starter but not able to keep the group going.

▓▓▓▓▓▓ is going to Indianapolis for his ▓▓▓▓▓ and plans to refuse to answer questions and fill out the questionnaire just as he has done before.

No information has been received by this source for any more local demonstrations this year and no word has been received concerning any demonstrations at the LBJ ranch in Texas during Christmas vacation.

DWIGHT WORKER sent his draft card back to the Local Draft Board with five $2 checks so that the members of the draft board could go and see a movie, name unknown, which was a propaganda movie for anti-draft activities. These checks were returned by the board stating that they could not accept personal checks. WORKER then sent the board five one million dollar checks for each member to spend on a vacation in Acapulco. WORKER was reclassified 1-A. WORKER told ▓▓▓▓▓▓▓▓▓▓ WORKER stated that ▓▓▓▓▓▓

▓▓▓▓▓▓▓▓▓▓▓ was identified by this source as ▓▓▓▓▓▓▓▓

According to this source, ▓▓▓▓▓▓▓ Bloomington, Indiana.

-4-

A page from my FOIA (Freedom of Information Act) which I finally received in 1998

# The Wild Years

to each of my draft board members. I wrote a note to them telling them to all take a vacation to Acapulco and relax a bit. They did not return those checks.

I dreaded the thought of going to court. My trial would only be about my actions that day, not about the war in Vietnam. I withdrew from about everything except school. I got more and more stoned. It was a momentarily easy way to get my mind off all the turbulence going around me. All I needed to do now was finish my final exams. I would be graduating a semester early, in January of 1968. After that, I would start my new life in Canada.

On the early morning of January 11, 1968, there was a knock on my apartment door. I quickly dressed and opened the door. There were two uniformed men standing there. They looked at a picture of me.

"You are Dwight Worker?"

"Yes."

"We are here to take you to the Indianapolis induction center."

I stood there for a moment, absorbing a full dose of this reality check.

"But I haven't even had my physical exam yet."

"We have orders."

"And if I don't go?"

"Then you'll be arrested for desertion."

They were dead serious. By the looks on their faces, they would have preferred to shoot me on the spot. I went upstairs and told my girlfriend. She looked horrified. I changed clothes, then grabbed a stack of anti-war pamphlets that we had been handing out at induction centers. I put the pamphlets in an envelop and got into the back seat of their car. I asked a few questions, but they were silent. Not a word more for the rest of the one hour drive to Indianapolis.

When I got out, they led me through the front door. There, they put me in the back of a long line of grim-faced young men. Draftees. After a bit, my escorts walked off. I walked to the front of the line and began offering anti-war pamphlets to the inductees. Just a few of them accepted them. My military escort came back and flipped out.

"GIVE ME THOSE PAMPHLETS NOW!"

I refused. He tried to grab them from me, but I turned and held them away.

"I am a civilian. You can't order me."

"I CAN HERE."

"No, you can't. You're violating my rights."

## The War is Over

"Your rights? Just wait until we induct you!" He went down the line, demanding that anyone who had taken a pamphlet from me give it back to him right now. I shouted that they didn't have to. But the few men who had taken the pamphlets all handed them back to him.

Then they ordered us inductees into a room. The uniformed man up front told us to all sit down and sign our loyalty oaths. I quickly spoke up and said that no one had to sign the DD-98 and DD-99 forms. It was not required by law.

"SIGN THEM!" he shouted. It looked like everyone but me signed.

Afterward he walked up to me and stuck his face into mine. "Just you wait until after you are inducted. You are *going to pay.*" Again, he looked like he would have preferred to shoot me on the spot. He ordered someone to stay with me at all times.

They told everyone to strip down to their underwear. When I pulled down my pants, they saw that I didn't have any underwear on.

"Leave your pants on!" some uniform shouted to me.

I saw long lines of semi-nude men, waiting to be processed. I remembered the photos I had seen when I visited Dachau Concentration Camp outside of Munich in 1965. When I finally reached the doctor at the front of the line, he searched for my medical records. He couldn't find them. He asked me if I knew anything about where my medical records were from my physical.

"I never had a physical."

"You can't be inducted without a physical. What are you doing here?"

"I don't know. Ask those two guys who brought me here."

I looked around for them, but I didn't see them.

"Go sit over there while we clear this up." The doctor pointed to a long bench where some guys were sitting. I sat next to them and offered them some reading material about the war. None of them wanted any of it.

A man in uniform told me to go into the room at the end of the hall. I walked in, and there was a man talking on the phone. He motioned for me to sit down. I did. I looked on the walls at his diplomas and certifications. He was a psychiatrist. I listened to him on the phone. He was honestly asking his broker whether he should buy or sell Xerox. The conversation continued for a while. Then, still holding the phone, he asked what I was here for. I told him I had no idea. He asked for my folder. I said that I didn't have any because I hadn't had any physical exam yet. He said that it wasn't possible to induct anyone without a physical.

"They brought me here."

# The Wild Years

He went back to his conversation. Then he looked up. "What do you think you're here for?"

"For resisting your bullshit war." Now I finally had his attention.

"I'll call you back." He put the phone down. "What did you say?"

"You heard it. You're just a pawn of the war machine. A well-enough paid one to being buying stocks while you should be working."

"You should watch what you say. You can get in trouble here real quick talking like that. What's wrong with you?"

"What's wrong with me? *What's wrong with you?* They pay you to justify what they're doing. Look at yourself."

"You are really showing anti-social tendencies."

That hit my final chord. "I am anti-social because ----" and I choked. I said something like "They had Nuremberg trials over doctors like you," and then my voice broke. I actually started crying, tears of rage. I figured that they would be locking me up for some reason or another real soon. I shouted at the shrink. He told me to sit down. I refused. He said I was out of control. I said this government and the military and he were all fucking out of control. The phone rang. He looked at it, then me. He answered it and began talking with his broker again.

I sat down and pulled out my handkerchief to wipe off my face. *Goddamn him, goddamn him, goddamn him. Goddamn me, for crying in front of this robot.* I listened and I could not believe that he could still continue his conversation about Xerox. I couldn't take any of it anymore. So I got up and walked out the door. Just like that. I did not look back. I had no idea where I was going, or what I was doing. I just wasn't staying in that room with him.

In the hallway, there was no one waiting for me. I kept walking until I got to the stairway. I went down to the first floor and walked past a few personnel, straight out the door. On the street I walked away fast. I glanced behind me, but saw no one following me. I headed to Kentucky Avenue and began hitchhiking back to Bloomington.

A few hours later, I got to my apartment. I packed my belongings into my VW van and drove it to a friend's home. I took off the plates so that they could not easily identify it. I told my friend what was up. He said I could crash at his place for a while. In the next few days I finished taking my final exams. Now I was done with school. I didn't go back to my apartment to get my mail. I figured they might be watching it. I had no idea that the Selective Service would eventually send my new draft classification to my parents' address. My dad had thrown me out of their home after he found out that I had been arrested in an anti-war demonstration. I respected his wishes, and would not be getting any of my mail.

I rounded up my last things and packed up my van. I was driving off to Vancouver, Canada. I wrote one last letter to the Selective Service Board. In it, I told them I had changed my name from Dwight to Adam, my address from 446 1/2 East 2nd Street, Bloomington, Indiana to Mountains, Streams and Forests, and my race from white to Indian.

I signed it, "Fuck You Paleface."

Then I headed off driving northwest to Canada. I never made it.

# Part 2

# On the Lam in the
# Land of Disenchantment

# 14

## How I Learned Mechanics

## The only known picture of Qaul

I left Bloomington, Indiana, in the winter of 1968 in my VW van on a slow trip to emigrate to British Columbia, Canada. I had decided not to fight in the Vietnam war, or go to prison. As I drove, my black Labrador retriever, Kingfish, sat upright in the passenger seat, intently watching for any animals. When I got tired driving at night, I pulled over and we slept in the back of the van.

On highway 70 in Kansas, we hit a massive blizzard just after sunset. Drifts quickly built up across the highway. I pulled off the pavement before I got stuck in the middle of the road. The temperature quickly dropped. I spread out my sleeping bag and Kingfish and I slept together. We appreciated each other's warmth. After a while, I noticed that there was no more traffic. The expressway was closed.

In the morning, all the windows of my van were frosted from our breath. I went to open the door, but the handle was frozen shut. I checked the other doors, but they were also frozen shut. I finally broke one loose by banging my shoulder hard into it while holding the handle open. I stepped into an alien world of blowing snow and gray rolling clouds. Snow drifts of up to three feet deep covered the expressway. I saw no other vehicles. Other than the power lines, I saw no evidence of human life.

I lit my double burner Coleman stove in the van and made a breakfast with hot tea while Kingfish gulped down his dog food. Then Kingfish hopped out and romped through the snow, running into it full speed with his lower jaw open, scooping up mouthfuls.

I melted snow and used the hot water to thaw out my other door locks. I scraped the windows and began digging out my van with a small folding army surplus shovel. I had just about finished the job when the first of the snowplows came along. It threw a wall of snow three feet high against my van, covering up all the shoveling I had done on that side. We weren't going anyplace soon.

Kingfish stayed outside the van and searched for wild animals in the snow. He seemed content to live along side this expressway forever, someplace west of Topeka, Kansas. I turned on the AM radio and listened to the weather reports. This highway would be closed for another day. That meant more cheese sandwiches, frozen apples, and tea. But if the Feds were looking for me, they would now need snowshoes. I put on my snow gators, then Kingfish and I took a long walk across the adjoining field. I read the fresh tracks of the animals. We followed them to a small stream that was still flowing under the snow. Mice, rabbits, and maybe a fox had all come here earlier today.

We returned to the van. I began digging out my van again with the shovel. I heard the rumble of the snowplow before I saw it. Another snowplow approached, with snow flying six feet high to the side. It threw a wall of snow against my van again. This time I just kept digging.

At sunrise the next day, I turned on the radio to find that highway 70 was now partially open. I dug around the van some more until I could see pavement around all my wheels. Then I started up the small air-cooled engine. I let it warm a bit, but it still blew no significant heat over the windshield. I put it in gear and rocked it back and forth until I broke loose the frozen brake drums. Then I gunned it and got back on the highway.

I drove slowly down the middle of the lane. No matter how I scraped the frost off the inside of the windshield, I still could not see out of it. So I put my ski mask on and rolled down the window. I leaned out to see down the highway. As far as I could see, I was the only vehicle on the highway.

In time, the heater melted small holes of visibility through the windshield frost. I pulled my head inside and drove faster. Finally I could

# How I Learned Mechanics

see. I passed disabled vehicles on both sides of the expressway. All of them were blocked with a wall of snow left by the snow plows. I had highway 70 all to myself.

Far ahead, I cautiously pulled into a truck stop. I stuffed my ponytail under my stocking cap before I entered. Then I had a hot, heavy breakfast along with coffee, coffee, and more coffee. All the truckers inside were waiting for the highway west of here to be cleared better before they departed. When I told them I was going to Colorado, they said I was crazy. The roads out west were still closed. I studied my maps. I decided that rather than wait a few days for the roads to clear, I would drive south to highway 40. It was not closed.

I plodded southward across icy roads in southwest Kansas, chugging along at maybe 35 mph. I was living on cheese sandwiches and fruit, while my dog Kingfish was content to eat the same dog food day after day. Late in the evening I pulled off the highway in western Oklahoma and carefully parked in a field of wheat stubble. I wanted to stretch out, so I laid out a tarp and rolled my sleeping bag on one side of it. Then I pulled the other side of the tarp over my bag. That would have to do. Kingfish crawled under the tarp and lay against me. After a few minutes, I was no longer shivering from the cold.

Later in the night it began to snow again. This time it was not the blizzard winds, but heavy, soft flakes. Still later, I heard a scratching sound on top of the tarp. Some small rodent was scurrying across the tarp above me. Instantly Kingfish bolted out of the tarp. I heard a squeal, and then the crunch of small bones. Kingfish then lay on the tarp above me and proceeded to eat whatever he had killed. After he was done, he nosed his way back under the tarp.

At sunrise I forced myself out of the warm bag. I shook another half foot of snow off the tarp and pulled up my pants. Cold. I saw no remains of whatever it was that Kingfish had eaten the night before.

The country road was coated with a glaze of packed snow. I drove at 25 miles per hour now."Don't go into a ditch," I told myself. At the highway 40 junction, I tanked up on gas, a hot breakfast, and coffee. While I was eating, a dark-complected young man came up to my table. He introduced himself as Maestos. He had a long, pointed mustache. He asked me what direction I was going. When I told him 'west' he asked if he could ride along. He was headed for Albuquerque, where he had grown up. I said yeah, and he grabbed his army duffel sack.

"What's your name?"

"Adam," I answered. That was one of the aliases I was using then. Now I would have to stick with it.

I finally hit better roads. The high New Mexico plains opened up with bright and clear. Far in the distance I saw the beginning of mountains. Maestos said he had just gotten out of prison in Oklahoma. Fourteen months for selling a few ounces of marijuana. He said he had just been back from Vietnam less then three months before he got busted.

"Ain't that the shits. I go and fight for them, then come back, and they throw me in prison." He shook his head. "You been to the Nam yet?"

"No."

"How come not? All my buddies been drafted."

"I'm going to Canada." The moment I said it, I regretted it. Too much information. Keep your mouth shut.

"Oh yeah. Some of yous can do that. But we can't."

Maestos said we should head for Taos instead. He had old friends there, and it was a really beautiful place. I had time to spare and it was more northerly. It wasn't like anyone in the world was waiting for me anyplace. So I veered to the northwest, through the austere high desert via Santa Fe, and then along the Rio Grande Gorge, climbing up to Taos.

In Taos, I pulled into a cafe. It just so turned out that a party was going on inside. Maestos came in with me. He stood alone in the corner and did not speak with anyone. He was the only Chicano in the room. He told me he wanted to walk down the road and see if he could find his old friends. He said he would be back in a bit. I told him I would stay here. He grabbed his duffel sack.

"I'll be back, man," he waved. "Thanks."

I never saw him again.

I was enjoying the party with friendly strangers. I stayed up late, and then crashed in my van again. I thought maybe I would stretch out my journey to Canada for a little while here in New Mexico. Those few days eventually became five years. I never made it to Canada.

Young people began arriving in northern New Mexico in the late 1960's. They staggered in from all over, without much direction, for many different reasons. The law, riots in the cities, personal visions of the apocalypse, deserting the military, serious drug problems, Indian and spiritual visions. They were refugees from a world that seemed to be going insane. Or maybe they were projecting their own insanities onto it.

# How I Learned Mechanics

I got to Taos with my great traveling partner, Kingfish, some mushrooms, and no money at all. It turned out that this would have to be enough. I heard of a room for rent nearby and checked it out. The landlord of sorts was Qaul. He described himself as an 'astral mechanic'. I guessed that he was about fifteen years older than me. Qaul stood over six and a half feet tall and had a three-foot long black ponytail trailing behind him. That was long hair, even for 1968. He stared intently at me when we spoke. I was not comfortable with that. Yet I felt I had to maintain eye contact with him.

Qaul introduced me to his wife, Zuannu. She was a beautiful red-headed lady with a ponytail even longer than Qaul's. They had a blond son, Dort, about four years old, who had a ponytail about a foot long.

"Where did you get your names?" I asked. "They're kind of strange."

Qaul grabbed me by the shoulders and turned me toward him, face to face. He silently stared into my eyes for all too long. Finally he stated solemnly, "We were given our names from the astral plane. We consulted with the spirits."

"Ohhhhh?" I nodded, waiting for him to let go of me.

Qaul showed me around the large adobe ranch compound they had rented outside of Ranchos De Taos. Surrounding all the buildings was a wall made of both adobe and stone. The main home had at least ten rooms. There were several out buildings, one of which held a great tool shop. Along one of the walls, Qaul had a large assembly of welding and metal-working gear. In the middle of an adjoining room was a large, oval-shaped frame, welded out of stainless steel.

"What's that?"

"We're building a space ship. We should have it done in a year or so."

"Uh huh."

"I have an extra room here, Adam. It's $35 a month rent. But you can work it off. You would be my apprentice. You'll have to work hard and learn quick. You want it?"

"Sure. But I don't have any money now."

"No problem. I accept mushrooms as currency."

How did he *know* that?

I followed Qaul around his shop. He had a problem. He could not figure out why the alternator he had installed was not charging the battery on this truck he was working on. All the individual components tested out fine. Qaul could find no shorts in the wiring. Yet the battery would not charge. Qaul muttered something, and then he began talking out loud to himself. He described the problem, inhaled on a joint, and then he shouted out, *"Now why the fuck would it ever do that?"* Then Qaul listed the potential reasons. He turned to me.

"I bet the engine is not completely grounded to the frame and chassis! Even though it looks like it is."

If he wanted my agreement, I was clueless. Qaul began installing grounding straps at a furious pace. A bit later he started the truck up and got out one of his meters.

"That's it! It's charging now." Qaul got out another joint. I asked him where he learned all of this. He was evasive.

"It's just *obvious* --- if you open your eyes and mind."

Then Qaul took a three pound steel mallet and **smashed** it full force onto the metal work table right next to me. I jumped back as boom echoed in the work shop.

"JUST PAY ATTENTION!" he stared down at me as I gathered up my nerves. Then he took his long Ichabod-Crane finger and stuck it to my heart. "Because *you have been chosen.*"

I stood there, flustered.

"Now let's go on to the next problem," he gleamed.

And thus began my apprenticeship under Qaul.

Under Qaul's tutelage, I learned how to grind valves, hone and bore out cylinders, press valve guides, measure crankshafts, torque engines to factory tolerances, rebuild clutches, brakes, front ends, and trace electrical shorts. I watched Qaul rewind electric motors, test voltage regulators, measure front-end alignments. Sometimes he even pulled out a slide rule.

For all of Qaul's assertiveness, I discovered that he and his family were completely committed to non-violence. No serious arguing, fighting, or weapons of any kind. They seemed to resolve everything with reason, humor, or just a twinkle in their eyes. And Qaul and Zuannu seemed to attract these kinds of people around them. Interesting folks were always coming by. I was living in the midst of a gentle, non-stop work-party.

About every week Qaul bought some broken down vehicle, usually from some itinerant California hippie whose knowledge of cars included turning the motor on, putting gas in, and nothing else. Fifty-dollar Volkswagens, one-hundred-dollar trucks, one-hundred-and-fifty-dollar jeeps. Then we would take two dead vehicles and combine them into one good, working vehicle. We dragged the carcass of the donor vehicle into the sagebrush field behind the compound. The place was quickly becoming a junkyard. "Parts inventory," Qaul preferred to call it. Sometimes Qaul

# How I Learned Mechanics

resold the working vehicle at a hefty profit. But other times, he sold cars cheap, or gave his labor away. Once I saw him donate a car away to a family in need. He adjusted his price to their ability to pay.

One day Qaul welded a mechanical engine hoist. He said that this time he would use the Archimedes principle. The business end of the hoist had all the normal chains to hook onto an engine block. In the middle was the fulcrum. But the other end had a twelve foot long, heavy iron bar with a steel plate welded to the end. Attached to the plate was an improvised rope ladder.

First, Qaul and I disconnected the engine from the vehicle. Then we wrapped the chains around it. Qaul told me to slowly climb up the rope ladder to the plate. I did. Qaul shouted for me to stop climbing, then start again, then stop. Slowly my weight brought the plate down. And in teeter-totter fashion, the engine on the other end slowly lifted out of the car and dangled in the air.

"EUREKA!" Qaul smiled through his greasy beard and windblown hair.

But the engine just dangled there. We had no way to turn the hoist to the side. Qaul mentioned that he had not thought about that. If I got off the plate, the engine would come crashing back into the car.

"Adam, we are going to rebuild the engine right here as it hangs. So I'll need you to stay on that plate for a few days while we work on it. I guess you'll just have to be some sort of industrial paperweight. Don't worry. We'll feed you."

??? as I stood on the plate.

Then Qaul shouted "But sometimes you must *move* the world." He had a mad look on his face as he leaned forward against the car. "But other times, you must just push the car." Qaul rolled the car out from under the dangling engine. Then Qaul pulled a small wagon under the engine. I slowly climbed down the ladder and we eased the engine into the wagon. Qaul stepped back from the engine hoist and studied it. "Tomorrow we will build a pivot for it, so we can turn it, and a counterbalance, so you won't have to stay up there for weeks."

One day a guy brought in his VW van to our shop. He told Qaul that it was losing power. Qaul walked around the van and examined it in detail. The van had the weirdest vertical stripes painted on it, like a rainbow of asymmetric jail bars. Just what had they been smoking when they painted it anyhow?

Qaul studied it intently. Then he turned to the van's owner.

"Those vertical stripes are causing *psychic resistance,*" Qaul announced. *"First, you will have to repaint it."*

The guy scratched his head, and handed the joint back to Qaul. He mumbled that he hadn't thought about that. Then he drove off.

A few weeks later, the guy pulled his van back into our shop to show us his new paint job. All the rainbow stripes were horizontal now. "It runs way faster," he yelled over the motor to Qaul. Qaul nodded knowingly.

So, under the guidance of Qaul, mushrooms, and peyote cactus, I learned mechanics and lived magic. We rebuilt and fixed everything we could, and took very zonked pride in our good work. At the end of the day, we washed the grease and filth from us and ate another one of Zuannu's delicious macrobiotic meals. It may very well have been bird food, but let me tell you, it was damned good bird food at that.

Then one spring, after a winter of shop and cabin fever, I left Taos for a while to visit some Indian ruins and national parks. I fully intended to come back directly. But I got waylaid on the trip by vehicle problems and a lovely siren. When I returned months later, I discovered that Qaul and Zuannu were gone. Others told me that some drunken locals had come by, threatened them, and shot some guns off. Then Qaul and Zuannu just disappeared, leaving many of their possessions behind.

I walked around the old compound. There were bullet holes through the main door. A few windows had been shot out. The few boxes of my gear in my old bedroom were gone. Whatever possessions Qaul and Zuannu had not taken with them had been looted by the locals. Even the space ship frame was gone. The only things that remained were the junk cars in the field behind – and my memories. Qaul did not leave a note or a message for me. Nothing.

No one seemed to know what had become of them. Some said that they went to back to California, or Puerto Rico. There was an unconfirmed story about them living on a spiritual commune in South America. And then, there was always the spaceship...

# 15

## Kingfish Loves Daisy

### Brave, Brave Kingfish

They rode into the Llano Quemado Hot Springs in Taos, New Mexico, with their Harleys roaring. My Nubian goats went running up the hillside. The colors on the backs of their vests said:

BROTHERS FAST
DENVER

There must have been twenty-five of them, all dudes, all dressed in levis and black leathers. Following up the rear were some guys driving a large stake bed truck. On the back of the truck were a number of broken-down Harley-Davidsons. I walked around the truck. It had a bumper sticker on the back that said

BIKERS HAVE MORE FUN THAN PEOPLE

A really big guy got off his Harley and walked up to me. He had a beer, a beard, boots, and a belly. BBBB. On the front of his vest the word

CRASH was embroidered. He pointed to CRASH. "That's my name." He handed me a beer. I opened it and it exploded in my face. We laughed.

"You in charge here?"

"I guess so. As much as anyone."

"You own this place?"

"We're buying now. We got a lease with an option to buy. We're raising the money now."

"Mind if we camp out here for the night? We'll clean up when we leave."

I nodded. Like I was going to throw all of them out anyhow. He walked over to his buddies. They pulled some coolers of beer from the truck and began drinking and wandering around. Beer went down fast in the hot dry air of the New Mexico mountains.

I heard some bikers shouting from the top swimming pool. There was some shoving going on until one of them fell in. "GODDAMNIT I HURT MY LEG! CUT IT OUT!" someone yelled. "I CAN'T SWIM EITHER!"

"HA HA HA. If you drown, I get your bike."

The wet one made it over to the side of the pool and got out. He threw a beer can at the guy who'd pushed him in. It splattered. "HEY! THAT WAS GOOD FUCKIN' BEER. NEXT TIME THROW AN EMPTY."

The wet guy pulled up the leg of his pants. Blood was running down his calf. Another guy came walking over to me. He was tall and had three gold and diamond ear rings in his left ear, a black leather vest, and a black handlebar mustache. He tied his black hair back with a bandanna.

"You got a first aid kit here?"

I nodded.

"What's your name?"

"The Indians call me Horsetail."

"What? What Indians? What you talkin' about?"

"The Taos Pueblo Indians."

"So what's your real name?"

"Leave it at that."

He looked at my hair. "I see why they call you Horsetail with that ponytail. You hiding out from the law or something? Don't want to use your real name?"

"So what's your name then?" I asked him. He pointed to his forearm. On it was a tattooed PIRATE.

"That makes it real easy for the law," I said.

We walked over to my home. It was an abandoned building next to the hot springs. I had put windows and doors in, plugged up all the holes with mud, put in a floor and built a fireplace. I had dug a small ditch from the hot springs that flowed past my front door step. So I had hot water year round.

"Kind of a nice place you got up here, all alone and all. But what the hell you do here for action?"

"People come here all the time. You want action, you just wait. They come. Like today."

I got out my medical suitcase and looked over the cut. It was nasty. My dog Kingfish tried to lick the blood, but Pirate smacked him before he could do it. Kingfish went running. I got out my suture kit.

"Hey. What you doin'? You a fuckin' doctor or what?" the biker with the cut said.

"You want stitches or not? You could use a few."

"Naw. Fuck those stitches. Just bandage it and stop the bleeding."

There was a loud knock at my door. Big Crash came in. "Hey man, we're running out of beer. We sent the truck in to get some, but every place was either closed or sold out. We can't have a Saturday night without beer."

"Yeah," Pirate said. He looked at me. "You got any cold beer? We'll pay you for it."

"No. I don't have electricity here to keep it cold."

"What kind of fuckin' place is this?" Crash yelled. "No beer – no electricity. And you? You got a job? What you do? Just live up here --- fucking your goats? Where can we get beer?"

"The Indians and Chicanos probably bought the stores out for the weekend. Happens all the time. You'll have to go over the mountains to Mora --- no, they'd be sold out too. Down to Espanola. But that's fifty miles away."

"FUCK! No beer, and the sun hasn't even gone down." Crash hit his fist on the table. "What do you do for women? Or do you just `hang out' like the rest of the hippies?"

"I'm a part-time ambulance driver."

"You?"

"I'm a certified EMT."

"Ease off," Pirate said. "He's on the lam from something."

"Oh?" Crash's face lit up. "Tell me, what'd you do? As long as it ain't child molestin', I don't care. Come on, what is it?"

I knew not to say anything.

"Come on. Tell me. Most of us are outlaws too." Crash unsnapped his

# The Wild Years

vest. "Here, look." His chest was covered with homemade blue tattoos. In the middle of his chest was a naked girl with blue-inked pussy hair. The name BOBBIE JO was crossed out below it. A dragon came out from under his arm, and MOTHER was on his shoulder. "I did two years for stealing cars for a chop shop. Half the guys here got rap sheets. What you runnin' from?" Crash pulled out a joint and lit it. He handed it to me. It was sweet and strong.

"I dropped out. Came out here. I'd been taking a lot of acid."

"How come they ain't drafted you for the Nam then?" Crash asked. I didn't answer him. "So you got busted for dope?"

"No. I just left. I don't know if they drafted me or not. I haven't checked my mail in a year."

Crash stuck his face into mine. "So you a *fuckin' deserting traitor*?"

"What about you then?"

He shut up for a bit. Then he said, "They wouldn't take me, with my police record and all. Said I was a bad apple. We're all bad apples here." Crash looked around my place. "You sure don't mind livin' primitive, do you? And you take that LSD stuff too, huh? I hear you get way out there on that shit. Makes you go real crazy. I'd never take any."

"I've taken it," Pirate said. "It ain't that bad. It can be far out man."

"No shit?" Crash looked at Pirate. "So you a fuckin' hippie too. What's it like?"

"You get way out there. Way farther than grass. It's intense--not like speed at all. I don't know if you could handle it, Crash."

"Bullshit. I can handle *anything*." Crash looked at Pirate. "So the President of The Brothers Fast is some acid-tripping hippie. Well, peace and love and *fuck you*." Crash put up the 'V' sign with a happy-face grin. Then he dropped his index finger. He turned to me. "Hey Horse ass, you got any of this here acid with you?"

"No. But a guy camping up the gorge in a tepee has some."

"*A tepee*. A real fucking tepee? You guys are getting fuckin' weirder by the minute, man. Go get us enough LSD to get everyone here high. The Brothers Fast are going to blow their minds tonight." He counted out fifty dollars for me. "Get going."

I stood there with fifty dollars in my hand, a bit dazed.

"GET GOING."

I hiked up the gorge to the tepee man and bought fifty dollars worth of LSD. When I got back, they had a fire going. In the distance I could see the Rio Grande Gorge and the mountains far away. I knew why I was living here.

I gave Crash a baggy full of blue tablets. He showed them to Pirate. "*Is this it?*" he asked. "I paid fifty dollars for this piss-ant little bag of pills? I think we been robbed. It better be good, or it's your ass --"

"You got no way of telling til you take one," Pirate said.

"You mean it could be shit? Or poison?" Crash looked at me. "Then you're takin' the first one, motherfucker." He handed me a tab. I looked at Crash glaring at me. I had had no plans on tripping tonight. What was I getting myself into?

"Well?" he barked.

I swallowed it.

"What you feel?" He asked me.

"It takes a while. You have to wait."

Pirate reached in and took one. So did Crash. "It'd better be good."

Crash shouted for all the bikers to come over to him. They were mostly younger than Pirate and Crash. Crash told them that they were all going to drop acid today. They'd love it. No big thing. Pirate knows all about it. In a minute, they'd all dropped. There were a few tabs left over.

My dog Kingfish came running over to me. He was carrying a young jackrabbit he had just caught. He tossed it up in the air and then jumped on it again and again. When I tried to take it from him, he danced away from me, teasing me with it. He always did that whenever he killed an animal. When Kingfish rode in the back of my pickup truck and saw a wild animal, he made flying leaps out of the truck at them. Lots of time he'd land right on them with his air attacks and kill them. He was part black Labrador retriever and part something else very wild. I'd had him for five years. He was the most consistent thing in my life. I didn't tie him up or even put a collar on him and I would not have thought to have him neutered. When I went to town, he always waited outside for me. Somehow, he never got lost. I swear he could follow my scent through the sidewalks. And if I couldn't find him in Taos, I'd just drive back to the hot springs. It was ten miles away and he always found his way back within a few hours.

Kingfish flung the jackrabbit in front of Crash and jumped on it again. The bikers were laughing at his antics. "Hey," Crash shouted, "What's your dog's name?"

"Kingfish."

"A black Kingfish. That's a good name for him. Hey Kingfish, where's Sapphire? This dog knows how to feed himself. He knows you can't depend on no fuckin' hippie for food or beer or anything else. Hell, he probably

# The Wild Years

brought back this rabbit just so Horse-ass can eat tonight." More ha ha ha's. "Why I betcha Horse-ass never even turns Kingfish on to dope. Ain't that a bitch, Horse-ass? Dog brings you food but you don't even give him dope."

"I gave him acid once before."

"*No shit.* What did he do?" Crash got out the plastic bag of LSD.

"No. You don't want to give him any."

"Hey man. It's my motherfuckin' LSD. I bought it. I can give it to anyone I want. *To anything.* Hey Kingfish, come here." Crash held his hand out with a blue pill in the center of it. "Come here and take this."

"No Crash. Don't."

Kingfish looked at Crash with his soft golden eyes. His ears dropped. Crash held his hand out like he had food in it. Kingfish sniffed Crash. One lick of his tongue, and the blue tab of LSD disappeared.

The bikers whooped it up. "THAT'S MY KIND OF DOG!" Crash shouted. "A HUNTIN' KILLIN' DRUGGIE! IF HE DRINKS BEER AND RIDES A MOTORCYCLE, I'LL MARRY HIM MYSELF!"

I had some things I had to do before --- *before I came on.* I busied myself with some chores until I started having trouble remembering how to do them --- until I couldn't remember what the chores were anyhow.

Crash came swaggering up to me. "Huh?" He put his face into mine. Acne poxs underneath his beard, gaps between his yellow teeth. *Dog breath.* "What you say?"

"I didn't say anything."

"Yes you did. Someone did." Crash turned around to the other bikers. "Who said that? Who's sayin' that?" None of them answered. He started asking all of them questions, but all he got back was laughter. When he told them to shut up so he could think, they laughed all the more. Then Crash looked around at everybody and nobody. His eyes were big and empty. He held his arms out like he was getting ready to tackle somebody.

"SOMEBODY'S SAYIN' THAT! I HEAR IT."

The other bikers just kept laughing. "You look like a mad dog hippie," one of them said. Then that guy got on his hands and knees and began barking like a dog. The other bikers fell over. I heard some splashes. Up above, some other bikers were going for a swim with their clothes on. Crash was yelling for everybody to come here *right now,* that he loved all his brothers and he had something important to say and nobody could go swimming. But nobody paid Crash any attention. There was screaming from the pool above that sounded like drunk hippos humping in heat. One of the bikers was grabbing another's ass, saying what they were going to do to their sweeties later tonight. "LIKE SHIT YOU ARE." They kept pinching each other and saying that again and again. Way more than I ever saw in any locker room. Another one of the bikers who was all wet from the hot springs stood behind the guy who was on his hands and knees barking. Then he got down on top of him and mounted him like a dog. A few pelvic thrusts and loud grunts and they were both rolling in the mud. Then the rest of the bikers were all falling down, flopping in the dirt and grass and rocks and mud, holding their guts and faces, choking for breath, laughing. One of them who was laying on his back started puking up some beer. He just kept laying there laughing between pukes.

Another one said he'd been laughing so hard he'd pissed his pants. Pirate shouted, "NO FUCKIN' BED WETTERS IN THE BROTHERS FAST, MAN. You're out, motherfucker. OUT!" They guffawed some more.

Pirate stood off to the side, grinning. He had taken off his thick leather belt and was busy working bits of broken windshield glass into it. The pieces were fitting in tight and glowed in the sunset whenever he moved. He saw me watching him work and he walked over. "This is good acid, man. Turning out better than I thought," he said with a distant smile. Then he pinched my cheek. "I sort of like you--kid."

One of the bikers got on his bike and tried kick-starting it.

"YOU WON'T BE ABLE TO DRIVE IT NOW!"

"SHIT I CAN'T!" He kept kicking it, but it didn't start. "YOU CAN'T EVEN START YOUR FUCKIN' BIKE!" they were shouting. Others got on their bikes, but all of them were having problems kick-starting them. They were laughing and falling over and shouting at the others. Somebody grabbed me and spun me around. It was Crash. He had dirt and spit all over his face. His mouth was moving up and down, but no words were coming out. Then sounds were coming out but his mouth wasn't moving. He was squeezing my arms hard. "WHAT THE FUCK YOU DO TO OUR BIKES!" He shook me. "OUR BIKES DON'T RUN NO MORE!"

Just then a motor revved up. A fat biker straddled his bike. It was a beautiful brand new red Norton, about the only bike here that wasn't a Harley. He revved the engine full blast. Everyone was looking at him. Then he popped the clutch raw. Dirt and gravel flew all over and the front end lunged up. The biker was only holding on by the handle bars when the bike ran over the leg of another biker who was laying on the dirt. He screamed. The Norton flipped back over and then onto its side. It spun around in a circle, its rear wheel spinning in the air, the engine screaming. The bikers all laid there laughing, except for the guy who was shouting about his leg.

# The Wild Years

Crash came at me with his arms out. I started walking backward. "NOW YOU WRECKIN' OUR BIKES! YOU MADE THAT HAPPEN, DIDN'T YOU? YOU'RE TAKIN' OVER OUR MINDS!" Pirate stepped in and grabbed Crash. He had finished his belt and had it on. It reflected rainbows. His diamond earrings were flashing in the sunset, his eyes as big as Crash's. "Hey man, cool it. Everything's okay." Crash stopped for a minute, panting and shaking. "Besides," Pirate said. "I like Horseass." Then Pirate reached over for me. I walked away from them.

Crash was nodding. He shouted, "HEY GUYS, IT'S SO BEAUTIFUL HERE. WE'RE GONNA LIVE HERE FOREVER. THIS IS IT, MAN. THE PROMISED LAND. WE AIN'T GOIN' NO PLACE."

"YEAH!" Some of the other bikers shouted.

Then the bikers began moving into my cabin. They were lying on my bed and floor, eating whatever they could find and still looking for booze. They figured I had it hid someplace. I lit a few kerosene lamps and pulled out some loaves of bread and a few pounds of goats cheese. It was all gone in five minutes. "Gimme more a that cheese!" Crash shouted.

"That's all I got till I milk my goats again and make some more."

"Well, go milk your fuckin' goats! I'm hungry. Starved like that motherfuckin' dog a yours. Go milk 'em!" Crash herded me out the door of my own home.

Outside, I saw a pickup truck pulling up to the hot springs. It was filled with Chicanos. They had open beers with them. They had come to drink and watch naked hippie chicks swimming in the pools. They never swam themselves. But this time when they parked their truck, some bikers ran straight up to them. The Chicanos did not get out. "Give us some beer," one of the bikers grunted. He reached in and pulled out a six-pack. The other bikers got a case and pulled it out. The Chicanos sat there without saying a word. They left the engine running. "Is that all?" another biker shouted. "Look, we'll let you swim here if you get us some more beer."

The Chicanos looked at each other, then the bikers. They were used to bullying and robbing the hippies at the hot springs. They even tried to rape a hippie girl a few weeks ago. But they hadn't ever dealt with a gang of bikers before. And now the bikers were opening the doors to *their* truck, searching them for any more hidden beer.

I knew the Chicanos had guns with them. They always did. But the bikers didn't look like pacifists either. The Chicanos let the bikers do what the bikers wanted. They just sat frozen still in their truck, watching these 250-pounders guzzling their beer, revving the motorcycles, popping

# Kingfish Loves Daisy

wheelies, and roaring around and hooting it up. Then Pirate came over and gave the Chicanos some money. "Thanks for the beer," he said. "We couldn't find any in town. Nice of you guys to bring us some."

"Yeah," said Crash. "Go get us some more, and we'll let you come back. We need smokes too." Crash reached into the driver's shirt pocket and pulled out a pack of cigarettes. "Thanks."

De-beered, the Chicanos had lost their reason for coming out to the hot springs. They backed their truck out slowly. Not a word from any of them.

In a few minutes, the bikers had guzzled all their beer. "When will they be back with more beer?" Crash yelled at me. "*When?*" He grabbed me.

"Well, I never seen them get their beer lifted like that. One time they came up here with guns to drive the hippies out of the hot springs. They shot my buddy Luke in the neck."

"*WHAT?*" Crash said slowly. "HEY EVERYBODY--LISTEN TO THIS. THEY'LL BE BACK WITH GUNS! EVERYBODY GET YOUR PIECES OUT. THEY'LL BE COMING!"

The bikers ran to their bikes and to the big truck and started searching into their stashes. They dug around until they found what they were looking for. Then Crash started telling them where to set up. I was telling Crash that they only shot their guns at the hot springs once --- that someone else could come driving around the corner, but no matter. They had their lines drawn in stoned-ass military fashion. Next vehicle pulling into the hot springs was getting blown away.

They waited and waited in the darkness, but nobody came. Then someone managed to light a few Coleman lanterns. Crash shouted that he was hungry again. He looked to me. "Hey, where's that goat cheese you said you were going to get me?" He pointed over to the stream where Daisy was grazing. "WE'LL EAT THAT FUCKIN' GOAT, MAN!" Crash shouted. "And where's my man, Kingfish?" Crash started whistling until Kingfish came running out of the bushes. In the gaslight everyone could see that his eyes were big, his tongue was hanging out, and he had slobber on his face. *Mad dog.* Kingfish came up to Crash. Crash grabbed Kingfish and began throwing him around. Kingfish loved playing rough, and soon he and Crash were at it. They seemed to hit it off in a strange way. Two wild ones. Crash bear-hugged Kingfish, and Kingfish started flea-biting Crash's beard. Crash was laughing, trying to push him away, but Kingfish kept coming back, licking his face and flea-biting him hard. Crash barked at Kingfish, and Kingfish barked back. Crash laughed some more, and then more flea-bites from Kingfish. Kingfish would not lay off Crash. Eighty pounds of dog determined to chew on Crash.

Then it happened, just like on Kingfish's only other acid trip. Out came his pink hard-on dick and he began humping Crash's leg. That's all Kingfish had wanted to do on the first acid trip too. Kingfish had his front paws hooked hard around Crash's thigh in dog-love embrace and he wouldn't let go. The other bikers were crying and rolling on the ground again, shouting for Crash to just bend over and take it up the ass like a bitch --- that Kingfish knows a good bitch when he sees one --- that they were made for each other. The the others bikers started calling Crash 'Sapphire'. Crash was pushing Kingfish away, trying to pry Kingfish's legs off. But Kingfish did not budge. Crash shouted and began smacking Kingfish on his head, but no matter. Kingfish was determined to hump Crash's leg *good*. When Crash finally broke Kingfish's grip, he sat down winded. Kingfish came right back up to Crash, mounted his leg, and started humping him again. Kingfish had worn Crash down and just wouldn't take NO for an answer. Each time Kingfish mounted Crash's leg, the bikers laughed harder than before. Crash was getting just too tired to defend himself. Kingfish had this waggle-assed, delirious look on his face, tongue out, mouth panting, eyes wide-open. He started looking more and more like the bikers. His hips were moving like one out-of-control piston. Finally, Crash rolled over and shook Kingfish off. He got up and staggered over to a motorcycle and sat on it. Kingfish jumped around him for a while, trying to get a good angle on him. The bikers were yelling about Crash being frigid and on-the-rag and just a plain-old bad fuck and a no-good fat-assed bitch to boot nohow. Crash was laughing and the bike was wobbling from Kingfish trying to hump him.

Some biker shouted "GODDAMN IT I JUST PISSED MY PANTS TOO!"

Pirate shouted "WHAT THE FUCK KIND OF MOTORCYCLE GANG WE GOT HERE? THE BADDEST BEDWETTERS IN THE WEST! THE BEDWETTERS FAST?"

Then Kingfish came back to the fire and looked all around. A strange silence sat in. "*You get away from me*," one biker whispered. ""Me too," another said. "You go fuck your old lady Sapphire." Kingfish was panting hard with his tongue hanging out and his pink dick waggling.

Then Kingfish did it. He ran up to Daisy the goat, hopped up, *and began humping her.* She spun around and butted him, but as soon as she turned around, Kingfish got right back on her again and start humping away. It went on and on, the humping and the butting, the butting and the humping. Kingfish just wouldn't stop. The bikers were rolling over on the ground like dying snakes. Finally Daisy couldn't take it anymore and she just went running up the hill into the sagebrush and pinyon trees.

Crash caught his breath from laughing, then he came running up to Kingfish with a piece of rope. He grabbed Kingfish and tied it around him while Kingfish was humping at his leg. "THIS IS OUR MASCOT! ANY DOG THAT GROSS HAS GOTTA BE OUR MASCOT!" All the bikers cheered. Before I could say anything, Crash stuffed something into my pocket. "Here's a hundred bucks. We're even."

"Hey, don't tie him up. He's never had a rope on him in his life." I handed back the money. Crash pushed my hand away. "Kid, we're takin' him *with or without* the money. Let's see you stop all of us."

I jumped in front of him. "You can't take Kingfish away."

Kingfish was leaping away from Crash, choking himself on the rope. Crash looked at me. "I'll take the rope off as soon as we get back to Denver. Then he'll run free with us. Hey man, I never seen such a beautiful dog. Big and wild, hunts for himself, gets high with you, fucks anything that walks, is crazy as they come. *I love this dog!*"

Crash tied Kingfish to the truck. Kingfish was leaping against the rope and barking. Crash petted him and said everything would be okay. Then he returned to the fire. I followed him. The fire was going out. Crash began talking to the fire. He said he was going to take acid every day for the rest of his life and live here forever. Just him and Kingfish and his Harley.

The bikers were passing out where they lay. Twisted in any position like pushed over statues that snored. Their faces looked like fossils, their bodies bent like the roots of old trees. These were not the lost boys.

Crash and I were the only ones up. I waited. He was talking to the fire calm and steady now, like he was preaching. I looked up. The full moon was in the west, in Scorpio. Good for night vision. In a few hours it would be getting light. Then the Sunday morning bathers would arrive at the hot springs and find all the bikers laying around like dead dinosaurs.

I waited until Crash leaned against a tree stump and started to snore. Big sloppy blubbers of a pig rooting in the mud. I crept over to him and stuffed the money in his vest pocket. Then I went over to the truck. When Kingfish saw me, he began whining and jumped all over me. I pulled out my hunting knife and cut the rope. He jumped straight into the air and banged his head hard into mine. He licked my face. I started heading up the mountainside to a shallow cave I knew. I stepped around the truck and bumped straight into Crash. He grabbed me.

"So you thought I was sleepin'?" he yelled.

# The Wild Years

I pulled my arms away from him, but he had me. We started wrestling around. Then Kingfish jumped in and bit Crash's leg. He was fighting Crash like Crash was a dog, growling and shaking his head. Crash screamed and let go of me. I jumped back and whistled Kingfish off. Crash held his leg.

"I'm goin' up the hill with Kingfish, Crash. I left your money in your vest pocket."

Crash stood there shaking his head. "He even fights for you, without even telling him to. Man, what a dog." I kept hiking up the trail to the ridge. "Hey, kid," I heard Crash yell. "You woke me up when you stuffed the money in my vest. I like that."

Kingfish led me on the trail, bounding ahead and coming back again. He was game for hunting any time. We climbed to where the gravel turned to rocks, and then the rocks to boulders. I got to the overhang where I had camped out before. I had found ashes here a foot deep, filled with arrowhead chippings and animal bones here from the ancient ones. From this point I could see beyond the Rio Grande Gorge. The whole hot springs were below me, sending mist across the high desert. From here I had seen mule deer come to the hot springs to drink. I thought of Indians lying under this rock in the wintertime. From here the world was mine.

It was a cool night. I laid down on the dirt and whistled for Kingfish. He laid down next to me. I curled around him for warmth. We slept.

# 16

## We Are All One Body

Buffalo came back to our cabin in the late morning. He had been out all night, again. He handed a smoking joint to me.

"You won't believe the new commune that's come to town," he breathed out a cloud of smoke. "They call themselves the New Family."

"Another commune? That's all Taos needs. And from California I suppose again?"

He nodded and we puffed.

"But this one is different. They're ain't a 'back to the land' one with a bunch of farming shit and hard work. And they don't do all that astrology and tarot card bullshit either. They say they're all about making world peace. They believe the Beatles are real prophets."

"Yeah. All the communes say they're about love. Big deal."

"No. Listen. They say they're gonna make world peace by *using* love."

"Big fucking deal. They all say that too."

"No. I mean, *by sex*. They believe that by having sex with everyone and teaching them about the power of love, they can change the world. I just stayed there last night, and I found out first hand what they mean. They have this big group sleeping room. And this girl April just comes and leads me into the room and lies next to me. Just like that."

"Just like that?"

"Yeah. Well, I mean, we talked some before, but nothing like a date. The weird thing was that there were other people coming and going into the room while we were in the sack. They were talking, getting clothes, doing anything and not paying attention to us at all. That bothered me. And when April and I were done, I'm lying next to April and two of April's girlfriends come and sit right next to us and start talking with her like I'm not even there. This really hot chick, Dawna, well she's just wearing a gown, but she's naked from the waist down and she's leaning against the wall with her butt next to my face talking away with April. She just keeps smiling at me while she's talking. She even started massaging me with her foot right in front of April, and April didn't seem to care. Man, I boinged right back! Was I embarrassed. But this Dawna, she laughed and said, "Don't worry. We're all just one body." Man, I gotta see this Dawna tonight. They don't believe in jealousy at all. None of that. And here's the final kicker, man. There's way more chicks than guys in the New Family."

"So are you going to join up and move in?" I asked.

"It ain't that easy man. Everyone has to give up all their property, money – cars --- everything --- to the commune. So like, this morning I had to buy breakfast food for 30 people. With that many people, all they got was pancakes and potatoes from me. And then they wanted me to drive them everyplace. To the free clinic, post office, food store. None of them had a car that was working, so they thought my truck was fair game. It took me most the morning just to leave. Then they wanted to drive my truck. On that one I told them to forget it."

He handed me back the joint. "But here's the worst part. No drugs. Not even one joint. The moment I pulled out a joint, they stopped me. Their leader, this black ex-con named Tyrone, he comes in and makes me take the joint out to my truck and promise never to bring any drugs here ever again, or he'll kick me out." Buffalo sat there shaking his head. "I knew it was too good to be true."

"So it's get high, or get nooky. You think this Tyrone just uses his harem for bait to get guys to join and then get their property?"

"I'm thinking that too. But he has just one girlfriend and that's it. He is a disciple of their love guru out in India. He even went to India to be with this here grand master guru Watananda, or some shit like that. They got lots of posters of him on the walls. He's some fuckin' old geezer who's smiling and got chicks all around him. I'd be smiling too if I was him. It looks like all he teaches and all they believe in is lovin' and screwin'."

Buffalo took another deep toke. "So you want to visit them later?"

"Sure."

Buffalo and I had arrived to Taos, New Mexico, in the winter of 1968. He first came up to me with his white Afro bushed out around his head and handed me a lit joint. Not one word from him. I inhaled and he introduced himself as Buffalohead. He said the local Tewa Pueblo Indians said he had a head like a Buffalo. He liked that name, and it stuck. About all he said to me that night was that he had just gotten out of the army. "I'm just taking *my* turn now," he said.

Lots of communes were moving to Taos back then. There were back-to-the-land agriculturalists, political resisters, an anarchist group, macrobiotic-fruitarian-vegetarian fooders, Edgar Cayce disciples, Scientologists, and our first feminist-lesbian collective. Wherever you looked, a commune was popping up.

I checked them out. Almost all of them were led by a the dominant older guy who said he knew the *complete truth.* Just listen listen listen to him and follow his vision and he would prepare you for the new millennium. Within

## We are all one Body

a week in any of the communes, I found myself questioning the absolute wisdom of their great leader. And then suddenly, it was, "get the fuck out of here right now and never come back or I'll beat your ass," to me. So I quickly packed up and left. So much for visions of Utopian non-violence.

But now we had a new commune based on --- Sex! For world peace, of course. Buffalo and I hopped in his truck and drove to it. Before we got there, Buffalo offered me a smoking joint. "If you want any of this, you better do it now. Cause this is going to have to last us a long time." I waved him off as he puffed up. When he was done, he brushed his teeth and put patchouli oil on. "They'll smell the weed on me if I don't."

We grabbed a bag of rice, potatoes, and pancake mix and walked up to the front door. From the outside, this house was an average three-bedroom, single-story adobe. The front yard was scattered with piles of wood, bricks, dead appliances, and just junk. It would take a few men a full day to clean all that crap up.

A heavy-set young woman opened the door. She was wearing a long sweat shirt that hung below to her thighs. We heard voices inside, and kitchen smells drifted out the open door.

"Hi. I'm Buffalo. This here's Adam. I was here yesterday. I met April. We're interested in joining your commune."

She looked at us a minute, then said she'd get Tyrone. A minute later, an older black man came to the door. He looked fit, with a gray and black goatee and an African robe. He gestured for us to step in. Buffalo repeated himself. He nodded slightly and then looked us over.

"How high are you?" he finally asked Buffalo.

"Oh, a little bit," Buffalo finally answered.

"Well, that's a little bit too much."

"Uh, that's why I'm here. I need to --- uh --- straighten out."

Tyrone nodded. Then he told us the ground rules. They were followers of Guru Watananda, of universal peace and love. No drugs or alcohol, all property was shared, they were all working together to save the planet from its imminent destruction because of greed, possessiveness, and lust for power. He said that if humanity did not change soon, the end was near. "We simply must save the world," Tyrone concluded. He pointed about the room, where maybe twenty-five kids, all of them white or near white, were walking about, talking, getting dressed, brushing their hair, doing ordinary things. "A year ago, they were all drug addicts. And now they have purpose and a mission in life. We expect the same of you, if you stay here."

"Well, we're not drug addicts, not we --"

"If you are smoking grass or drinking every day, *then you are a drug addict,*" Tyrone shut Buffalo off. "I have been there, so I know. We take in active users only under the condition that they stop using the moment they enter. Are you ready to agree to that? Because if you are not---"

Just then an attractive young lady stepped out of the bathroom and walked by us, her hair all wet, with only a dripping towel around her.

"Uhhh -- yeah. We're ready. Just understand, this could be hard on us -- at first."

"It is on everybody."

Tyrone leaned forward and hugged both of us. "Welcome. Bring your stuff in."

We grabbed our bags and followed him. Tyrone led us to a bedroom. The floor was covered with mattresses. On top of them were blankets and sleeping bags in disarray. I stepped between the mattresses and got to the closet. I opened it. A box fell out on me. The closet was overflowing with clothes, backpacks, suitcases, and junk. I looked around, then laid my backpack in the corner, next to a mattress. Buffalo went to the other corner and propped his backpack up. "I ain't sleeping with you," he smirked.

A woman came into the room and hugged Buffalo. "You came back!" She kissed him. She was young and plump, looking like she was fresh out of high school. "My mattress is over there. Leave your backpack on it."

Young people walked in and out of the room as we chatted. Girls coming from the communal shower, changing clothes. One young guy came in looking for a winter coat. "You going outside very soon?" he asked me.

"I don't think so" I said.

"Then can I use your coat?"

*What? Get your own fucking coat.* "No. I'll be using it soon. Plus I have all my stuff in its pockets."

He gave me a dirty look, then asked Buffalo if he could borrow *his* coat. Buffalo tilted his head. The guy said he needed it to carry firewood in.

"Then you won't need it. You'll be warm soon enough."

The guy walked out, pissed.

"Next time he'll ask to borrow your pants," Buffalo grumbled.

Tyrone came into the room. "Either of you guys know anything about plumbing?"

"Sure," Buffalo said. "I've built houses before."

"Good. We've got an overflowing toilet. Can you help?"

## We are all one Body

Buff gave me a funny look. I followed him to the bathroom. Inside the bathroom, everything was covered with wet clothes, towels, wash cloths, panties, everything, all dirty or drying. There were a dozen bathroom shaving and personal kits laying about. We had to clear things out just to get at the toilet. And there, sure enough, there was an absolutely full toilet bowl with a half a turd floating in it, and the other half on the floor.

"Goddamn," Buff muttered.

"Can you fix it?" Tyrone asked from behind.

"Only after whoever flushed it cleans the floor up first. Then I'll bring my tools in." This time Tyrone gave Buff a funny look. "That's real cheap for a plumber," Buff added. We went out to his truck to get his tools.

Tyrone shouted for Baby Anne to come here. This really young girl appeared. She looked too young to be on her own. Fifteen --- maybe sixteen max. She had runaway written all over her. But I figured she was a lot safer here than on city streets. Tyrone asked her to clean it up first.

"How was I supposed to know it was going to overflow?" She complained. But she finally cleaned the floor up just enough to keep us from vomiting.

We got out the pipe snake, plunger, pipe wrenches, and long rubber gloves. Ten gross minutes later, Buff had the smelly culprit in his hand, a turd-stained tampax. Someone had tried to flush it down the toilet.

"Goddamn," Buff repeated. He called Tyrone and showed him the mess. "You gonna have to train your crew better."

Tyrone called Baby Anne in and asked her if she had tried to flush a tampax down. She looked at Tyrone, then Buff and me, then the mess in Buff's rubber gloves. She started crying and ran out of the bathroom.

"Well, we know what her time of month is, so her mood shouldn't surprise us," Tyrone said in his baritone voice. We shared a laugh together.

I helped Buff carry his tools back to truck. Tyrone followed us. "Hey guys. Thanks for fixing that. You know, they're kind of young kids here. They've been messed up. A man's gotta help them." Buffalo nodded to Tyrone. "You guys know much about fixing cars?" he asked us.

Buffalo looked at him and barely nodded.

"Well, cause our van's not running. And me, I know about fixing people, yes. But cars, that's totally another thing."

Buffalo paused for a moment. I knew he was a great mechanic. He had been doing it with his dad since he was a boy. They had built up race cars before he was drafted.

"So when you need this van looked at?" Buff finally said. "'Cause I'm hungry. I haven't eaten lunch yet."

Tyrone put his muscular arm around Buff. "Oh come on in and eat first. If you could have it running this afternoon, that would be great. Think you can?"

Tyrone walked ahead of us.

"Jesus Christ," Buff whispered to me. "I haven't even looked at it yet and in his head, I've already fixed it."

We sat down at the corner of a cluttered kitchen table. There was a large pot of something steaming on the stove. Another pretty young girl ladled out bowls of it to us. It was oatmeal.

"Hi Dawna! Remember me?" Buff lit up when he saw her.

She smiled warmly at Buff. "Oh yeah. We're out of toast. But we still have some milk --- I think."

We ate it. Afterward, Buffalo looked at me funny. When the girl left, he whispered. "Oatmeal? I ate the whole plate and I'm still hungry. This is fuckin' bird food, man. I want some bacon and eggs. Let's go eat."

Buffalo waited in line for the bathroom. He came back a little while later. "You wouldn't believe it, man. I was in there shitting, and two girls come straight into the bathroom. I shout, "OCCUPIED!" but that don't stop them at all. One of them says, "that's okay," and begins brushing her hair! The other one looks around for some stuff. Right when I was shitting! What the fuck?"

"So what'd you do?"

"Well I kept shitting, man! I mean, what the fuck else could I do? Stuff my shit back up my ass?"

We walked out to the truck. Tyrone followed us. "Guys, you think you could look at our van before you leave? Where you going anyhow?"

Buff glanced at me. "Okay then. But I'm not guaranteeing anything." Tyrone went back in.

We got out our tools and climbed into a Dodge van. The engine sat between the two front seats and had a shroud over it. We pulled it off. The engine was really dirty. I disconnected the fuel line to the carb and turned the engine over. Gas squirted out the line. So it was getting fuel. We pulled off a plug wire, held it next to metal, and then turned the engine over. No spark. Buff pulled the distributor cap off. We turned the engine over a few times until the lob on the camber should have been opening the points. But it did not. Now we knew that the points were simply out of adjustment. And without that, there could be no spark to the plugs. Buff quickly adjusted the gap by eye. "Go ahead and try it now."

## We are all one Body

I turned the engine over, and after missing a few times, it started up. "Bunch of dumb fucks here," Buff said to no one. We let the engine warm up a bit, but it would just not idle smoothly. It was missing on at least two cylinders. Buff bet that the plugs hadn't been cleaned or changed in years. We turned the engine off and did a fluid check. Every last fluid was low. The engine was two quarts low of oil, and what little oil we could see on the dipstick was filthy.

"Let's take it for a ride." We sputtered out onto Highway 64. Even though it was missing badly, it accelerated enough to move us along. A car pulled out in front of us. "Goddamn!" Buff shouted as he hit the horn and brake. But no horn. The brakes pulled severely to the left, putting us next to oncoming traffic. Buff corrected and found the emergency brake in time to slow us down.

"Fucker's barely got any brakes. I can't believe they drove it like this." Buff turned it around and we limped back to the New Family house. Tyrone was waiting when we pulled in. He slapped us on our backs. "Wow, you guys are talented. Just what we need here. It'd been sitting there a month. We thought we'd never get it working again. I see there's a place for you here for sure."

Buff turned to Tyrone. "But you can't drive that van. The brakes will kill you. It needs a major tuneup too. Probably a hundred bucks in parts alone."

"Not even drive it to the food store?" Tyrone wanted us to say, "Well okay, but just for that."

"Nope," I said. "Not even a little bit. And we're not driving it any more till it's fixed."

Tyrone stood in bare sleeves in the cold, holding his muscled, prison-tattooed arms for warmth. "Well, I'm expecting some money soon. Then we'll buy those parts. You guys will fix it for me, right? But in the meantime, I got to get these kids some food. We're running low. Can I borrow your truck?"

I had already learned NOT to loan your vehicle to anyone in communes. They drove it hard, put more miles on than they said they would, returned it late, and didn't take care of it. And if it broke down, they came back saying they were sorry, told you where they parked alongside the road, and were gone out the door before you could punch them out.

"I don't loan out my vehicle. But I can pick up the food for you," Buff said.

"Good enough. I'll get a list." Tyrone ran back in.

We sat in Buff's truck and waited --- and waited. Tyrone finally came out. "Hey guys, get twenty pounds of rice and potatoes, five pounds of pinto beans, a big, five-pound box of instant pancake mix, three-dozen eggs, three gallons of milk, and five loaves of bread." He handed us ten dollars. That wasn't enough. That wasn't *nearly* enough.

"We'll need more," I said.

"You think?"

"I know."

"Well, maybe you fellows can chip in too. After all, you'll be eating it too."

We started to pull out. But before we got onto the road, we heard voices yelling for us. I stopped, and two girls came running to my side of the truck. One of them was Dawna.

"Wait! Get us a box of tampax."

"A big box. And some maxipads too."

"Yeah. Maybe two big boxes. A few of the other girls---"

"Thanks. Brrr, it's cold." They ran back inside.

"All of that, out of ten dollars," Buff wheezed. He pulled out a joint.

"How much those things cost anyhow?"

We both shrugged.

Then we took off. Buff lit a joint. First thing we did is pull into a diner. We stuffed ourselves with the combination plate covered with mole and green sauce, with homemade tamales wrapped in corn husks. "Gotta make up for that sludge oatmeal shit they flung at us this morning," Buff mumbled between bites.

We wiped our plates clean. I leaned back, stuck my skinny belly out, and slapped it hard. "Ahhhhh. *Bien invertido* (well invested)." My Spanish was improving. Then off to the food store.

We loaded up the food and it was twenty-five dollars worth. Then we found the feminine products section. We picked up the boxes and looked at them.

"I mean, what's the cashier gonna think?" Buffalo grumbled.

"Well, whatever she thinks, she sure ain't gonna think that it's for you. That's for sure."

We stood there in the aisle, holding boxes of sanitary napkins and maxipads. A woman passed by and noticed. Did she wonder whether we were having trouble making up our minds? Did she think that she should advise us on each product's merits? Neither of us wanted to find out. We put the boxes back.

"I think twenty-five dollars is enough to spend today. If they want them

# We are all one Body

so bad, they can just get them theirselves," Buffalo grunted.

"The New Family is gonna be one mess then --- with a lot of upset girls."

"Well, maybe so. But at least the toilet won't be clogged."

We drove back to the New Family house. They were waiting for us when we pulled in. A few young guys carried the food in.

Dawna was waiting. "Where are the tampax?"

At the same time that Buff said, "We ran out of money," I said "Ohhh. We forgot."

Disappointment on the faces of two women. Not a thanks for what we had bought for them and brought to them.

We walked in. The house was really crowded now with over thirty people milling about, in a house that was built for one nuclear family. I went to the bathroom, but there was a line again. Someone was playing a guitar, singing some John Denver folk music. Buffalo went out to his truck and returned with his violin. He began playing along with the three-chord-kid. Buff suggested some songs that the guitarist did not know. A few of the girls there had noticed his violin virtuosity and were smiling at him. So, for Buff, this was not in vain.

It got late and I got tired. When do these people sleep around here anyhow? I went into one of the communal bedrooms where I had left my back pack. The lights were on, several people sitting around talking, and a few were asleep. No one was on my mattress yet. I quickly claimed it. I didn't see any pillows, so I rolled up my pants into my shirt and used that. I stripped to my under-ware, pulled my sleeping bag over me, and shut my eyes. But there was no way I could sleep until the lights were out and and they stopped talking. After a few minutes I was thinking, *SHUT THE FUCK UP!* But I didn't have the nerve to yell it. The worse part was having to listen to every word of their conversations. They gossiped about people I did not know, and about the teachings of the guru Wuwu what-the-Fuck-is-his-name-anyhow. I just wanted to sleep.

Much much later, the lights finally went out. With it, the chatting ended. In the distance, I heard a couple making love. This time I listened. Then on the mattress right next to me a young couple began to make love. I looked, but I couldn't see anything. They had a sudden beginning, a quick crescendo, and an abrupt ending. So that was it, huh? I had never slept in the middle of live, stereophonic love-making before. Wall-to-wall fucking. I was going to have trouble sleeping tonight.

Later the door opened. I heard Buffalo's voice. The lights turned on for a moment. I saw Dawna beside him. Then the lights went off. I heard them stumbling through mattress-land to their corner. Then the rustle of clothes coming off. There were some whispers. I heard some rolling and wrestling about.

Then I heard Dawna distinctly say, "WHAT?"

"Well, you said that we were all one family --- all one body---" Buff whispered.

"Yes, that is right," Dawna whispered back.

"So, uh, I was just trying to feel my pussy," Buff mumbled.

I heard some giggles. Then more sounds rising in the darkness.

Next morning, we managed to get a few pancakes. They were out of syrup and butter, so I ate mine plain. Buff sat on the floor next to me. They were out of silverware, so he rolled up his pancake and ate it like an empty taco. Tyrone came up to us and asked if we would finish fixing the brakes on the van today. Buff was very careful not to speak with his mouth full.

Then Dawna came up to Buff and handed him a list of things they needed. He looked at it and nodded silently. When we got up, I noticed Buff stuffing all his things into his backpack. He grabbed it and his violin and carried it out to his truck. I gathered up all my things too. We double checked to make sure we hadn't left a thing behind.

We were getting ready to pull out and have some real breakfast when Dawna came running up to the truck through the snow half naked.

"We almost forgot these." She handed Buff another piece of paper.

"Okay. I'll get them," Buff took the paper without looking at it.

Dawna waved, then ran back. She turned and shouted. "And this time don't forget the tampax!"

Buff started the engine and pulled out of the lot. He stopped at the main road and lit up a joint. One big puff, and he handed it to me.

"Sure baby. Sure. After all, we are all one body."

# 17

## Dale Marley Loses It All

I first saw Dale sitting by himself in the corner of The New Family commune in Taos in 1969. I was visiting there only because of this stunning young lady, Helene. I was bird-dogging her, trying to convince her to leave this crazy commune and live with me. My home wasn't as crazy.

Dale looked lonely, so I sat on the mattress next to him. We began to chat, and without much prompting, he told me much of his life story. Dale had been a senior in high school when both of his parents were killed in a car accident. As the only child, he eventually inherited a lot of money. Then Dale got strung out on drugs, and arrested for it. Dale met Tyrone at a drug rehab center. Tyrone invited Dale over to The New Family Rehabilitation Commune that he was just setting up. Dale said that either with, or without, Tyrone's encouragement, the New Family commune girls began seriously bedding Dale. Dale smirked as he said that he soon discovered that this pussy therapy did wonders for his kicking drugs. So Dale quickly moved in with The New Family.

Tyrone made sure that Dale also quickly moved his bank accounts into The New Family. Tyrone explained that they had to pay for food, vehicles, rent, and the hundred other needs that a crew of fifty near-teenagers had. These were recovering teenager-addicts, who lacked any visible means of support. Tyrone told Dale, "These are merely needs on the material plane. All the truly important challenges in life are always on the spiritual plane." I guess Dale nodded in agreement. Just sign here.

I was getting ready to leave the Family that day when Tyrone put his hand on me and spun me around. "Don't walk away when I am speaking to you. I will be speaking tonight. It is important, so you will stay for it." Then he walked away.

I wanted to split right then. But I stayed, maybe because Tyrone intimidated me, but definitely because I wanted to see Helene again. Before I left, I spoke with Dale outside. Alone, I told him I didn't trust this place. Something didn't seem right about it.

"Better watch what you say here," Dale whispered.

"That's what I mean."

After I left, I could not recall what Tyrone's lecture was about. A few days later, I received a message from Helene. Tyrone wanted me to know that I was prohibited from ever setting my foot on any of the family's premises. If I ever came back, Tyrone would deal with me "severely, and on the physical plane."

I wandered about the west and the national parks for the better part of a year. When I came back to Taos, I parked near the The New Family home to check on Helene. I figured Tyrone couldn't drive me off from a public street. I saw Dale Marley sitting on the front porch and I waved for him to come to me. Dale walked to my car and gave me a hug. He told me not to worry, because Tyrone wasn't in town. Great. Dale wanted to talk in private, so he hopped in my car.

"Don't tell anyone," Dale said, "but Tyrone and Vania went to Las Vegas to win a half million dollars by playing keno. They said they knew they were going to win, because they had consulted with the spirits for the winning numbers. They had used Ouija boards and other kinds of good magic to get these numbers." Dale went on to say that Tyrone had promised to pay Dale back all of his inheritance plus interest, after they won big in Vegas.

"Pay back?"

"Yeah. They took the rest of my inheritance from my bank account to win with. They've done this before. I know they won the last time. But as soon as I get my money, *I am getting the fuck out of here.*"

"About time." I hugged him and wished him well. "Is Helene here?"

"Oh no. She left a long time ago. Actually, Tyrone threw her out. She had a big fight with him. She called him a dictator. So he threw her out in the middle of the night, into the snow. She had to beg just to get her backpack. I haven't seen her since."

Shortly thereafter, The New Family mysteriously split from Taos in the middle of the night, leaving a load of unpaid bills. I guess Tyrone did not win at keno this time. The members of the New Family all went in different directions, never to reconstitute again as The New Family - Version II. Taos may have missed all those pretty women of the New Family's collective body, but I doubted if they missed Tyrone's orders. I was missing Helene, and I had a good idea of what Dale Marley was missing.

A year later, I was walking down Telegraph Avenue in Berkeley,

# Dale Marley Loses it All

California, when I passed a bearded, robed man. Nothing unusual for back then. But we each caught the other's eyes and did a double take. There stood Dale Marley, now full-bearded, tanned and muscular, wearing an off-white robe with a rope belt and straw sandals. We hugged.

"You finally got out of The New Family?" I asked.

"Yeah. After they got everything they could out of me," his grin tapered off. "You were about the only real person I met there."

That was a strong statement. But then, I had resisted Tyrone's intimidation.

"So what's with the robe?"

"I am a *certified* Kundalini Yoga instructor," Dale beamed. "And I have started a school."

"Great. Where is it?"

"Well, right here." He gestured to the concrete patio in front of the bookstore. We laughed. "What you doing tonight?" he asked.

"Seeing a few friends."

"Come to my class instead."

I hesitated, but Dale insisted. So I agreed.

I arrived at the room in the bookstore at the appointed hour. There were four women, a guy, and myself waiting. Dale showed up in a shiny new robe. "We're going to wait a little bit until everyone else arrives."

So we waited for about a half hour. But no one else showed up.

"This is strange. I was expecting at least twenty more people. I guess we'll just begin then."

We all got on our yoga mats. Dale explained the critical importance of breath and breathing in Kundalini Yoga. "After all, if it is not important, just stop breathing and see how well you do."

I went through the positions and stretches and breathing exercises. I didn't know anything about chakras, much less that I had any. But in the end, I felt relaxed and stretched out. I had worked up a sweat too. The only bad part for me was just having to sit still and empty my mind and do nothing. I didn't know how to do nothing. I had to do something in order to do nothing.

"All right," Dale summarized. "I hoped you enjoyed it. The first lesson is always free. But after this, we have a membership. I can work out payment schedules with you."

I rolled up my mat, like everyone else was doing. Dale talked with a few of the students. I said good bye to Dale and started to leave.

"So when will you be back?"

# The Wild Years

"I don't know---"

"You need this class, man, with all the drugs you do."

"So you want me to join right now?"

"Yes. We can work out a payment schedule. These are merely needs on the material plane. All the truly important challenges in life are always on the spiritual plane."

"Well, I'm just passing through Berkeley now, Dale. I'll have to think about it."

I started to turn away, but he grabbed my elbow and spun me around.

"Don't walk away from me while I'm speaking to you. This is more important for you than it is for me."

I slowly freed his hand from my elbow.

"What do you mean?"

"I mean I am doing this for you. For your good. This is the way. I will be speaking tomorrow night. So you will come for it."

"But I have other plans."

"*Everyone* has other plans," Dale's voice rose. "Everyone walks out on me. You use my class, and then you walk out."

"Dale---"

"Goddamn you, you are all fucking alike. All of you. You take what you want and then you split. All you assholes. You're just like Tyrone."

At the mention of Tyrone, I saw tears in Dale's eyes. I promised Dale that I would show up tomorrow for his lecture and enroll.

"Bullshit. You'll skip out on me just like everyone else." he shouted. One of the women who had attended the class looked at us.

"Go on. Get out." He pointed me to the door.

I left Berkeley as I had planned, and I never saw Dale again.

# 18

## Save the Witches!

I saw both of them in the supermarket in Taos, New Mexico, on a cold winter day in January of 1969. They were wearing full-length brown robes with hoods that covered everything except their faces. Each wore matching rope belts. The older one, perhaps in her late thirties, might have been attractive, but I could not really tell --- *because her face was covered with paint*. On her cheeks were precise diagonal markings that mimicked Navaho blankets. From the center of her forehead a small, bright cadmium yellow sun glowed, just like the one on our New Mexico license plates. The younger woman with her also wore a similar pattern of facial paint.

In the coming weeks I often saw both of them walking about town. They were always together, on Taos Plaza, at the post office, in the food store. And as always, they wore the same brown robes. I stared at them, along with everyone else. Dress like that, and eyeballs follow. I only saw the older one talk to anyone else in public. Her words seemed limited to buying or paying for something. Whenever they talked between themselves, they whispered with their heads close together.

One day in the food store, I found myself again staring at the two women while trying not to be conspicuous about it. A tall skinny white guy who was standing next to me was also watching them. This guy had long, curly light-brown hair flowing far down his back. Feathered earrings stuck out through his hair. Streams of colored cloth and feathers were woven into his mane. Intricate bead work with Pueblo Indian motifs covered his buckskin jacket. Bright rainbows, eagles, and corn depictions. His jacket was a masterpiece. He wore buckskin leggings that flowed down to his handmade moccasins. This man was Buffalo Bill on some serious peyote.

We watched the two women move slowly toward us. They examined everything in the aisle.

"Man, them chicks are weird!" Peyote Bill whispered.

"What religion are they?"

"Their own, man. No one else is like them. I seen 'em around here a lot. They show up at gatherings and do their own chants and rituals and shit. We were having a big winter solstice celebration down at the hot springs last month and they just showed up. Their faces was all painted up black and white, weird as shit. They stood around quiet for a while, just hanging out. But then all at once they both started screaming and shrilling as loud as they could – louder than coyotes – all high-pitched and scary, like they was being killed or raped or something. Their faces were just all lit up and crazy. All the hippies just stopped talking and and watched them. You couldn't do anything else. The two of them were looking at each other all weird-like. It went on and on. And hey, I been stoned outta my fucking head lots of times, but never seen anything like this. Well then, after a while they stopped – I mean that was the only way they could go – they couldn't of got any louder or faster. Then I remember them smiling all crazy-like at each other, like there wasn't a person else in the world. Then they stepped back into the shadows, and they were gone. No one saw them again."

"Wow. What's their names?"

"Vania and Gupti. Or something like that. Vania's the older one, the boss. They live south of here, maybe a mile out of town. They walk everyplace – they don't got a car."

I watched them approach us down the aisle. The other local Chicanos and Indians in the food store were watching them too.

"I'd stay away from them, man, if I were you," Peyote Bill advised.

"Huh? How's that?"

"'Cause they hate---"

Both of them stepped in front of us. Vania, the older one, stared directly at Peyote Bill. She did not take her eyes off him. He stopped speaking. After an awkward pause, he turned to me and said "I'll see you man". He walked quickly off.

The older one parked their cart in front of mine, blocking me. From

# Save the Witches!

under their brown hoods, they stared at me. Vania's face was severe. I felt uncomfortable. I finally backed my cart up and walked away. I checked out of the store and pushed my food cart outside into the blowing snow. As I returned my cart, the two robed women stepped in front of me.

"What were you saying?" the older one spoke gravely.

"Uhhh – nothing."

"That is not true," she spoke deliberately.

"I wasn't saying anything. That guy was. He started talking to me about both of yous. I never saw him before. I'm new here."

"You believe everything you hear?" Vania intoned.

I shook my head. I felt like a school kid being disciplined. *Who are these women*? She looked around and saw the blizzard blowing.

"I gotta get going. You—you want a ride home?"

Vania paused, and then barely nodded her head.

An older Chicana woman pushed her cart slowly past us. She stopped and looked Vania in the eye. Vania turned to her and stared back.

Slowly, the Chicana woman spoke. "*Brujas*," she slowly hissed. "*Putas del diablo*."

They stared at each other for a long moment. And then Vania turned and pushed their cart to my van.

I opened the door and helped them with their bags. Vania gave me directions to their home. While I drove, they said nothing. When I had to make a turn down one of the many irregular roads that surrounded Taos, Vania just pointed. Finally, we arrived at a small, isolated adobe cottage at the end of a long drive. I carried their food bags to the front door. Vania took them from me. She stared into my eyes. She was older than I had thought. Still attractive, but with lines on her cheeks and around her eyes.

"Do not talk about us again," she said. Then she went into her home. Not a thanks, or anything else.

I stood outside the door, next to the younger one, Gupti. She took my hand.

"She's not really like that. You would just have to understand." I looked into her eyes. Her face was soft, not severe like Vania's. She was young enough to be Vania's daughter. "Thank you for the ride." She squeezed my hand. "Maybe you can come by some time."

I sincerely doubted that as I left.

But I was wrong. A short while later I saw Gupti food shopping at the Safeway. She was of course wearing the same brown robe, but I did not see Vania. I had never seen them separate from each other. Gupti came up to me and grabbed my hand.

"Oh, I am happy to see you," she said with an uncharacteristic smile.

"Yes. You can have a ride home again."

"Oh I know that already." She looked through the window at the bleak winter weather. "But I am still happy to see you."

We walked up and down the aisles and shopped together. I noticed the local people staring at us. Gupti's robe may not have been such a deal to the Taos Indians. But by the stares from the Chicanos, it sure was to them. One squat Chicana woman hissed at Gupti as she passed.

Gupti chatted with me about nothing in particular. Without Vania, Gupti seemed, well, almost normal, whatever that meant anymore. I gathered from Gupti's references to Vania that she was Vania's apprentice. But as to what she was apprenticing for, I had no idea.

I drove Gupti home. She asked me to come in. I sat on the living room floor, as there were no chairs. Gupti excused herself to the kitchen to make tea. I looked around. The inside of their home was arranged with Asian and native American art on the walls and shelves, desert wood and cacti, tapestries and blankets hung in the doorways, bright colors from traditional art. A small kitchen adjoined the living room which doubled as a dining room. I got up and walked around. There were two other rooms. One was used as a studio. There were paintings and clay sculptures in various stages of completion.

I stepped into the next room. It was a bedroom. On the floor in the center was a large king-sized mattress. It had two neat Navajo blankets covering it. There were two pillows, each with head prints in their centers. There were women's clothes on either side of the mattress. The room smelled of incense. Opposite the mattress was what looked to be an altar. On it were clumps of sage, incense, dried bunches of flowers, many polished stones. Toward its center were numerous clay figurines, almost all of them of nude females.

"*You are not supposed to be in here*" Gupti commanded from behind me. I jumped. She stood at the doorway with two cups of tea. "Please leave now. Vania would be very angered if she found you in here."

I quickly passed through the beads and tapestries that hung in the doorway, back to the living room. I sat on a large cushion. Gupti sat on the other edge of the cushion, next to me. She lit a joint, inhaled, and then handed it to me. We passed it back and forth.

"So, tell me, what is it you – do with the robe stuff and all?"

Gupti looked at me funny, and then blew a puff of smoke into my face

## Save the Witches!

with a burst of laughter.

"Vania received a message that she was to do this. You see, Vania knows things. She teaches me these things. Like how to tell the future, how to know what someone is actually thinking, how to make people do things for you."

"What do you mean, like control people?"

She nodded. "Well, remember that first time we saw you at the food store? After Vania stared at you, she told me that you would give us a ride home. And you did. She said that from now on you would give us a ride to anyplace at anytime we needed one."

Now Gupti was staring intensely into my eyes.

"But if you recall, I asked *you* if *you* wanted a ride," I objected.

Gupti shook her head while still smiling. "You don't get it. But you will, if you spend time with her. She is my teacher now."

"Are you like, a disciple?"

"You can call it that if you want. Other people feel that they have to call it something. But I don't."

Then she leaned forward and put her head on my shoulder. She nuzzled against me and kissed my cheek. I turned to her.

"I suppose you are making me do this," I said.

"Now you are starting to understand." She laughed.

We kissed. She pulled me to her.

We heard the door abruptly open to our side. Gupti jumped up as Vania stepped in, with her brown robe covered with snow.

"Where were you?" Vania snapped at Gupti. "You were supposed to meet me."

Vania saw me stand up. "And what are you doing here?" She glared at me. I told her that I gave Gupti a ride home. "Well, you should have picked me up too." Vania looked at both of us. "As for Gupti, she is spoken for."

I gathered my things and quickly stepped out of their home. The last thing I heard was Vania scolding Gupti. As I drove off, I told myself to stay the fuck away from here, and never come back again.

And then the attacks began against the hippie newcomers in Taos. VW vans smashed in the streets, hippies beaten up in the Taos Plaza, gunshots through the windows of rented houses, hippie women raped at the hot springs. And the cops did nothing.

The locals saw it as driving back an invasion of drug-using, disease-carrying outsiders who would turn their kids onto drugs and then get their daughters pregnant. They said these hippies burned furniture in rented houses for firewood, poached cattle and sheep for food, and practiced black magic. The locals in northern New Mexico had been invaded many times before, by roaming Kiowa and Comanche bands, then by the Spaniards, then Anglos, cowboys, and most recently, Texans with money. They had a long history of resisting outsiders.

Now I just went into town in the daylight to quickly do my business. I only spoke with them in Spanish. If it were possible, I always left someone with my vehicle when I parked it. I tried to never leave my house alone. I wasn't too sure what I would do if a mob of drunk thugs came after me, but I didn't want to give them an easy chance to smash my van or burn my home down.

I ran into Peyote Bill again while shopping at the Safeway. I asked him how he was doing, like I might ask anybody. I almost didn't notice the "Not too good, how about you?" response. I stopped. I asked him what was wrong.

"They shot the windows out of my truck. By the time I came out with my gun, they were gone. Next day, my dog was dead. They'd poisoned him with antifreeze."

"I'm sorry man. Your dog too. Real sorry." I put my hand on his shoulder.

"I catch them coming around again and this time it's my deer rifle. They taught me how to do it with the Gooks. This time it'll be easy."

"Careful man. There's way more of them than you. Plus they got the cops and courts."

"I'll have a better chance of winning my appeal then they will of coming back to life."

I couldn't argue that. I started walking away, but Peyote Bill grabbed me.

"What are you doing about tonight?"

"Huh?"

"Didn't you hear --- the locals say they're going to drive out all the hippies this weekend. The sheriff has let guys out of jail to drive us out. I know that."

I told him I had been out in the desert for a few days and didn't know anything about it. I didn't mention that I had been eating peyote by myself, on a vision quest. I think Peyote Bill would have understood. But the vision quest I was on did not include being attacked by locals.

"Well, you better watch yourself," Peyote Bill commanded. "We're ready at my place with our guns if they try to break in."

# Save the Witches!

"I'll think about it."

"And hey, you hear about what happened to the witches? I heard this from people who saw it. A few days ago on the Taos Plaza, a drunk Chicano pulled Vania's robe off --- in front of anyone standing around. I guess all she had on was black tights and underwear stuff. She had to run after him in the snow and beg for him to give it back. Then I heard that when the two of them were walking home, someone came driving by and ran them off into the ditch. And when they got home, their home was all messed up. On the door they had painted the number 666 and mean shit on the front. I guess there was a bloody goat's head on the steps."

I told him I didn't know anything about it.

He said it looked like to him that those witches' magical powers weren't working so well just right now. "Serves the bitches right, weird as they act. You don't go bringing black magic to a Penitente Catholic community like this and act as fuck-face-weirdo as they do and not expect some shit to happen." Peyote Bill shook his head and rolled his eyes. His feathered earrings rocked with him. His eyes glared back at me, gaunt and burning.

"You be careful," I told him and spun out the door.

As I carried my groceries out to my van, I got a few catcalls from some young Chicanos. Two of them followed me to my van. But when they saw that I had two people waiting in my van, they drifted off.

I had a few guests staying at my home. They professed good intentions, but in the end, all they did was lay around, smoke my dope, eat my food, and then say, "thank you bro." Normally I would have thrown them out long ago. But in these times, I could use some company for protection. Safety in numbers. I quickly drove out of the parking lot to my home. I went inside and gathered the crashers together. I told them about the threats this weekend. One of the guys had just gotten back from Vietnam. He was jumpy and stoned most the time but--- I showed him where my guns and ammo were. He nodded silently. I told them I would be back in a bit.

Then I drove over to Vania's and Gupti's place. I didn't know why. I arrived there in the middle of the long winter sunset. An eerie orange and pink glow pierced the cold blue-gray clouds on the horizon over the Rio Grande Gorge. When I parked, I saw Vania and Gupti standing out front. Vania was painting over the front door while Gupti scraped at the words painted on the adobe. I could still read "WE BE BACK WITCHES WE FUCK YOU BOTH." Vania stared at me as I walked up to them. This time I did not see the stern glare. I was going to say something like, "I heard what happened," or "I'm sorry about all that." But nothing came out.

# The Wild Years

"The hatred from them," Vania's face broke. "I thought they were going to kill me."

"One of the guys at the plaza shouted that they were going to come back and get us both if we did not leave," Gupti spoke rapidly.

From their looks, I guessed that this just did not happen to them in the hip San Francisco Haight-Ashbury where they were from. All I saw now in their faces was fear. If the Penitente Catholics here could climb up Mount Truchas on their bloody knees to give penance to Jesus, what else might they do to protect themselves from the witchcraft of the whores of the devil himself?

"Could you stay the night?" Vania asked. I was not expecting that at all. But Vania and Gupti lived on an isolated road without any neighbors or a phone. They had no protection, and they knew it.

*What? To stay in the house of the witches, on the night of the revenge, when the avengers would come speeding in with their hatred and guns and lust all rolled into one sick fireball, to defend these two psuedo-psychic psychotic self-professed servants of the dark arts, to protect them against an armed posse who believe they are doing what is in the word of God --- while I myself am unarmed? What kind of dumb fuck do you think I am?*

"Sure. I'll stay."

Vania imperceptibly smiled. She took my hand and led me into their home. It was lit only by candles, and smelled heavy of a mix of incense. In the middle of the main room now stood a small altar made of stacked stones. On it stood a few Kachina dolls and Virgin Mary statuettes. Some were of painted plaster, a few were plastic, and one was of carved wood. In the center of the altar was a brass crucifix of Jesus. There was a large glass of what looked to be wine in front of the crucifix, and crackers next to it. None of this had been there the last time I visited. *Hocus-fucking-pocus.*

"What should we do if they come?" *We?* Vania asked me with the queen's "we," as if I actually had any idea in the world of what to do. Now I knew what *I* might do. I just might run outside the back door and hide, or try to drive away. But I did not know what *we* should do.

I went outside to my van and drove it behind their home. I wanted it out of eyesight --- and gun sights. When I came back in, Vania snapped, "Why did you do that? Now they won't know that someone else is here."

*Well, bitch, maybe it's because I don't want them shooting holes through my van, or lighting it on fire. Maybe it's because I value my van way more than your weird ass.*

But I didn't answer her. What had I gotten myself into, defending these bitch-witches? Why I had come here had everything to do with Gupti and nothing to do with Vania. In a town where I might see ten hippie chicks swimming naked all at once at the Llano Quemado Hot Springs, I found Gupti's long robe more interesting. But -- *What to do what to do what to do?*

"You got some planks -- building wood? Any of that white paint still left?"

Vania nodded. "But what for?"

"You'll see."

Gupti led me out to behind their home with a flashlight to a pile of wood. Before I could look through the wood, she put her arms around me and kissed me passionately on the lips.

"Take me from here," she whispered.

I glanced back at the door. I did not see Vania watching us. She couldn't have seen anything on the outside anyhow. It would be the same for us if they attacked us here tonight.

"Later. Let's see what you got here."

I took two old planks, one about seven feet long, and the other four feet. I got my tool box out of my van. I nailed the two planks together into a crude cross. I told Gupti to get the white paint. In a few minutes we had a dripping wet white cross that would never dry in this freezing cold. By the looks of it, we had more paint on us than the cross. I stood the cross up against their front gate and told Gupti to get me some rope. With the rope, I secured the cross to the gate. We went inside, looking like a mess to Vania. She asked what we were doing. Gupti pointed to the cross out front. Vania looked, and said no more.

I bent a few wire clothes hangers into the shape of cups. I put two of the thick burning candles into the wire cups and hung them on the arms of the cross. But the wind blew the candles out as soon as we hung them. I came back in and got two empty tin cans. I pounded holes through them and then hung the cans on either end of the cross. I lit the candles from inside the cans. Spots of light glowed through the holes in the cans. The cold mountain wind rocked the tin cans, causing the beams of light to flicker eerily across the cross and walkway. But the candles kept burning. On her own, Gupti painted PEACE ON EARTH on the front gate. I told Gupti to get the large brass crucifix of Jesus from their altar. I tied it upright in the center of the cross. I figured all of this was a first for these witches. We checked over our work, and then went back in. Once inside, we locked the doors.

# The Wild Years

"You think this will work?" Vania asked me, as if I were an expert on what a drunk, raging Chicano mob would do on this night of the exorcism.

"Yes," I answered her with no basis at all. Anything to get those creepy eyes off me. I wanted to leave now, right now, but their expressions – actions, everything about them were pleading with me to stay.

We sat around their altered altar. Jesus was conspicuously missing from the center. Vania said it was getting late. What did she mean --- that it was past their bewitching hour?

"What if they have guns, walk straight through the gate, ignore the cross? What do we do then?" Vania asked yet again.

*Well bitch, I myself am out the back fucking door, into my van and driving off. And if I can't do that, then I'm running across the field. But I don't know about you. Maybe you could cast one of your fucking magic spells at them, and then they would all become angels -- or better yet, your servants in darkness. But you don't seem so confident that you can do that right now, do you? Or you could come running with me, I guess. If you were quick enough and didn't panic and trip over your fucking robes. But I am not planning on fighting a group of drunk men with guns or carrying your sorry ass out of here.*

"They won't do that," I answered.

But Vania just got more and more nervous, with her twitching, asking more questions, wanting to know what I thought, what I'd do. She kept repeating herself. I stopped answering her, as it did no good.

"I can't take it anymore!" Vania shrieked, then ran into their bedroom. A minute later she came out and sat in the middle of the floor with a tray in front of her, oblivious to Gupti or myself. I watched her with growing fascination as she meticulously prepared her kit. The spoon, the candle, the cotton, the needle, the tourniquet, and finally, the brutal act of penetration itself. I had never before seen this done in my life. Mushrooms, cacti, five-leaved stems, yes. But they were all plants. I had no idea what Vania had just injected.

Vania looked at me with a cool, satisfied smile. She pointed to the tray and gestured for me to come closer. I shook my head. She sat there smiling at nothing or no one in particular. Then she got up and slowly flowed back to her bedroom.

Gupti got up and filled the fireplace with wood. Then she leaned next to me. "We're alone now." She kissed my cheek. She opened a small vile and carefully stuck the long painted fingernail on her little finger into it. When she pulled it out, it was filled with a light-colored powder. Gupti sniffed it.

She repeated herself with the other nostril. Then she filled her fingernail again and held it to my nose. "Take it," she commanded. "It'll help us to sleep."

I looked at her in the candlelight, her cheeks rosy from being outside in the cold with me, but her eyes now dreamy big. *"Come with me,"* she whispered. *"Don't leave me alone."* She beckoned with her finger. I leaned forward and inhaled...

I recall us falling back onto the floor together in each other's arms. Dream state, sighs, then sobs. Trance-walking. Then, later, the sound of vehicles pulling up, doors slamming, men's voices shouting in Spanish. Sounds of footsteps out front of the house...

It was late morning when I awoke in a cold house. I had a terrible headache. Gupti lay sprawled out on the floor next to me. She was breathing, but not much more. The clothes on both of us were in disarray. Gupti's face paint was all smeared. There were granola crisps in the corners of her eyes, while her mouth hung open with a bit of spittle on one corner. The hood of her robe was pushed back, revealing a head full of dull blond hair. Her robe was up to her hips, revealing more hair of a much darker shade. In the bright morning light, Gupti looked decidedly un-witchlike.

I staggered up and looked out the front window. It was bleak and cold. No one was there. The cross was still standing. I tiptoed to the back door and looked out the window. My van was still there. I saw no damage to it. My head throbbed.

*Coffee... Coffee...* I started to look about their kitchen for coffee – tea, something. But then I stopped myself. I did not want to wake them. I gathered up my shoes and jacket.

I quietly opened the back door of the house. As I was stepping onto the stairs, I stumbled over something and fell. I looked behind me. There lay a baseball bat that I had slid on. It wasn't there the night before, and Vania and Gupti did not seem like the types who played Little League baseball. I got into my van and drove away. I never returned to the house of the witches again.

I left Taos shortly after that, afraid for my own safety. I thought the saga of the witches was over. But a year later, I found myself driving back to Taos again to visit friends. First, I went to the Llano Quemado Hot Springs to bathe. There were a number of people in the water splashing about. As I started to strip down, a young, wet, naked woman came running to me with a smile.

"Hi! How are you?" She hugged me. I leaned back to look into her face. I had to pause.

"Gupti! I didn't recognize you with your clothes off."

"And Adam. I didn't recognize you with your clothes on."

We laughed.

"I'm not Gupti anymore. My name now is Wild Blossom. I left Vania long ago, just about right after that night. Oh that seems like forever ago. I tried to find you, but everyone said you had left."

I nodded. "Yeah. It got too violent for me. I've been camping out and hiking a lot in the national parks."

"That sounds like fun."

I looked at her, naked in all ways. Tan, fresh, lush, bursting with fecundity. I watched the water drip from the point at the bottom of her delta of pussy hair. Now she was a flower child, defrocked of robes, intrigue, mystery. Just another California hippie running wild before the apocalypse.

"Well, what are you doing now? Let's get together."

She told me how to find her and invited me for dinner. I fumbled around my clothes and wrote her address. I told her that I would come by. She hugged me again.

"Good. I'll be waiting for you."

I went back into the pool. I soaked and enjoyed the cleansing warmth of the springs. I thought of the Gupti I had known, and the Wild Blossom I had just met.

Later, I got out of the pool and dressed up, purified and relaxed. I walked back to my van and watched the others frolic in the springs.

I never visited or saw Wild Blossom again.

# 19

## Hot Springs Shootout

The Llano Quemado Hot Springs
Ranchos de Taos, New Mexico -- January, 1969

"YOU LEEEEAVE NOW!" The Chicano grabbed my arm with one hand and pointed down the road with his other arm while holding a half-empty bottle of Tokay. Behind him in the pickup truck sat two other Chicanos, one of them cradling a shotgun in his lap. "You fuck-eeng heep-piees, go! You shit and piss in the water. It drain down to Ranchos de Taos and we get your fucking disease. So you go NOW!"

He stuck his face into mine -- bloodshot eyes, purple lips, and the stink of way too much cheap wine. "I MEAN YOU!" He pushed me. I stepped back. "We live here hundreds of years, and you think you can come here and take the hot springs from us. FUCK NO!"

I watched his lips move without speaking. Words came from him when his face was still. Waves of purple and green rippled across his cheeks. Behind him, the pinon trees on the mountainside moved in unison to the wind. "When you leave? ANSWER ME!" he shouted at me. No words came from my mouth.

The Chicano staggered back to the pickup truck and got in. One of them held the shotgun out the window, pointed it upward, and BOOM! Gun smoke wafted into the air. He revved the engine and they peeled out through the gravel down the road, kicking up a cloud of dust down the mountainside.

*What?* We stood around looking at each other dazed. No one said anything. We had sure picked just a great Sunday afternoon at the Llano Quemado Hot Springs in New Mexico to eat peyote. Some vision.

No one said anything coherent. Whatever we had wanted to achieve that day now lay shattered amongst us. I looked at the people around me. We had come from all over the United States to the mountains of northern New Mexico in this spring of 1969. Army deserters, bail jumpers, urban refugees, pacifists, spiritualists, draft dodgers, pleasure seekers, mystics, dopers, vision seekers, common criminals --- the poor huddled masses of dropout America. Somehow we had ended up here with all our different stories. And now we were camping out on this mountain side, living for the moment, while the apocalypse did whatever it was going to do.

We heard another vehicle coming up the hillside. Stoned, we watched a police car bounce over the rough road and skid to a stop at the main pool of the hot springs. Two Chicano cops hopped out with their guns out and ran to the edge of the deep pool. They looked at the people swimming in it. "YOU ARE UNDER ARREST FOR SWIMMING NUDE! COME OUT WITH YOUR HANDS UP!" The smaller cop waved his gun across the pool.

I grabbed the bag of peyote, ran up the hill, and hid it under a rock next to a juniper tree. Below me, I watched two young men and a woman get out the pool, butt-naked, while a cop held a gun toward them. These three had just arrived here today after driving non-stop from California. Then they had stripped down, jumped into a hot springs, and now gotten arrested. Welcome to New Mexico. Wow. After they dressed, a cop handcuffed them and opened the back door of the police car. But first, a white-haired old man with a cane got out. He was wearing a black suit with a white shirt, a turquoise bolo tie, and silver-toed armadillo cowboy boots. The cops then directed the three arrested bathers to get into the back seat.

Zonked

I recognized the old man as Faris Elias Martinez. He was a small and thin, in his eighties. His family and he were the principle owners of these hot springs. I knew I would have to talk with Faris, so I came down the hill. As I approached, I watched Faris beat his cane on the ground. "EVERYONE LISTEN!" Faris shouted. "LISTEN!" A cop repeated. He yelled for everyone to get closer and hear what Faris had to say. Some people stepped closer, and others stepped further back. Faris held a paper in the air.

"I have a court order here, a court eviction, that says that you have to leave the hot springs immediately. Today. No one can live up here--or swim either. Tomorrow the police will arrest anyone who is still here. So everyone start leaving. *Now.*"

The cops walked through the hippies and began pushing them, shouting, "*Vaminos Vaminos.*"

I ran to my cabin and started going through my papers until I found our signed contract. It was the only paper I had that was of legal size. I looked at the paper. The letters were crawling over it like nervous ants. I put my sun glasses on and ran to the police with this letter. I held the it up to them.

"Here is our lease to the hot springs," I managed to say. I folded it to the second page. "If you look here, you can see that both Mr. Martinez and I have signed it. It says we have a lease with an option to buy. We paid him five hundred dollars cash. The lease is good for two more months. After that, we have an option to pay him $50,000 for the purchase of the springs." I said this out of memory, as I could not make out a thing on the paper.

The cops took the contract from me and read it. Grim faces. They asked Faris in Spanish if that was his signature. He said nothing. They turned away from me and spoke amongst themselves in hushed Spanish. Then Faris took the lease from them and stuffed it in his sports jacket pocket.

*"No importa,"* Faris shouted. "You have to leave, and that is that."

"May I have the contract back?" I held my hand out. The cop waved me back. *"Vete, cabron."*

I stepped back and turned to Faris. His face was cragged like the rocks around us, with creases in it like erosion gullies. One eye was black, the other frosted with a cataract. The pattern on that eye was moving for me.

Words started coming from me. "You can't do this. We signed a lease with you. We paid you three months rent. We've cleaned up tons of garbage from this place--cleaned out the pools, rebuilt the buildings, built new bridges. You know that."

*"No importa!* You hippies pollute the water. People downstream will get sick from you. So get out. With or without lease, it makes no difference. You will leave. This is not your land. Leave now."

Patterns swarmed all over his face. He changed from rock to reptile to human and back again. His mouth moved independently of his words, like a badly synched movie.

*"Faris, in the eyes of God you know that you are breaking your word,"* I stated. I had never uttered those words previously in my life. So pompous and absolute, and hypocritical for someone whose only previous use of the word 'God' had always been in vain.

Faris waved me off with his hand and walked back to the police car. The cops turned toward us. "All right, all of you people, get out of here now. We be back here tomorrow and we arrest anybody who is here. So start packing."

We stared at each other. No one else spoke. The cops walked back to the car. Faris stood there pointing his cane at us, waving it back and forth in a slow oval motion to include all of us. Then the cane fell out of Faris' hand. Faris leaned against the police car. He put his hands across the hood. Then he slowly slid down against the car. His face hit hard against the ground.

The short cop stood over him and spoke in Spanish. Faris didn't answer. The other cop leaned over and reached under Faris' shoulders, while still holding his gun in his hand. Faris slipped from his grip to the ground again.

The cop put his gun back in the holster and lifted Faris over the hood. Faris lay there with his mouth and eyes open. Spittle came from his lips, but he did not move or speak. The cops spoke to each other in hushed Spanish.

I was a certified Emergency Medical Technician in the state of New Mexico. I knew what I was supposed to do. But I froze still. *When a man dies, does his spirit leave through his mouth? Would I be inhaling Faris' spirit?* This was the same Faris who had smiled at me when he accepted the $500 after we had signed a contract a month ago. The same Faris who had demanded that the earnest money for the hot springs only be in cash. The same Faris who insisted that we only speak in Spanish. The same Faris who now told us to leave these hot springs at this very moment. And now this Faris lay unconscious. I did nothing to help him.

The cops now spoke to each other in rapid Spanish. They opened the back door of their squad car. The three arrested hippies were sitting there. "Get out!" the small cop shouted to them.

They stumbled out, their handcuffed arms behind them. The cops quickly laid Faris on the back seat. Then they hopped in the front, slammed their doors shut and started the engine.

"Hey, what about these handcuffs?" a guy who had been arrested shouted. He was waving his arms up and down from behind him like the tail of a bird. "HEY!"

The cops slammed on the brakes. One of them quickly took off all the handcuffs. Then the cop car disappeared in a cloud of dust around a curve.

The cabin I was living in once had been the business office for the Llano Quemado Hot Springs Company. These springs were south of Taos, New Mexico, at 8000 feet altitude, on the west slope of a mountain. Legend had it that the Martinez family had, via hook or crook, swindled it from the Taos Pueblo Indians. They had then tried to make a go of it as a business. But because of a complete boycott by the Indian pueblo, bloody family feuds, and the lack of sufficient paying crowds, the venture went bankrupt. The crowning event was supposed to have been when one of the Martinez clan accused another of robbing the business. Shots were fired, with one less Martinez was the result. Or so they said.

And so the hot springs sat idle for decades. The road to it eroded and gullied out. It was passable only on dry days, or with four-wheel-drive. On weekends, crowds of locals gathered with cases of beer and gallons of wine. They threw the bottles wherever they finished them. Broken glass covered the grounds. Eventually, they filled up the pools with so much trash that they were unusable. All the while, the Taos Pueblo Indians continued their boycott of the hot springs.

But the beauty of the location of these hot springs still overwhelmed me, despite all the trash. From these hot springs I could see the Rio Grande Gorge and the next mountain range far in the distance. I imagined what these springs would look like if they were cleaned up. And with that vision, several friends and I began working on raising the money to buy the land, restore the springs, and live here. We would make it publicly accessible to all. Somehow that became our implausible grand vision.

One day at the springs, I met a muscular young man named Luke. He had just arrived and wanted to camp here for a while. After a few days he told me that he had just deserted the Marines. He had been gungho, all ready to go to Vietnam and fight the gooks. But then he dropped LSD. And that was that. He didn't want to fight anymore. So here he was, on the lam like me. I told him my background. We compared false ID's and laughed about it. Both of us figured that they wouldn't be searching for us up here. Luke looked around and also thought this place was worth saving.

After we had signed the lease, we began cleaning it up. Teams of hardworking guys hauled truckload after truckload of trash from the pools and the grounds. Daily for a month we ran loaded trucks to the county dump nearby. We patched up the pools until they held water. The grounds began to show their beauty again.

After Faris Elias Martinez died at the hot springs, the cops did not return as promised to evict us. So out of inertia, we stayed there. One evening, a few weeks after the Faris incident, there was a knock on my cabin door. I opened the latch and in the kerosene light, I saw two old Indian men. Long gray braids, black hats, beads, blankets, leather clothes. I recognized them. Their names were Tell-Us-Good-Morning and Little Joe. I had listened to them sing at a peyote meeting last year.

"Hello, father. Please come in."

Tell-Us-Good-Morning nodded and held my hand. I got seats for them and we sat at the table.

"I want to tell you this story," he said. "Please listen." The orange light from the kerosene lamp reflected from his dark eyes. "Long ago the Chicanos stole this hot springs from us. It had always been a healing springs for us. Whenever we were sick in the winter, we would soak here and cure ourselves. We allowed everyone to use it. But they stole it from us with paper. They had learned well from the Anglos. We refused to pay admission to something that had always been ours. We said that no one could own it, or live here either. It was a healing gift from the Great Spirit and it would always be that. Then our spirit men put bad medicine on it." Tell-Us gestured with his arm in the direction of the pools. "Now I look and I see what you are doing and I see good. You have cleaned up all of this trash that has piled up here. You have moved thirty years of garbage in one month. This is very good. But do not forget what we have always said, that no one is to own this land --- or live here. That is the way it should be."

"What about the lease, and the five-hundred dollars we gave the Martinez family?"

Tell-Us-Good-Morning looked at me for a long time.

"I do not know about papers and contracts and these things. But I know that this gift from the old people is greater than any contract."

"I also know about the Martinez's," Little Joe said. "And you will never see that five-hundred dollars again. It is not the first time that they have taken money to sell this land."

"We know that Faris died here last week," Tell-Us-Good-Morning said. "Powerful medicine. Some people believe you did bad magic against him. Some people were happy about his death. That is not good. Again, we are very thankful that you have cleaned these hot springs up so well. But I say again. *No one is to own this land. No one is to live here.*"

Tell-Us-Good-Morning squeezed my hand again. Then they stood up and left. Afterward, I spoke with my friend, Luke, about it. But still, neither of us was in a hurry to move out.

As the spring of 1969 rolled on, the hot springs became more of a carnival than a healing spot. Every day was another party, with people rolling in from all over the nation. There was smoke and drink and homemade music and dancing around bonfires every night. More pickup trucks bringing fresh garbage for us to gather up and haul away. All of this in my front yard. And yes, there were lovely young women, women who needed food and places to stay. Long-haired women with beads and peasant dresses, big eyes and smiles, and no bathing suits or panties. So we stayed on at the hot springs. It was living in a party, living in a dream. How could we leave?

Luke and I tried to run the place, as much as one could do that while stoned. One thing we did not pay attention to was the fact that most of the Chicanos stopped coming to the hot springs after Faris Martinez died. We did not miss them. Maybe they now believed we had magical powers to strike people down. If that was what kept them away, then let them believe it.

Many times when I returned from town to the hot springs, there was a new surprise waiting for me. Ten new people from the coast, or somebody who just broken his arm, or more runaway teenagers needing food, or some wandering European hippies setting up their tents. Most of the new arrivals were penniless, food-less, and homeless, living only on their visions. They treated me like I already owned the place, and that was my plan. So we fed them. Each afternoon I started a large pot of stew to feed them all. Pinto beans, salt, vegetable oil, corn tortillas, chili peppers, water cress from the stream, young prickly pear cactus strips, and anything else we could gather. It all went into the big kettle. By the time it was finally ready, we were hungry enough so that it tasted good.

Occasionally, someone shot a jack rabbit or poached a mule deer and gave us some meat. Then I would have two pots going; one for the vegetarians, and the other for the carnivores. And occasionally the carnivores got greedy and put meat conspicuously into both pots. That way the vegetarians wouldn't eat, and the meat eaters would have more for themselves. So I had to sternly patrol the pots.

One afternoon, a feral-looking guy came up to me.

"Wanna buy a gun?" he asked. He was jumpy and nervous.

"No. I don't believe in them." I gave my stock answer.

"Well, I need the money. I jumped bail and I'm going to Mexico. They can't get me there, and I don't dare cross the border with a gun." He pulled out a small black automatic and handed it to me. I saw how it had an external hammer. With a flick of my thumb, the barrel popped up and open. It was a 6-shot Beretta Jetfire automatic that fired 22 shorts only. This was the weakest shell on the market. But it was a Beretta, and they made good guns.

"How much?"

"Fifteen dollars."

*A giveaway*, I thought. He *must* be on the lam. I bought it on impulse. The first pistol I ever owned. I suddenly felt dirty owning a hand gun. I knew I would not be hunting animals with it. Later that day I went into town to buy ammo for it. When I got back to the hot springs, I saw two new arrivals, teenie-bopper girls who said they were from Odessa, Texas. Everything about them said runaways. They had hitchhiked all the way here, and then hiked in the last five miles to the hot springs. They had set up a cheap army surplus tent across the stream from my cabin. All they had between them were a few clothes, a tent, and a meager backpack. Nothing else. They were hungry and broke.

That evening we fed the two girls. They unconvincingly claimed they were eighteen and nineteen years old. They said they were sisters, and they looked it. They told stories of their fundamentalist parents beating them and sending them to psychiatrists and religious camps. So one day, rather than go to mid-week church, they started hitchhiking on an expressway ramp. They got rides very quickly. They said a lot of the drivers had tried to force sex on them. But together, they had resisted the come-ons.

Later that night, the girls went back to their tent. Luke came over to my cabin with some of this Panama red marijuana. We smoked it, and I was immediately zonked.

I looked at the moon rising over the mountain. A full moon in Scorpio. April 2, 1969.

In the background, we heard a vehicle drive up to the hot springs and stop. Some doors slammed and there were loud voices. We paid it no mind and went about smoking and talking.

Then we heard a girl scream NO.

"NO. NO NOOOO!"

I jumped up from my reverie.

"Huh? What's that? Who's that?" Luke was muttering something.

`I unbolted the door. The girls' screams were much louder now. Across the way in the full moon I saw a small crowd near the place where the two runaways were camping. One of them was holding a flashlight. Luke and I stood at the doorway. In the moonlight in the distance, we saw several men standing around the two runaways on the other side of the hot springs.

"Take your clothes off!" one of them was shouting.

"No please no. No no no!"

Luke grabbed my arm. *"They're trying to rape her."*

The girls kept screaming. I had never witnessed anything close to a live rape in my life. I had no idea what to do. But even in the fog of being completely stoned and lame on marijuana, I couldn't just stand there.

Luke shouted, "HEY STOP THAT! LEAVE THEM ALONE." Then he ran down the hill toward them. I followed him. One of the men turned toward Luke.

BOOOOM! Orange flame from a barrel. Luke spun around. He stopped for a moment and then began running back to our cabins. One of the two runaways ran behind him. I retreated with her. We bolted the door behind us. I shouted to the girl to hide on the floor in the kitchen. She was gone in a moment. There was a banging on the door. Luke was shouting. I opened the door and he rushed in. I rebolted the door and held the Aladdin kerosene lamp up while he took off his shirt. There was blood on his shoulder and neck.

"I got some pellets!"

I looked at them. He had maybe ten speckles on his back and shoulders. Painful yes, but it did not look like anything real serious. We heard the girl scream again. I ran to my bed and grabbed my pistol. It was loaded with six in the magazine and one in the chamber. I cocked the external hammer with my thumb. Luke grabbed a leg from the kitchen table and pulled on it as hard as he could until it broke off. Then he ran out the door with it. In front of our cabin were a few men in the darkness. Luke ran straight up to one and swung the table leg full force baseball-bat style against him. The guy went down. Then he swung the table leg into another guy's chest. Mixed with the thud of the impact was the sound of the table leg breaking.

In the moonlight, I saw a man coming up behind us. Someone hit me in the face. He and I both fell and slid down the rock slope. I heard another gunshot, and then noises coming from above me. Another man came running down the hill at me. He was carrying something long in his hands--

-

Just before the man stopped running at me, a fireball came out of my Beretta as I was pointing it at his  midsection. He was no more than ten feet away. BAM. He stood still. I ran from him, back up the hill. I passed two men on the ground fighting. Luke was on top of a guy, pummeling him with his fists. I heard another gunshot. I had no idea where it came from.

"LUKE IT'S ME!"

Luke jumped up and kicked the guy hard in the gut and chest and head. The man did not move.

"IS THERE ANY MORE?" Luke bellowed.

We looked around. There were four Chicanos laying on the ground, moaning and muttering. The other girl came running up to us, shreiking.

"Get in the cabin!" Luke yelled. She ran to it.

Luke grabbed a shotgun laying on the ground. We ran to their truck where the last guy was standing.

"DONT SHOOT!" He begged. "PLEASE DONT SHOOT!"

Luke waved the gun at him. "IT'S OURS NOW!"

"Get all your guys into your truck and get outta here!" Luke shouted.

Two of the three guys on the ridge came stumbling down the hill carrying the third guy.

"DONT SHOOT!" They put one guy into the bed of the pickup, and then another one. Only one of them seemed fit to drive.

He fumbled around for a long time, then started up the truck engine. He turned it around and began pulling out.

"WE BE BACK LATER TONIGHT WITH MANY MORE AND WE KILL ALL YOU FUCKIN' HIPPIES!" one of them shouted. I shot my pistol in the air.

Then they were gone and there was silence in the moonlight.

"What do we do now?" I asked Luke.

"They ain't coming back tonight. They ain't no organized army. Just a bunch of street punks. Maybe in a week or so, but not now."

"We gotta prepare for if they come. They could bring their cops out for sure."

"Yeah," Luke agreed. "I think we should get away from the buildings. That's where they'd be looking for us."

That made sense to me. As I limped up to my cabin, I felt something wrong with my knee. It was stiff and swelling from a fall I had taken. Blood was running from it. My dog Kingfish began licking the blood.

I looked around my cabin. *What to take? What to leave? Where to go?* This marijuana I had smoked did not help any of my decision-making. *Did I just shoot somebody?* I wasn't sure. What if he died? No matter, the law would be back, looking for everybody – anybody. *Looking for somebody like Luke or me.* I wouldn't stand a chance in their courts. They'd get to me in the holding jail before it ever went to trial. Time to leave.

I began packing all that would now be useful to me: tools, food, kitchen gear, my tent and sleeping bag. I took large armfuls and piled it into my van. Then I scanned and double scanned the cabin, making sure that I hadn't left anything that I would need later --- or would reveal who I actually was. I found a stash of all my papers and letters. Some of them had my alias names, a few had my real name. I stuffed them in the van. I looked at my marijuana and peyote stash. I'd need a clear head, and I couldn't give anyone another reason to arrest me. So I left it by the pools at the hot springs. Anyone who found it could have it.

I walked outside to the hot springs pool. I saw friends carrying their things out of their cabins. A day before, no one could have gotten me to leave here. And now, no one could have gotten me to stay.

I whistled for my dog Kingfish. He jumped into my VW van. It was maybe four a.m. Time to go.

Years later, friends who worked at the Taos Hospital told me with confidence that the local police had let the attackers out of the jail to drive the hippies from the hots springs. One local man had been shot. He spent a few days in the hospital. A few others were treated for bad bruises and cuts. The two runaway girls did not get raped. Word had it that they promptly returned to Texas.

Friends also told me that a few Chicanos from Taos came to hot springs asking for a 'Luke' or an 'Adam'. That was one of the aliases I had used then. They left messages that they wanted to take us drinking. That would have been our last round.

# 20
# Mormon Health Care

I packed up my Volkswagen van as fast as I could in the moonlight. Then I counted my money. If I camped out all the time and cooked over a fire, I had enough money to get me to California, and maybe even to Canada. Some people owed me money, and I was waiting for a check. But now I had no time to wait and collect.

My dog Kingfish hopped in the van and I took off driving in the darkness --- to get out of this town, this county, and this state, this country --- before the law ever figured anything out. There was no way I could ever get a fair self-defense trial in this county where the jury would be related to the plaintiff and figure me to be the intruder --- if they didn't kill me in a holding cell before that.

By sunrise I was in Rio Arriba County, heading toward Navaho country. I was doing 50 mph on the flats, and 30 miles per hour up the mountains. Suddenly this 44 horsepower, 1500 cc air-cooled engine no longer seemed so glamorous to me. Frugal, maybe, but it sure was a terrible getaway vehicle.

At the next general store I bought two metal five-gallon gas tanks and filled them up along with my van's tank. I filled up five gallons of water and bought bulk food and dog food. Then I set off again, driving toward Shiprock, New Mexico. That sounded as good as anyplace to get lost.

Late in the afternoon, I saw the red sandstones of Shiprock Monument in the distance. I had not slept at all last night, and the fatigue was finally setting in. I turned off the paved road, down a little used gravel road. I drove on it for miles, until I spied a rocky trail veering to the left. I slowly turned off down it. I was very alone now, but still within view of the gravel road. I did not want anyone to be able to see me or my van from that gravel road. I idled down the trail until I came up to a lonely dry arroyo. On either side of it was an erosion ridge about ten feet high. If I pulled into it, no would be able to see my van.

I turned off the trail onto the dirt. Immediately I felt the rear wheels start to sink into the sand. I floored it, but the van did not pick up speed. I struggled up the arroyo, and then tried to turn around to get back to the hard gravel trail. But as I was turning, the van bogged down in the sand and stopped. I tried reverse and first several times, until I finally proved to myself that I was dead stuck. I was out of anyone's sight all right, and completely stuck in the isolated high desert.

Kingfish and I got out. While I examined my rear wheels, he sniffed around. Then he began digging for something. To Kingfish, this was a perfect place to camp. Stuck or unstuck meant nothing to him. Roaming and hunting in the outdoors was his only world.

I studied my rear wheels. I was nearly up to my axles in sand. I walked out to the hard gravel trail. I saw small plants beginning to sprout on it. It looked like no one had driven on this trail in months. I was also several miles from any pavement. Maybe I could walk to the pavement, then hitchhike to the nearest town, and then try to convince someone to drive all the way back here and pull me out. But I didn't have enough money to pay them. I needed what little money I had with me for gas and food. And what would I do with Kingfish? I figured I had gotten stuck here by myself, and I would just have to get unstuck by myself.

I took inventory. Besides the regular VW wheel jack, I had a forty inch Bloomfield Hi-lift jack, a twenty-foot, two-ton hand winch, and maybe fifty feet of nylon rope. Pretty good by most people's preparedness standards. After getting stuck a few times in the winter around Taos, I had learned to be prepared.

But there was nothing in front of my van for me to latch my winch onto. No trees or rocks, just sand and gravel. I didn't have a dead man to drive into the ground. I walked about and gathered some large rocks. My knee had swollen up from the fall at the hot springs. It now really hurt. Something was wrong inside it. Then I jacked up first one rear wheel and put rocks under them. I did the same with the other side. I got in, started the van, floored it, and popped the clutch. The van moved forward maybe two feet before it stopped. Fifty more times and I might get to the hard trail.

But it was sunset and I was already tired from no sleep. So I built a small fire, cooked some food, fed Kingfish, and called it a day. I lay under the springtime stars in the high desert and marveled at the magic of the light show. Kingfish roamed around, chasing after the rodents that came out after sunset. Later that evening, he came up to me on the tarp. He was panting and happy as he drank. This was as good as life got for Kingfish, give or take a bitch in heat. For me too. We were now down to four gallons of water.

I awoke in pain in the morning. I wanted nothing more than to stay in my sleeping bag. Strange for me, as I usually popped up before dawn and started off full speed. I crawled out of my sleeping bag and built a fire for coffee. It helped a little, but I had no appetite for food. I noticed that Kingfish was limping. I called him and checked his legs. His paw was covered with cactus thorns. He resisted as I pulled them out with my pliers.

# Mormon Health Care

I had to bull him down to get the last few out. We were both panting afterward. This had worn me out.

I examined the van wheels. I could jack them up fifty times, make two feet at a time, and get to the hard trail --- maybe. I jacked the wheels up again, put the rocks beneath them, and set the rear wheels down on the rocks. Then I lunged forward two more feet before I stalled. But on the third time I tried it, my front tires sank deep into the sand and the spinning rear tires just threw the rocks behind. This was not working.

I was already tired and hot, But I had the chills too. I thought about walking to the paved road and ask for help. But what if they were looking for me? What if that guy I shot at-----*It was self-defense, wasn't it? He had a gun. They had actually shot one of us. No matter.*

I walked down the gravel road toward the Shiprock monuments looking for something, anything, to put under the wheels. In the distance, up a slope, I saw a glint of metal. I climbed up the hill toward it. I had to stop a few times to rest. When I finally arrived, I found an old, collapsed metal shack. It covered the remnants of a shaft. It was an old, abandoned mine. The shaft did not look very big or deep, and the tailings pile was small. It must have been a failed exploratory shaft.

The roof of the shack had been covered with sheet metal. Each piece looked to be about ten by three feet. Some of them had rusted through. I managed to pry one of them loose. The rest were nailed on to the roof too tight for me to break loose by hand. I grabbed the piece and dragged it down the hill. I rested, and then pulled it behind me back to my van. The pain in my knee got worse. For the first time in my life, I was limping in a major way. I needed to rest when I got there.

After I awoke, I grabbed my claw hammer and tire iron. I returned to the abandoned mine and broke three more pieces of sheet metal from the wooden beams. I dragged them all behind me. Kingfish accompanied me enthusiastically. He never got bored exploring the same trail a second time.

By the time I got the sheet metal back to the van, it was sunset. I still had no appetite, but I forced myself to eat cheese, tortillas and fruit. Kingfish gulped down his dog food.

I lay in my sleeping bag and stared at the stars. Although the evening temperatures were moderate, I was shivering. My teeth chattered and my hair was soaked. Later in the evening I woke up to piss. I was so tired that I just half-unzipped my sleeping bag, scooted to the edge of the tarp, and pissed onto the sand while lying on my side. I looked up and noticed that the sky was now covered with clouds. What if we had a heavy rain? A flash flood might come down this arroyo and wash my van away. And me with it. I lay in my sleeping bag telling myself that I should get up and move my campsite up the hill. I kept telling myself to do that, again and again. But the bag was just too warm and I was just too tired.

When I awoke, it was cold and gray. A light rain was falling. It was a few hours after sunrise and I was still tired. I did not want to get out of my warm sleeping bag even though I was getting rained on. Kingfish stood over me and nudged me with his nose. Let's go hunting, he was saying, and while you're at it, I'll take some dog food too. I got out of my bag, dressed, and put on a coat. I put my sleeping bag in the van to keep it dry. Then I pissed. I noticed it was dark orange. I wasn't drinking enough water. But we were down to two gallons and I was conserving it. I still had no appetite.

I slowly jacked up the rear wheels and put the roofing metal beneath each wheel. Then I started up the engine and floored it in first gear. The rear wheels spun and threw the roofing behind the van. It didn't move an inch. My front wheels were now buried in the sand. I realized I would have to jack up all four wheels, one at a time, put the sheet metal beneath each one, and then try to drive forward. This would take twice the time.

I was jacking up the last wheel when I heard a rushing sound behind me. I turned to see a flash flood coming down the arroyo. I quickly ran up the side of the canyon and watched a wave of dirty brown water filled with wood and brush rush by me and hit the van. The water rose above the bumper and flowed around the van. The van moved a bit, and then turned sideways. I watched as the water rose higher, to the floor level of the van, into the engine compartment. Kingfish stood at the edge of the floodwaters and drank from it. I sat on the ridge and watched. There was nothing I could do.

The water subsided within an hour. I walked over the sand. It was firm now. The flood had deposited sand on top of the sheet metal. I had to dig around to find my tools. I opened the engine compartment and cleaned the debris out of it. The water had covered the cylinders but had not risen to the distributor cap or air filter. Nevertheless, I still took the distributor off and dried out the inside. I climbed into the driver's seat to start the engine. I was fully expecting nothing to happen when I turned the key. The starter could have water in it and be shorted out. But the engine turned over and started. I let it idle for a while to warm it up and dry out.

When I could wait no longer, I put it in first gear, revved the engine and quickly released the clutch. The van lunged forward and began to speed up.

## Mormon Health Care

As soon as I was off the metal the wheels slowed in the sand, then stopped. I made about fifteen feet before the van bogged down again.

I did the whole process over again. Jack up a wheel, put the sheet metal under the wheel, drop the wheel on the metal, and then repeat, repeat, and repeat. Then lunge forward the body length of the vehicle before it buried into the sand again and stalled. Again and again. With each time, I was one more van length closer to traction. But by mid afternoon, I was too exhausted to go any further. I did move my tarp and sleeping bag to higher ground. Before it was dark, I crawled into my sleeping bag.

Later in the night I suddenly awoke. I was shivering violently. Kingfish was lying against me, so I hugged him for warmth. Then I realized I had not fed or given him water since morning. I found my flashlight and poured him a large bowl of food. He drank all of the water first, and then ate all the food. I had less than a gallon of water left.

I crawled back to my sleeping bag on the ridge above the arroyo. I was too tired to walk. I snuggled into my down bag and covered my face. I breathed on my hands to warm myself up. I zipped the bag open and nudged Kingfish in. He worked his way to the bottom of the sleeping bag. I stuck my feet against him. Although he warmed the bag and it was not very cold outside, I still shivered. I slept in a daze.

Morning came and Kingfish tunneled himself out of the sleeping bag. He wandered about the arroyo, and then came back to me. He sat and waited. Finally I could wait no more. I got up and walked to the soft sand. I dug a hole in it and crapped. I looked at my stool and it was gray-colored. I stared at it. Was I hallucinating? I buried it. When I pissed, it was now dark brown. I fed Kingfish and forced myself to eat some cheese. But I just could not swallow it. I poured half my water into Kingfish's bowl, and drank the rest of it. We were now officially out of water. This was it.

I jacked up the van wheels again. Either the van was getting heavier, or I was getting weaker. Then I lunged the van forward. I finally got the front wheels onto the trail before the rear drive wheels sank back into the sand. Just one more time. But I fell forward with my face in the sand. I lay there a while.

I recall Kingfish sticking his wet nose against me. I got up and jacked the rear wheel up and slid the metal beneath it. The front edge of the metal now reached the trail. I rested, and then did the same with the other side. Then I climbed up into the driver's seat and started the engine. After it warmed up, I revved it and slowly eased out the clutch. The van hesitated, and then pulled forward. I turned quickly to the right to stay onto the trail. I

# The Wild Years

had made it.

I leaned over the steering wheel and rested. I looked to the ridge where all my stuff was spread out. I saw trails of footsteps and knee prints connecting the different spots. I gathered up all my camping gear and tools and threw them into the van in one big lump. Any other time I would have sorted everything out neatly. But now, I just didn't have the energy to care.

I remembered to double check the site. I found my Swiss army knife half-buried in the sand. What about the four pieces of sheet metal? Should I drag them away? I did not have the energy for it. I left them next to the trail road.

I idled the van up the trail to the paved road. I did not recall driving this far before. When I finally hit the pavement, there wasn't a car in sight. I sped the van up to forty miles per hour and drove on and on. I got low on gas and poured one of my five gallon cans of gas into the tank. We crossed into Arizona before we finally came to a trading post. I ran in and drank some water first. The locals stared at me. Then I filled up my gas tank and the five gallon tins. But when I started to fill up my five-gallon water can, the woman charged me fifty cents for it. "We have to haul it," she said.

I ordered a sandwich and went to the bathroom to clean up. I really needed it. While I was washing my face, I noticed how dark I was. Darker than ever before. The whites of my eyes were yellow. Was that what they were staring at? I put my sun glasses on before I went out. Maybe the Chicanos were right – that I was a dirty hippie. What if I had not gotten my vehicle out this morning?

Would I have been a dirty, *dead* hippie?

I forced myself to eat the sandwich. When I finished, I rested my head on the counter.

"You okay?" the waitress twanged. I nodded, got up and left.

Kingfish and I rolled on out of town. I pulled off at a scenic view on a hilltop. I let Kingfish out. Then I crawled into the back of my van and slept, despite the midday heat. I woke late in the afternoon. Kingfish was waiting outside with a dead kangaroo rat in his mouth. When I came out of the van, he threw it up in the air and jumped on it. His perfect toy.

We drove on across northern Arizona. I slept in the van all night and part of the day. Drive, drink, sleep, and try to eat. We passed through the beautiful western desert, only I was too tired to hike any trails.

In the morning while driving through the beauty of the Vermilion Cliffs, I heard a noise in the back of the van. It started out as as a rapid clicking.

But it gradually picked up as I drove west. While rolling along at 45 mph, I shifted in neutral. I still heard the noise. It varied with the speed of the engine, so it was not transmission or wheels. Then while still coasting, I turned the engine off. The noise immediately stopped. Bad news. The sound was coming from the engine. I stopped and opened up the rear engine panel. I saw fresh oil splattered around the engine shroud. Worse news. I checked the engine oil and it was really low. I added two quarts of oil before I could finally see oil on the dipstick. Two days ago when I had checked the oil, it was fine. More worse news. I started the engine up, and immediately I heard the loud knocking sound. I had thrown a rod. *Oh fuckkkkk*. Had dirt and sand from the flash flood gotten into the engine or carb? It did not matter now. The truth now was that I had a rapidly dying engine.

My van limped into Kanab, Utah, driving at 25 mph. I parked in the center of town next to a small plaza and walked to the rear of my van. Oil was dripping onto the pavement. It was engine rebuild time. But I had just rebuilt it 3000 miles ago. Apparently, not well enough. And now, here I was in perfectly manicured, Mormon Kanab, Utah, on the lam with a broken down van, a dog, almost no money, and dead sick. I looked around. Everything was ordered and neat. The town plaza reminded me of my mother's living room. I crawled into the back of the van, watered Kingfish, and rested.

I woke up in the early afternoon. Kingfish was lobbying me to take him hunting. I stepped out of the vehicle and was blinded by the light. I saw a few old men sitting on a park bench. I limped over to them and asked where was a clinic or hospital. They looked at me, but did not say a thing. I stood there a moment, then walked to a woman sitting nearby. She looked at me nervously. Then she pointed down the street and told me it was just a few blocks away.

I moved the van to under a shade tree and locked it with the windows partially open for Kingfish. He wanted so much to come along with me. Then I walked down the street to the hospital and into the waiting room. I was with three pregnant women. I went to the bathroom and looked at myself. Yellow-brown skin, yellow eyes, and brown piss. I was gaunt and dirty. I revulsed myself. What would my mother think? I washed myself as best I could in the sink and then sat in the corner of the waiting room, away from everyone else.

# The Wild Years

The nurse came and escorted each woman, one at a time, to their appointments. It was toward the end of the day when she came into the room and looked at me.

"You don't have an appointment. Why are you here?"

"I'm sick."

"Do you have insurance?"

"No ma'am. I got a little bit of cash, but not much. I'm sicker than I've ever been."

"We accept traveler's checks."

I shook my head.

She looked at me impatiently. "I'll go check with the doctor." She left. She returned a bit later. "The doctor will see you now."

She led me to a small, clean examining room. The doctor was sitting there. He looked me over severely. Then he said "You have hepatitis." He took my arms and looked up and down them. "Where are the needle marks?"

"I've never used needles in my life."

"Where do you inject your drugs?" He raised his voice.

I shook my head. He examined my body. He asked the nurse to help him find the injection tracks. They searched in vain. Then he conferred privately with the nurse.

"Well, you do have hepatitis. That is clear. Normally, I would give a patient a program of gamma globulin. But I don't think we have any on hand. And you have no insurance."

He stood up and gathered his things. "I advise you to get lots of rest, eat well, and drink lots of liquids. And stop using drugs."

They walked to the door and held it open for me. The nurse led me through the front door. I heard the handle click behind me. In the bright afternoon light I was disoriented. I walked down the sidewalk toward the road. I suddenly felt sick. I turned to the manicured lawn and sunk to my knees to vomit. But I had nothing inside me to throw up. My head swirled with fatigue and nausea. I collapsed and lay in the grass on my stomach. I must have passed out because I dreamed that I had lost Kingfish and was trying to pick up his trail. But he was gone. In my dream I panicked. I felt a tugging on my shoulder. I heard voices. I rolled over and looked up at the nurse. She continued shaking me until I responded.

"This looks terrible. Could you go lay someplace else? Anyplace else. But not in front of our hospital."

# 21

## Busted in Berkeley

I got in the right lane to turn onto Telegraph Avenue in Berkeley, California. My plan was to visit a few friends in the Bay Area, and then head north to Canada. Ahead of me, I saw two California State Police cars parked at the ramp. Four officers were standing beside them. As I slowed down to pull off, they looked at me. Both of them quickly raised their arms and motioned me to stop. I pulled off to the side of the ramp. A muscular cop walked up to me.

"Where you going?"

"Berkeley."

"You here for the People's Park thing?"

"No. What are you talking about?"

He looked at my New Mexico license plate, my long hair and garb.

"Let me see your ID's."

I reached under the seat for my wallet that had all my false ID's. I searched around but I couldn't find my wallet! Where was it? In front of the cop I panicked. I checked over and over, getting more flustered as the cop waited. I was positive that I had put it there. That was where I always kept it while I was driving. But now, when I needed my false ID's the most, I could not find them.

The cops were getting impatient. I recalled that I had picked up a hitchhiker yesterday near Bakersfield. He was an older guy without much to say. Homemade blue tattoos covered his arms. When I gassed up last night, I went inside to use the bathroom. When I came back out, the guy was pulling his backpack out of the back seat of my van. "This is good enough," he quickly said to me, and walked off. Not a word of thanks. And now, my wallet was missing.

"Someone stole my wallet!" I told the hitchhiker story to the cop.

"Step out of the van and put your hands on the roof. Do not move. We are searching your car."

I did as they told me to do. Both of the cops opened each door of my VW. One of them jumped back as Kingfish, my big black Labrador Retriever, jumped out.

"He won't bite," I shouted. "Don't hurt him."

"You'll have to tie him up to the van." The cop looked at Kingfish. "Where's his collar? All dogs have to have a collar and leash in Berkeley."

## The Wild Years

"Uhh—he's never had one."

"That won't work here," the cop answered.

I told Kingfish to lay down, and he did.

The cops resumed the search. One of them stuck his hand into the door pocket. OH MY GOD! That was where I kept my loaded Beretta pistol! They were going to get me carrying a loaded gun and I would go straight to jail for that one.

The cop pulled some things out of the door pocket and continued searching. The other cop opened the dash of my van. They searched through my luggage and boxes. They opened my tool boxes.

"That's a good set of Craftsman tools. You fix cars?"

"Yes, officer. I'm a mechanic." I would do anything for empathy now.

"Where did you get these tools?"

"I bought them --- I didn't steal them." The moment I said that, I felt guilty. And I had bought those tools. They continued with the search. Then one searched in the lining of the driver's seat. He pulled out a wallet. My *real* wallet. And I thought I had hidden it well.

"Here it is." He held it up to me and then opened it up.

"So... you are 'Dwight Worker'?"

Oh no. They had my *real ID's*. That was the name I was wanted on by the law.

They conferred among themselves for a moment. "Well, we are taking you to our central station to do an NCIC on you. We'll hold you until we get your results. Hold up your hands." he handcuffed me. "My partner will drive your van behind us to the police station."

"What's an N-C-I-C?"

"National Crime Information Center check on you. If you have any warrants, we will hold you."

"And my dog?"

"Tell him to get inside your van."

Kingfish jumped into my VW. They locked me in the backseat of the police car and drove to the police station. On the ride to the police station, I grew furious at the thought that the hitchhiker I had picked up had stolen my wallet with my false ID's. I helped him out on the road, gave him some food, took him in the direction he wanted to go --- and he steals my wallet. Now the police are going to check my real name and arrest me. *Goddamn him.* What a low-life betrayal. I started running fantasies of revenge, but then panic set in. The cops had not mentioned the gun yet. Were they going to check and see who was the real owner? Or run ballistics tests to see if it had been used in a crime? I had absolutely no idea about the background of that gun. My first handgun, and now I was in major trouble because of it. What had I gotten myself into?

When we got out, they led me into the Berkeley central police station. I asked the other cop to please open the window of my van so my dog could breathe. He did, and I thanked him.

We went inside and they booked me and locked me in a cell. As they were leading me, I looked out the door. And there, waiting at the door, was Kingfish! He climbed through the window of my van and was waiting for me in front of the police station door. With no collar or IDs or anything. What would happen to him? I panicked even more.

They were going to arrest me for a loaded pistol or figure out that I was wanted for walking out of a draft induction center, and lock me up. And Kingfish would be waiting patiently for me in front of the police station until they called the dogcatcher. And then--- Pure panic.

When the jailer walked by me, I told him that was my dog out front and asked if I could call a friend to have him pick him up. The jailer said that I had not been charged yet with a crime. If or when I was charged, they would allow me one phone call. He reminded me that most people called attorneys, and not for people to take care of their dog.

The thought of my dog being caught and euthanized sickened me. I no longer cared so much about my freedom, but Kingfish's life. He had always been a free, unleashed, un-collared, un-neutered dog. Although he was very well-trained and disciplined, he had run free his whole life. To be locked up in a pen would panic him – as badly as I was panicked now. I turned to the corner of the holding tank and started to cry. I covered my face so that no one else could see.

A bit later, across the holding tank, someone said "You get tear-gassed at People's Park too?"

I looked up and there was a long-haired man among several others whom they had just put in the holding tank. His eyes were red.

"No. What happened to you?" I asked.

"We were protesting the University destroying People's Park and the fucking pigs shot tear gas over our heads as I was running away from them. I ran right into the cloud and couldn't see a thing. Then they arrested me."

"Did this protest just happen?"

"No. We had planned it for weeks. They were ready for us."

So I had accidentally driven into Berkeley at the very beginning of the protest. The cops were stopping all suspicious-looking vehicles, and that included mine. Wrong place, wrong time.

I started to tell him what happened, but then I stopped myself. I had heard that jail houses were filled with snitches who got special privileges and reduced sentences if they spied on other prisoners. Then I thought that, if he were a snitch, I would just tell him the truth anyhow. If that got back to my jailers, it could not hurt my situation. So I told him about my bad timing. I did not mention my lost wallet or the pistol.

I listened to the young guys talk about their tactics against the police at People's Park. Any other time, I would have been interested. But now, I could only think of Kingfish. I sweated and my heart pounded. *So this was it.*

Some time later, a guard came up to the holding tank.

"Dwight Worker," he called. I had not heard my name called in public for over two years. He opened the gate.

"You can go now."

"You didn't find---"

"Find *what?*" he looked at me funny. You dumb fuck Adam, no Jimmy, no – now your name is Dwight.

" -- my dog. Did you find him?"

"Oh he's been waiting out front the whole time. You'd better get a collar on him. You're not wanted for anything. And you had better keep it that way, or we'll bust your ass."

The cop handed me the keys to my car.

"Thank you."

I stepped through the door and Kingfish jumped up against me, almost knocking me over. I put my arms around his neck and held him to me. I cried into his neck. Before we got into my van, I poured him a bowl of water. He drank it all up. Then we hopped in and I took off.

Why hadn't they arrested me for walking out of an induction center? I couldn't believe that the Selective Service had not charged me with any crime. And I had been living for two years like I were a fugitive. *I was no longer wanted by the law?* I could call my parents now? And what about the gun?

A few miles away, I pulled over and parked my van on an isolated street in Oakland. I quickly searched every place in my van where I might have hidden my pistol. I could not find it. It was gone. Did the cops find it and keep it? No. They would have no use for such an under-powered pistol. And besides, California cops were too professional to do that. They would have arrested me for the possession of a loaded weapon. *But the gun was*

## Busted in Berkeley

*gone from my car.* The hitchhiker-thief! He had stolen my gun and along with my wallet full of false ID's.

I sat there shaking my head. My dog was getting restless. Nearby, on Telegraph Avenue in Berkeley, people were getting arrested. *And I was not wanted for anything.* I was now 'Dwight Worker' for the first time in years. I had sort of gotten used to living on the lam. On the lam, you traveled different circles, met different people, and living a different life. But now, I could get a passport. I could travel.

I started up my VW. I had had enough of Berkeley already. I took off driving straight for Yosemite. When all my other chips were down, the wilderness always made sense to me.

# 22

## Here Comes the Motherfuckers

In a snowstorm on a bitterly cold winter night, at 9000 feet in the Sangre de Cristo mountains of north central New Mexico, in the winter of 1969, a large U-haul truck struggled up an icy road. Only the driver knew where he was going, and he was lost. He finally stopped in front of a small adobe house to ask for directions. There was no place to pull off, so their truck blocked the road. But there was no traffic at this time of night, not in these mountains with these road conditions.

As the driver gets out, he hears pounding from inside the enclosed cargo space. He opens the cargo door. Young men and women jump out, shouting that they are freezing, hungry, thirsty, and have to shit and piss. The guys walk over to the snow piled alongside the desolate road and urinate. A few young women look around for a flat spot off the road. But it is all deep snow piled up from the snow plows. So, after hesitating, they lift their mini-skirts, pull down their pantyhose, squat, and pee on the road. They squeal at the cold. Their thick streams splash on their platform shoes and stockings. They cuss about it as their pee runs down the road and quickly freezes.

"How far more?" a few men shout. "Hurry up and get there."

The driver answers that he is almost there, but that he must ask for directions. A light turns on in the window of the small adobe home where they parked. The driver walks up the pathway and knocks on the door. Then

# The Wild Years

the door slowly opens. A man is barely visible, with a rifle hanging on his arm. The driver steps back, apologizes, and then asks for directions to Ojo Sarco. But the man does not speak English. The driver shouts out for Lobo to come quickly. Lobo comes running up. He speaks to the man in fluent Spanish. They finally get their directions, thank the man, pile back into the rental truck, and take off.

Several miles later, following directions, they turn onto a snow-covered dirt road. It descends quickly and the driver panics. He hits the brakes and then throws the truck into reverse. But the dual rear wheels just spin. There is no getting out of this road. He sits there for a moment cussing while another man in the cab says "This had *better* be it."

In the headlights beams, they watch the snow blowing violently across the road in front of them. The driver shifts into first gear and continues his downward descent. They flip on the cab light and study the crudely drawn map again. Then they count the adobe houses on the right as they drive slowly. After about a quarter mile, they come to the third house. "This must be it," the driver says.

"It better be," the man next to him answers.

They get out of the cab and leave the engine running. This time they ignore the pounding coming from the inside of the cargo area of the U-haul. They trudge through the foot-deep snow in their street shoes. Their shoes quickly fill with snow that packs into ice. The house appears unlit. They cautiously knock on the door. This time, before the door opens, they step back with their hands up. The door opens with a crack. Again they see a man who looks like he has a rifle.

"Two Bears? It's me---John-John. Is that you?"

There is a long pause. "Yeah man. It's me."

"We're here, from New York City. Finally made it. Half the family too."

Two Bears opens the door. "Come on in."

John-John runs back to the truck and opens the cargo door while the driver steps into Two Bears' cabin. In a few minutes, more than twenty people come staggering into Two Bear's place. Young men and women, dressed in New York City street clothes with winter coats and no more. No one is carrying any children. One woman has lost a shoe in the deep snow and a man wearing platform shoes has slipped off the steps. As soon as the last one is in, a woman shouts "Shut that door and turn up the heat and turn on the lights!" Two Bears tells her he doesn't have electricity here, and that the fireplace is the only heat. The woman's face is incredulous. Two Bears lights several more candles and puts more wood in the fireplace. They crowd around the fire and push for space. They hold their hands out to the growing fire in worship to the heat goddess.

"I'm starving. What you got to eat?" the same woman asks.

"Where's the bathroom?" another asks. Two Bears points outside, and gives directions to the outhouse.

"Outhouse! A fucking outhouse! I'm not using that."

"Just don't shit on the floor then," Two Bears says.

Someone goes out to the outhouse. In few a minutes, he returns. "That seat was so fucking cold I thought my ass was going to freeze to it!"

Others reluctantly walk outside to use the outhouse.

Then Two Bears tells them that he has no running water, only a hand pump well.

Another woman shouts, "What the fuck kind of place is this anyhow?"

Two Bears shows them a twenty-gallon water container. A woman begins washing her hands and face. She shouts that the water is freezing. Two Bears says that he 'll get a fire going in the cooking stove to heat some hot water, but that will take a while.

"*Heat water up*? You mean it's not hot already?" another woman shouts.

"Where can we sleep?"

"On the floor," Two Bears answers. "Wait a minute and I'll get out all my blankets. Two Bears comes back from his bedroom with a large armful of blankets and lays them on the floor. The new arrivals bring in all their blankets and sleeping bags from the truck and spread them out. They try to arrange themselves on the floor so that everyone is covered, but they just don't have enough blankets.

"How do you ever keep warm here, Two Bears?" a woman asks in the candle light.

"I got good wool blankets on my bed," Two Bears calls out from his bedroom.

"Fuck this shit. I'm coming in to sleep there too." A woman gets up and walks across the bodies. "Make room."

"Me too," another woman seconds. She follows the first woman.

"Don't worry about me," Two Bears says from the bedroom. "I won't bother you."

The two women get into bed with him. "I don't give a fuck if you do. I'm still getting under covers," one of them answers. "I'm freezing."

Two Bears did his best trying to accommodate over twenty hungry, freezing New York City street kids who had mostly never been out of the city's limits. They were loose members of an anarchist street gang who called themselves *The Motherfuckers*. One of their band, Lobo, idolized Billie the Kid. Billie the Kid was also from New York City and he had holed up one winter in Ojo Sarco, New Mexico. So the Motherfuckers came in Billie the Kid's tracks. Many of them could no longer stay in New York City anyhow. They had warrants for robbery, assault, drugs, prostitution---even an attempted murder. And maybe there were other warrants they didn't know about. They had no money, attorneys, driver's licenses, or futures there. They figured anything, *just anything*, had to be better than what they were facing in NYC. Besides, the city was going to burn down and fall into the ocean anyhow. Just like California. Hadn't you heard? Everybody knew that. So, after a few successful drug deals and drug ripoffs, they managed to raise enough money to rent a U-haul truck, pack themselves in and take off, driving non-stop across the USA in the winter. Those in the cargo box only saw walls for the whole drive. So much for seeing the good ole US of A.

I was visiting a friend down the road in Ojo Sarco when Two Bears came knocking on our door in the morning. He was a short, stocky guy from back East with long curly black locks and a beard. He had gotten his name by shooting a mother black bear and then her cub.

"I got unexpected company show up," Two Bears said. "Lots of them. I need to get them some food and blankets until the roads clear up and we go get some supplies. You got some stuff I can borrow? I'll make it up to you."

Two Bears had always been square with me on money and trade matters. So my friend and I gave him some bulk food and loaned him my two sleeping bags. I told him I would be needing the bags back tomorrow when I left for home.

I came by Two Bear's cabin next morning to find a group of people crowded around the fireplace. They were eating out of a large bowl. A few were using spoons, while the rest ate with their hands. Two Bears introduced me to them as Jimmy. No one paid any attention.

I pointed to the bowl. "What is that?"

"Cornmeal, molasses, and water."

"Grits?"

"Naw. They didn't let the water boil first. They were too hungry."

I found one of my sleeping bags wrapped around a guy's shoulders. I started to take it from him, explaining that it was mine. He resisted. Two Bears had to intervene before I got it back. When I got the other one from another guy, I saw a big hole burned in its bottom.

"What's this?" I held my burned sleeping bag up to him.

# Here Comes the Motherfuckers

The guy looked at it slowly. "Oh. I must of got my feet too close to the fire last night. They were cold." And with that, he turned back to the fire. The bag was ruined, unless I sewed the burned end together. And if I did that, the bag was going to be a foot shorter. I glared at him, but it didn't do any good. I grabbed both bags and walked back to my VW van.

When I tried to pull out, I got my van stuck in the snow. So I jacked up a wheel. Then, while I was laying in the snow, I put the tire chains on that wheel. I had to take off my gloves to hold cold metal and snap the chains together. My fingers almost stuck to the metal. I needed fifteen minutes for one chain. When I finally got it on, I tried to drive it out with one chain on. But then the other wheel just spun. So I had to repeat everything with the other wheel. Finally, I shifted my van into first gear and managed to climb out of the driveway onto the road. Two guys who were watching me the whole time now came running up to me. A woman followed them.

"Hey!" one guy shouted. "When you come back, bring some cigs---"

"---and some food!"

"---lots of food. And some wine---"

I put my open hand out the window. "MON----EEEY. MON—EEEY!"

"We'll pay you when you get back."

*What?* Oh, a year or two ago and I might still have fallen for that bullshit. But I had been conned and ripped off enough to now dismiss them point blank. I let the clutch out in first gear and felt the chains slowly chew away the hard pack snow under me. I started pulling away when I heard a loud pounding on my passenger door. A girl was waving frantically to me.

"Where you going?" she shouted. Then without waiting for an answer, she opened the door. "Can I come along? I'm starving and freezing." Then she just climbed in. "Hi. I'm Slinky. You Jimmy?"

"Yep."

"You got a smoke?"

I told her I didn't smoke tobacco. She groaned. This girl was tall and skinny. Her makeup had long ago smeared all over her face. Slinky was very pale, even by winter mountain standards. Her dark hair accentuated her whiteness. Her lips were bluish and chattering, and she was shivering. Her hands were inside her winter coat. She was still wearing a mini-skirt, bright stockings, and platforms. Except for a few crooked teeth, she could have been really pretty.

"It is *really* fucking cold here!" she repeated. "Turn the heat on."

"It is on." Back then, air-cooled VW vans were one of the few vehicles in the US where you needed an ice scraper for both the outside *and* inside

# The Wild Years

of the windows. I reached back and handed her my burned up sleeping bag. She wrapped herself with it.

I told her I was going to Mora. "Where's that? Do they have a restaurant there with a heated fucking room?" Yeah. "Good then. I'm going with you, okay?"

"I'm not planning on coming back here any time soon."

"Well then, I'll just have to figure out how to get back when that time comes. What the fuck kind of place got no electricity, no running water, no heat, no bathroom?" she said to no one. "I tell you, this is fucked, man." She leaned back in the seat. She was twitching and couldn't sit still. "You sure you don't have any more heat in this van? No cigarettes either?" As the engine finally heated up, it blew a feeble stream of warmish air across the front windows. Just enough heat to maintain visibility.

I drove slowly to the main highway, listening to the chains slapping on the pavement. When I finally got to the top of the mountain pass, I stopped to take the chains off. Slinky got out with me.

"It sure is beautiful here. I never seen anything like this in my life. But it's just too fucking cold," she repeated. Then she suddenly pursed her lips and leaned forward. She awkwardly ran to the edge of the road, leaned over the safety railing, and began vomiting. She continued for a bit. There's nothing a man can do when a woman's vomiting.

"That cornmeal crap. It was terrible," she mumbled as she was catching her breath. "Never eat that shit again. You got any water?" I handed her my canteen. She opened it, but the water inside was frozen." "Shit!" she exclaimed.

She washed her mouth out with handfuls of snow. Then she reached into her purse and pulled out her toothbrush and paste. With a combination of snow and toothpaste, she brushed her teeth. She spit out and brushed again. Then she repeated, "Whoa this is cold!"

She walked up to me on the road and started to slip. I caught her and stopped her fall. She held onto me. Then I felt her shuddering. She was crying.

"I'm sorry. But I'm just not used to this. They didn't tell me it would be like this." She held onto me until she had stopped crying. "I'm sorry, Jimmy. Thanks."

I helped her back into the van. Those platform shoes of hers were less than useless here. We rolled slowly down the mountain pass to Mora, dropping some 2000 feet. The roads got better and it was no longer so cold. I told Slinky there was a great little local Mexican restaurant up ahead with

# Here Comes the Motherfuckers

wonderful posole and home-made tamales. Slinky said she didn't know what that food was, but as starving as she was, she'd try anything.

"But hey Jimmy, I don't got no money," she blurted out in a pure NYC street accent. She reached over and slapped her hand on my knee. "Jimmy. Jimmy Jimmy Jimmy Jimmy," she repeated. "Tell you what. If you buy me a good meal, I'll give you a blow job." She laughed and rubbed my leg again. "I like you anyhow."

I was *not* expecting this, or anything like this. This was a first for me.

"I was going to buy you food anyhow, Slinky."

She kept smiling at me, and I sort of awkwardly smiled back.

"And I was going to blow you anyhow, Jimmy. So that makes us even."

After a strange pause, we both burst out laughing. Mine was out of awkwardness, and I had no idea what hers was out of.

We stopped and ate. She said the food was weird but really tasted good. When we were done, she asked me where I was going.

"Home."

"Can I come?"

"I guess. Sure."

"At least you got electricity and heat and a bathroom, right?"

"No, but I have plenty of food and firewood and blankets."

"Shit, you're almost as bad as Two Bears. But I guess I'll come anyhow. I don't have much other choice, do I? I gotta live up to my part of the bargain anyhow." She laughed at that.

We stopped at the turnoff to my road. Slinky tried to help me put the chains back onto the rear wheels of my van, but mostly she just got in the way. Then we made the long climb up to my cabin. When we got there, she said this place was just beautiful too.

She would stay far a while. But after a few days, she got bored with doing nothing but work. No television or stores, and she hated reading. She was also shaking and sick. But by then, I had noticed her forearms. She had to get back to her friends, wherever they were. And could I loan her some money? When I handed her some dollars, she said, "I need *more* than that."

For a while after that, I hardly saw the Motherfuckers. I never heard them call themselves the Motherfuckers either. But their stories carried over to my side of the mountains. I heard that more of them arrived from New York City, that Two Bears quickly ran out of firewood for them, and so they burned his furniture for heat. Then Two Bears threw them out at gunpoint. The Motherfuckers ran out of food and money too, so they took that U-haul

# The Wild Years

rental truck down to Albuquerque, found a chop shop, and sold it for cheap.

So the Motherfuckers needed a place to stay. They heard that Jack Nicholson had just bought a large section of land above Le Doux, New Mexico, with the money he had made from the movie, *Easy Rider.* So the Motherfuckers scouted out the land for a campsite. In the past, in New York City, the original Motherfuckers had regularly occupied abandoned places to live. So why not just occupy Jack Nicholson's land too? *What private property rights anyhow?* the street communist Motherfuckers asked themselves. *If Jack don't like it, he can just come out here himself and drive us off himself. He's too busy in LA with his movies to have time for it, and he's too cool to get uptight about it.* And on that one, The Motherfuckers turned out to be right.

More stories came over the mountain to me about the Motherfuckers. I heard that a lot of them were abandoned street kids, who lived in the same rooms where their junkie prostitute mothers shot up and tricked. Some of them had become junkies by stealing heroin from their mothers and her tricks. Soon they were doing anything they could to get more drugs. Some of them were born practically homeless. Feral kids, like you might see in the barrios of Colombia or the favelas of Brazil. Only they were here in the USA. By the time other kids were thinking about the prom and sports, they were getting arrested for theft, drugs, robbery, assault, and prostitution.

There was revolutionary politics in the air in New York City in the sixties, from the shutdown of Columbia University to the civil rights, anti-war, and anti-draft movements. But for these street kids, they didn't need any lectures to tell them that life was stacked against them. They had known that from day one. From that first cold wintry night when they climbed out of the stolen U-haul truck, they looked around and began doing the only thing they knew how to do. Survive, by most any means possible. Soon they began doing things that would cause everyone to stop calling them 'The Motherfuckers'. Their new name became 'the Banditos', and they earned it.

Some of them began their very first detox in their lives in the back of that stolen U-haul truck and in freezing cabins in the mountains. Some couldn't take it. They commandeered a vehicle and headed to Albuquerque. A week later they returned with cash, marijuana, heroin and a few guns. From their New York City days, they knew that the best ripoffs were dope deal ripoffs. No cops to worry about, and they could score from both sides; cash *and* drugs. When they returned to the Nicholson land, in true

# Here Comes the Motherfuckers

communist fashion, they shared their loot with their family in crime. They bought camping gear, tents, tepees, horses, and especially, rifles and pistols,. They preferred the older models; Winchester lever actions, single-action Colts, double-barrel shotguns. The kind of guns they had seen in western movies and thought that Billy the Kid might have used.

The Banditos expanded their raiding forays to include Santa Fe. Those mellow hippies there were just no match for them. Occasionally, they hit a gas station or restaurant. Once they even got a bank. Since they had no addresses, phones, utility bills, or local history of any sort, the law was clueless as to who they were. They hadn't dealt with people like this in 80 years.

But the word about the Banditos spread among the hardcore drug dealers in the nearby cities. One Bandito named Maxie went to Albuquerque to set up another drug ripoff. His plan was the same as before: do a small buy to set them up for the next big buy. Then get the draw on them and take all the money and drugs. Maxie set up a buy on Albuquerque's tough south side. The Banditos waited for him to return, but no one ever saw or heard from Maxie again. A few Banditos went down to Albuquerque to look for him, but they were met with drawn guns. They returned and mulled about what to do about Maxie. In the end, they divided Maxie's remaining possessions of saddles, tack gear, and guns among themselves.

Another story that filtered down to me was about an apparently successful heroin ripoff in Albuquerque. Before returning to the mountains, the bandito stopped at an abandoned house to sample the product. Sidestep was the first one to shoot up. He passed out and died on the spot. What a bummer. Was this just such pure heroin, or had they been set up with poison? After thinking about it, none of the other Banditos wanted to try the next hit. They sat around in their private withdrawals wondering what they should do now. They couldn't rightly return the heroin to the people that they had just ripped off and demand better product, could they? None of them knew Sidestep all that well either, as he had just recently come out west from New York City. He wasn't part of the original band. So they stood around in an abandoned house in Las Vegas, New Mexico, wondering what to do? Always the important question in life. So they left the stolen heroin on the table and Sidestep's body under it and split. They would have to find somebody else to rob.

Sometimes the Banditos stopped at my small ranch on horseback, always with guns. Inevitably they needed something from me. As I was five miles from the nearest paved road and without a telephone, I tended to be friendly with them. You want some antibiotics, a few shotgun shells, some feed for your horses? Sure. I even included some food with it. They usually did not take too much from me, and they promised to pay me back later. Sometimes they even did. But when I asked the Banditos for specifics about what happened with Maxie or Sidestep, at first all I got got was silence. When I pressed on, their answer was, "What the fuck you wanna know for? Don't ever ask again," or "None of your fucking business," or a kinder, gentler, "He's gone. We can't bring him back. So drop it." And so I did.

So the Banditos stopped going to Albuquerque. They could only rip off the drug dealers there so many times before the word was out on the street about them. Then the Banditos went to Espanola. This was a dumpy little town north of Santa Fe that was loaded with heroin. Espanola had a history of generations of drug addicts and drug dealing. But when Roger of the Banditos tried to pull off their drugs-and-money ripoff, an Espanola home boy shot him dead on the spot. Somehow, the Banditos managed to get Roger's body back without going through any of the coroner, autopsy, and death certificate BS. They carried him up to the Jack Nicholson land on horseback, buried him, and then had a big party. They would talk about that party for years.

Newly minted Banditos continued to arrive from New York City, unknowingly replacing their fallen soldiers. Many of them loved the mountains at first sight. For the first time in their lives, they felt truly free. The Bandito women who kicked heroin stayed on at the camp. They dropped out of prostitution too, because in sixties, even if they had wanted some extra cash, how could they compete with free-love market? The Bandito men divvied their women up as they might their loot from a successful ripoff. If these women resisted or even complained, I never saw any of it. Perhaps compared to what they had been doing on those New York City streets, the Bandito camp was a major improvement.

When I finally visited the Bandito camp, I saw that many of the women had really taken to horseback riding and wilderness living. Some looked like they were becoming strong and healthy, for maybe the first time in their adult lives. These women doted over their horses better than any cowboy did. Daily groomings, rubdowns, and bucket feedings. It seemed that any money they got went to their horses.

The Bandito women also watched over Melody's daughter, Rain. Melody always had a dozen volunteer babysitters. Some of them talked of having a baby of their own. I doubted that any of them was using contraception. But in the coming years, there were very few pregnancies amongst them. I only knew of one child carried to full term.

Around a fire one night, I heard Bandito women joking that maybe their *old man* was infertile, or too stoned to do it. They laughed hard among themselves over their wisecracks. I heard that the Bandito women would casually bed other outside men, on the sly or not so sly. Maybe they were loving these passerbys as sperm donors for their real task at hand --- of having a baby doll of their very own. More than once I heard one of their women say, "I'll quit smoking, drinking, and drugs the moment I find out I'm pregnant." They didn't seem all too concerned about who the father would be, so long as they were the mother. After all, what had men been to them in their previous lives, but powerful, dangerous creatures who came, took what they wanted, and then left.

Later, I met a guy who had stopped over at the Bandito camp for a few days and had a dalliance with one of their women. A few weeks later this same guy showed up at the health clinic getting treated for some painful STD. Young men soon learned not to party with the Bandito women.

By the late summer of 1970, the Banditos were getting good at poaching mule deer, elk, and any other wild game they could find. Hunting licenses were like driver's licenses to them: they never had or wanted any. Within a year, there was little game to be had around their campsite. Local Chicano hunters were the first to notice. They reported this to the New Mexico Department of Game and Fish.

When the Banditos couldn't find wild game, they knew of another sure source of free meat. They simply rode to an isolated pasture in the late afternoon, found a yearling steer, and shot it in the head. They had it field-dressed in an hour. Then they carried the carcass on horseback back to the camp for the feast. Within a week, there would be nothing left of the steer. Then they dumped the bones and fur deep in the mountains, where the wild animals quickly finished it off.

But the entrails that they left in the high pastures drew vultures. For centuries, the Chicano ranchers had been following the flights of vultures to find out what had died. When they arrived to a pile of putrid, half-eaten guts, they knew this could only mean poaching. They checked amongst their own first, to see if any local might have done it. This was highly unlikely, as their culture had many generations to learn the serious consequences of cattle rustling. Then to them, everything pointed to that gang on Nicholson's land. If that was true, they knew what to do. They would take a mounted, well-armed posse to the campsite and *get those*

## The Wild Years

*motherfuckers.* Little did the Chicanos know that this had been the preferred name of the Banditos while incubating in New York City.

Sheriff Sanchez of Mora County tried to contact this Jack Nicholson guy about driving those trespassers off of his land. But he had no luck. Jack was never in and his secretary simply did not know what to do. She dealt with meetings and schedules and offers. Not banditos in the mountains. New Mexico was just too far away from the LA movie business.

And so it began. New Mexico had seen more than its share of outlaws in its day: Indians bands marauding the pueblos, the Spanish attacking the Indians, Indians attacking the Spanish, Indians then attacking the covered wagons, the highway robbers attacking the stage coaches, the range wars with the cattlemen and the farmers, the Indian-Chicano-Anglo shootouts, and Pancho Villa raiding across the border at Douglas, New Mexico. But never in New Mexico's history had their people seen anything remotely like that band of heroin-addicted, gun-toting, nothing-to-lose New York City street toughs who jumped out of the backs of rental trucks and charged out onto an unknown land.

# 23

# How I Got My Winchester 38-40

"Take a look at this Winchester 38-40 carbine, son." I handed the rifle to my son. It had a hexagon barrel, rear adjustable sites, and a black-stained stock from gun powder, dirty hands, and a century on the trail. "This is the story about how I came upon this gun."

I had bought a small ranch for a pittance in the Sangre de Cristo Mountains in northern New Mexico, near the little town of Mora. The locals called the place '*La Sierra*'. Spanish was the first language here, and it sure helped that I spoke it. The place was up at 8800 feet, with a year around flowing stream and a well that never went dry. It was at the end of a five mile long dirt road and was without any utilities. On my 24th birthday, on September 17, 1970, I camped outside. When I awoke, I had over a foot of snow on the tarp covering my sleeping bag. I had just discovered that this place had only a 75 day growing season, maximum. This was going to be a tough place to survive.

When we had a three-foot snow drift over my only access road in late November, I learned I had better get my firewood in early. I would now be using Pharaoh, my Spanish Mustang stud horse, to get in and out. Snow plows were unheard of around here. But if someone wanted to get snowed in and lost for the winter, this was the perfect place. My only contact with

# The Wild Years

the outside world was the post office, and that was six miles away.

By January, I had cabin fever bad. Since my job as an ambulance driver did not begin until they finished remodeling the clinic next summer, I had no work to keep me here. As the winter wore on, thoughts of camping out in the Sonoran Desert dominated my days while I chopped wood and carried water. Most of my activities related directly to keeping myself warm, fed, and alive. My big joy at the end of the day was crawling under thick blankets with my Aladdin lantern burning brightly and reading the stack of good books and magazines I had with me. Even then, my fingers got cold holding the books.

Finally I found Cheryl, a hardy mountain woman who was looking for a place to stay. She had a reputation for honesty and hard work. I offered her the place rent free if she would keep the horse fed and take care of my home. I had enough feed and firewood for her to last the winter. She accepted and moved in. She promptly cleaned the place better than I ever had.

I waited for a break in the weather. Then I loaded up my four-wheel drive pickup truck with all my camping gear and my dear dog Kingfish. I reminded Cheryl to guard the place well. Then I began my drive down the mountain. When I came to the snow drifts, I gunned the truck. Snow flew onto the windshield, blinding my vision. If I slipped off the road here down the hillside, this truck wasn't going anyplace further until springtime. Only the gravity of driving downhill and my momentum kept me rolling. I was sliding to either side, but to stop now was to get stuck. I finally made it to the base of the mountain and to paved highway. I first stopped at my friend's place, Ronald and Rosa, and left Kingfish and my 22 rifle with them. Now I began a long slow drive to the southern desert, and to warmth.

I spent the winter camping out in the Sonoran Desert of the USA and Mexico. In sleepy border towns and abandoned mining camps, in Mexican cantinas and villages, with trips to Puerto Penasco, Santa Ana, and Tucson for supplies. My major expenses were bulk food, gas, beer, some smoke, and auto parts for whenever my truck broke down. In those days, you used to be able cross the border without much fear of getting killed....

Come springtime, I began the drive back north. When I arrived in Mora, it was green. There was plenty of water in the valleys below from the mountain snow melt. When I turned off to La Sierra, I switched the front wheel hubs to four wheel drive, and began the long climb up to my cabin.

The road was muddy and slippery in places, but at least the snow had melted. I was worried because I had not heard from Cheryl, even though I had sent her several letters. When I drove around the bend and saw my cabin, I was relieved that it had not burned down this winter. Smoke was coming out of the chimney and my horse Pharaoh was roaming a pasture. Good. I would have to break him in for riding again, as I had to do every every springtime. He was a stud horse who went wild whenever he hadn't been ridden for a while, or when he caught the scent of a mare in heat. I could understand that.

I started to park my truck in a little pull-off next to my barn. But in front of me I saw a stripped-down frame of a vehicle. It wasn't there when I left. The frame looked new. I parked next to it.

I walked into the kitchen and saw Cheryl standing in front of the wood stove. With her were two young women. They did not look like they were from around here. Their faces were grim.

"Have you seen Two Braids?" Cheryl almost shouted at me.

*This is the first thing Cheryl says? Not a hello, welcome back, or anything.*

"Who is Two Braids?"

"He would be driving a 65 Plymouth," one girl says.

"A blue one. Two door," the other girl adds.

"What's going on here?"

We sat down at the table and I listened. The two women told me that they were driving from Boston to LA. They picked up this guy and woman who were hitchhiking, Two Braids and Meadow. When they got to Mora County, Two Braids asked them if he could borrow their car to get some medicine. The women said okay. Then Two Braids and Meadow dropped the two women off at my place and told them to wait. They said they would be back in a few hours.

"And that was two days ago!" One girl blurts out, in tears.

"And what's with this stripped down car in my parking spot?"

"Oh yeah. Just after you left, Two Braids brought it here. They had a mechanic take all the parts off it to sell."

"And they left it *here*? Whose is it?"

"It was a rental car. They didn't return it."

"No shit."

"And who is this Two Braids?" I almost shout at Cheryl. "You let him come into my home to do all this?"

Cheryl shook her head at me like I didn't get it at all. "Two-Braids is this bandito from New York City. He's been living in the mountains this winter, robbing the Texans' cabins. He's hurt a few people too. There's been a few gun fights up in the mountains, you know. He's a big guy and he's always got a gun on his hip when he comes here. How could I throw him out?"

At this point, the other woman begins to cry. "They've got our purses and money and credit cards. Everything," she says. Then she asked me to drive her to town so she can call her parents. I agree, and we leave.

I first stop at the Mora County Emergency Care Center to tell them I am back and I will be able to begin working shortly. Then we drive to a pay phone. I give the women money for the call as they have nothing at all. I watch one of them make a call. In a moment, I hear her crying. She talks for a while, then waves for me to come to the phone. I do. She says that her mother wants to talk with me. I take the receiver and listen to a frantic woman. She does not completely trust me and asks me to take her daughter and her friend to the police. I tell her I know sheriff Sanchez personally and I will do that. I also explain that I have never met this Two Braids and I have no idea who he is. The mother asks me if I will loan her daughter and friend money to get to LA. She promises again and again to repay me. I tell her that I will do that. I spend a lot of time assuring the mother that her daughter and friend are now safe. But she was still very worried when we ended the conversation. I found myself feeling enraged at this whole mess.

We go to Sheriff Sanchez's office. When I enter, he has his chair tilted against the wall, chatting with a few Chicano friends of ours. Sanchez seems young for a sheriff to me. Maybe ten years older than me. He has the mandatory mustache and is wearing a gray stetson hat.

"Finally back, huh?" We shake hands. I speak Spanish with him. He says I am the only hippie here who speaks Spanish, and the only hippie who has a job. My speaking only in Spanish to them was my way of showing respect to these people who were here long before I. I look at the gun on Sanchez' hip. It is a double-action, stainless steel Colt 357 magnum. What stands out is the silver handle with turquoise inlays. It is one of the most beautiful hand guns I have ever seen.

There is a pause, and then the young women repeat their story. Sanchez apologizes for what has happened. He has the women sign papers reporting the stolen car. I stress to Sanchez that I have no idea who this guy Two-Braids is. Sanchez tells us that the robberies and break-ins and even cattle rustlings have really increased ever since these banditos came here. The New Mexico State Police sent a mounted posses into the hills this winter looking for them, but did not find them. Then Sanchez leans forward and his voice drops. "We heard that those banditos killed two of their own this winter. Tell me whatever you can find out about it." Then Sanchez says, "Personally, I don't care if they kill themselves off. We'd like that. But in the meantime, we're hunting them down."

"What should I do if a group of them come around my ranch packing guns?"

"You got a gun?"

I nod. Sheriff Sanchez looks right at me and says, "If they are trespassing on *your land*, and they come *with guns to rob you*, then *shoot them dead*. You are way up there. No one is going to be able to help you in time. I assure you that there is *no* jury in this state of New Mexico that would ever convict you. But personally, I can assure you that we would make sure that it would *never* get to a jury here. We'd give you a medal first."

I nod. Then I look at the girls. Now they are really panicked. I guess the cops in Boston don't talk like this. I ask Sanchez where is an inexpensive, secure place nearby where the girls can stay. He directs me to a motel down the road. We shake hands and leave. I take the girls to the motel and and pay the seven dollars a day for the room. I give them a hundred dollars as I had promised their mother and I tell them I will check in on them tomorrow. Then I drive back up to La Sierra.

When I pull up to my place, I see a 1965 blue Plymouth parked there. Cheryl comes running out. "THEY JUST LEFT!" she shouts. "Two Braids and Meadow came back with the car and unloaded a pile of stuff they bought in Santa Fe. It's lying all over your bed room. They used the girls' credit cards to buy it all. They say they're done with the car and left me the keys for it. Two Braids said to tell the girls that they just need to report the credit cards as stolen and they won't have to pay a thing." Cheryl was puffing. "They're gonna come back soon and get the rest of their stuff."

My adrenalin was going. I dug up my only pistol, a terribly weak Beretta 25 caliber that I had bought after my first Beretta had been stolen. The only thing it was better than was no gun at all. My 22-LR rifle was in storage with a friend. I first decided to return the car to the girls. I drove it down to Mora and found them in their motel. They were excited to have their car back. They wanted nothing more than to get on the road and out of here forever. They checked their purses. Their credit cards were missing. I told them of the loot that Two Braids and this Meadow had been buying with their cards. They grimaced. But they thought they could get to LA on a hundred dollars. We exchanged addresses. Then I asked the girls to drive me back to my home. They were hesitant. I asked them to just take me close to my home. We got to within a half mile when I hopped out. As we shook hands, they kept repeating to me to be careful. I got off the road and walked through gambel oak stands to my home. I carefully crept up to my home. I saw Cheryl waiting outside.

"What are you going to do when they come back?" she asked.

"You just stay away when they come," I answered.

I went into my bedroom and checked the gear that they had bought with the girls' credit cards. A new tent, an ax, hatchets, buck knives, cast iron skillets, horse bridles, a western saddle, new boots, fishing poles, lots of outdoor gear, and boxes of ammo. Ammo? I looked around. There in the corner was a rifle leaning against the wall. It was a Winchester lever action type. I checked it out. It had 38-40 stamped on it. I had never heard of that caliber before. I took the gun and ammo out to the hay loft in my barn. I loaded the 38-40 and walked up the hill. I aimed at a tree and shot it. BOOM! It worked. I decided to keep that rifle and the Beretta with me.

I moved my truck off the road so that no one could easily see it. That night I slept in the hayloft of my barn with the loaded guns to my side. I told Cheryl not to mention a word to Two Braids that I was back.

"What do I say when he finds his gun is missing?" She asked. I didn't have an answer for that. Then Cheryl said she would be leaving today 'for a while'. I didn't blame her.

Two Braids did not come back that day, or the next either. On my third day home, Ronald visited me. He had heard that I was back. Ronald was a Nam vet, recently back from the war. He had been an infantry grunt who had seen it all, and did not talk about any of it. He returned to me my 22 long rifle. It too was underpowered. But at least it held 16 under-powered rounds. Ronald broke out a joint and we smoked. I told him about the incident with Two Braids and I showed him the rifle I had confiscated. Ronald admired it as a gun-guy would. We talked a while about my trip to the Sonoran Desert. But Ronald did not have my dog Kingfish with him. I asked him where Kingfish was. Ronald shook his head. "The ranchers set poison out near my place for the coyotes and feral dogs. And Kingfish ate it. Sorry about that. I buried him near our cabin."

There went my best companion --- my *only* companion --- for the last five years. The smartest dog I have ever had. I didn't know how to take it. We sat there silent.

There was a loud knock on the door. Before we could answer, a big guy stepped in. "Where's Cheryl?" he asked.

# How I Got My Winchester 38-40

"She's moved away," I answered.

"What?" he looked directly at me. "*Who are you?*"

In my own home --- *who are you?*

He was broad and tall. His face was weather beaten and rough like a ranch hand. He had *two long braids* down his back. But what got my attention was the long-barreled large caliber pistol hanging reverse holster on his hip.

I looked over to Ronald and --- maybe I sort of nodded. But I felt the adrenalin going off. I didn't say anything as I stood up. Later I would think what I did was out of panic. But I don't know that I would have done it if Ronald weren't there. But what I did do was charge Two Braids with a few running steps and hit him with my shoulder directly into his chest. Two Braids fell back halfway out the door. I quickly got hold of his braids and began banging his head hard as I could against the wooden steps. I was head-butting him too as he tried to get my hands off his hair. But he couldn't. His braids made for perfect handles. I maybe let one braid loose and elbowed his face again and again while banging his head on the stair. I must have knocked his head good because he didn't have much fight left in him. It all happened so fast. Then I panicked about his gun and reached down for it.

"DONT WORRY! I'VE GOT IT!" I hear Ronald yelling.

"STOP IT!" I hear a woman's voice shouting.

I look up and see that that Ronald is holding Two Braid's large single action pistol.

"What you doing? What you doing?" Two Braids is yelling. I jump up and step back panting, completely out of breath. I am shouting at him full force as he is sitting on the floor, telling him if he ever comes around to my home again we'll shoot him---that I've reported him to Sheriff Sanchez and they are looking for him --- and to get the fuck out now!

Then Two Braids leans forward and actually seems to sob. *No? What?* I did not expect that. Later I remember feeling really good about this.

"We only came for our stuff. Just let us get it and we'll leave."

"Not the gun or ammo. We're keeping the gun."

"But they're---"

"FUCK YOU! Not anymore. Get your shit and get out. Come back again we're shooting!" I am near out of my mind.

Ronald keeps the pistol in his hands as Two Braids and Meadow get their remaining loot and tie it onto their horses. I look over to Meadow. She is a tall, attractive young woman, sun-burned like Two Braids from living outside. She must be Two Braids' partner in crime. Later I'll wonder how she got there. Was she just another passive woman, easy to lead on?

As they ride off, I shout again that they better never come back. Ronald seconds it. Then I shout that they'd better get out of state, because I'll be joining Sanchez' posse. At this point, I am talking totally out of my ass.

Only when Two Braids and Meadow are completely out of sight, do Ronald and I go back in. Ronald congratulates me on doing a number on Two Braids. Any other time I might have felt heady about it. But now, still under the heavy influence of marijuana and adrenalin, I am feeling completely unnerved and freaked out.

"What should I do with this?" Ronald holds up a Colt single action 44 magnum pistol.

The barrel must have been close to nine inches long. I have shot that caliber pistol once before and it was simply too powerful for me. One blast from it and I had a flinch reaction from it for all the following shots.

"Looks like it's yours now," I say. We look strangely at each other. Then we begin laughing hysterically and cannot stop, for whatever reason.

"You want to smoke some more?" Ronald asks.

"Fuuuuuuuuuccccccccck no!" I shout, and we laugh some more.

Ronald and I decide to sit outside, away from the cabin. In case Two Braids comes back with some of his banditos to settle a score, we will see them first.

Later, Ronald takes off home to his wife Rosa. I make it a point to not sleep in my home, but on the hill above it. I build a small campsite and cover it with brush so that no one will find it unless they stumble right upon it. I keep the 38-40 with me, along with my 22 rifle and the Beretta. But I knew that these were really the wrong guns for self-defense.

About a week later, a lone Bandito on horseback came riding up to my home. He waved a white bandanna from a distance. I recognize him as Texas John. His arms were covered with cheap, faded, blue, homemade tattoos. He was long, skinny, and gaunt-eyed. They said he had done a lot of speed and time in his life, and they both showed. Cheryl said there was talk that it was Texas John who had killed another Bandito last winter. I had once treated Tex at the clinic for a bad cut that sure looked like a knife stab to me. Since then, Tex and I had gotten along well enough. But not well enough for me to put my gun down.

"Two Braids sent me to tell you he'd like to buy his 38-40 back from you."

"So he could shoot me with it?"

# How I Got My Winchester 38-40

"It dont hafta be that way." Texas John drawled out as he got off his horse. "Two Braids just loved that gun. He'd like his Colt 44 back too."

"Ronald's keeping that. And I don't think Two Braids wants to deal with him, cause Ronald's still in Vietnam, you know. He loves hunting --- animals --- people --- it don't matter. Ronald's got something else Two Braids don't got either. A lot of US army training and field experience."

"Look," Tex answers slowly. "It ain't like I'm a friend of Two Braids. Or that anyone else is either. Two Braids gave me some money and gear so I'd come here and tell you this. This time I'm just the messenger."

I put my Beretta back in my pocket and Tex and I sit down. I pull out a joint. He nods. Maybe we both could use relaxing a bit. As we're smoking, I give Texas John maybe a quarter ounce of good smoke. Up in the mountains, all isolated, I know he could appreciate that.

"It's like this, Tex. I gave those girls money to get to where they were going. I went through a lot of shit dealing with the mess Two Braids made *in my own home.* So I deserve something. You tell this to Two Braids. We can meet at some safe place and fight it out *mano a mano,* no weapons. He can bring a backup. Ronald'll be mine. If Two Braids wins, he gets the 38-40 back. But if I win, I get to cut off his braids and wear them on my war bonnet."

Texas John broke his deep inhale with a smoky cough that turned into laughter. His smile showed broken and missing teeth. He sat there shaking his head. And this was from a guy who never showed much feeling at all. Real slow he said, "I sort of like those terms. I might like to watch this one myself. Y'all could sell tickets." He got up and went to his horse. "I'll tell him what you said --- and thanks for the smoke." With our goofy, smiling faces, we didn't *feel* like violent men right then.

I never saw Two Braids again. I wrote a letter to the girls and the mother telling them not to send me money because the gear I had confiscated from Two Braids was worth more than a hundred dollars. They answered my letter and thanked me for whatever help I did for them. Much later, the rumor in the valley had it that Two Braids had gone to Montana to rob there.

In the fall of 1971, I drove back to Indiana from New Mexico to visit my parents. Before I left, I also bought an ancient Winchester 25-20 rifle at a pawn shop for a good price. It looked just like the 38-40, except it shot a much smaller bullet. This time when I returned, I had a short haircut. That was much easier on my parents. I also had some polished lies in place so that they did not know the true nature of my life. My parents greeted me warmly, but with suspicion. I am sure that they wondered whether I had really changed? After we talked a bit, I said, "Hey dad, I got something for you."

I went out to my truck and brought in the two Winchesters and laid them on the kitchen table. My dad and my brother gathered around and looked at them. Only a family of hunters could appreciate guns like that. My dad studied the two rifles like a mother might her new-born baby.

After a long inspection, my dad looked up from the table and said "These are some hell of a guns, son. Thank you." That was one of the few times in my life that my dad ever said thank you to me. So I knew he meant it. The rest of the times he said that whatever good deeds I did were simply to be expected of me in the first place. I think those guns were the third best gifts I ever gave to my dad. And what were the other two? Handing to my father his newly born grandson, and dedicating a book to him.

I returned to my old home in New Mexico 25 years later and I spoke with a long-time resident named Amara. She told me that Two Braids did return once, briefly. While he was back, he gave her teen-aged son a terrible beating. Amara cryptically stated that she wished that I would have 'solved' the Two Braids problem once and for all back then.

I lost all contact with Ronald. I have tried to find him, but without success. I heard he and Rosa later had two children, and then divorced. He moved to Las Vegas, then returned to his home back east. But all of our mutual friends have since passed away. I feel a sadness at the thought of time gone by and never having seen such a good friend as Ronald again.

I don't know what ever happened to the Winchester 25-20. My brother Kenny said that dad traded it away for another gun. That surprised me. After dad died, Kenny stored the 38-40. When Kenny died, his son Greg inherited it. When I told Greg the abbreviated history of this 38-40, Greg immediately gave it to me. What a kind thing for my nephew Greg to do.

I handed the Winchester 38-40 to my son.

"And that, son, is the story about how I got this gun. You will inherit it when I am gone. May the gun and the story stay with you."

# 24

# Crossing the Border

Drug dealing: The most addictive habit of them all

On the table in front of us sat a one-kilo brick of marijuana. Terry pointed to it and said he had just flown a planeload of this very marijuana up to the Mexican side of the border. My old college buddy Mark and I examined it closely. Its quality was superb, and the price was right. In the past, Terry had always been fair and honest with us about any marijuana he brought into the USA.

But this time, Terry said it would be our job to get it across the border. Terry said that he was finished smuggling by land. Too risky. But he would show us where and how to smuggle it by land. Then Terry gave us directions to the abandoned mining town of Ruby, Arizona. He told us to bring everything we would need including water for the two days we would be there, because Ruby was empty.

"You want us to pick the marijuana up on the *Mexican* side of the border?" I was incredulous.

"Yes. Just follow my directions and it will be easy. And much cheaper."

Much cheaper, yes. But I doubted it would be easy.

Terry was a big, jovial man, twenty years older than me, who grew up at the border and spoke English and Spanish interchangeably. He moved transparently between the cultures too, switching languages in mid sentence

The Wild Years

One kilo of Mexico's finest

and never missing a beat. I wasn't sure if he was citizen of Mexico or the USA, for he revealed nothing of his personal life to us. This time Terry brought with him Billy the pilot. Billy was an Anglo man, maybe ten years older than I. I knew Billy wasn't his real name, but then, I did not use my real name, either. Both Terry and Billy looked and talked as normally as any of the ranchers or construction workers around here in southern Arizona.

Terry rolled a joint from the kilo in front of us and lit it. I had never smoked marijuana with men so much older than me. I was still naive enough then to believe that only young people smoked marijuana. Through a puff of smoke, Terry said he had been smoking marijuana since he was 15 years old.

"And I smoked it most every day in the Nam," the pilot said.

"Did you fly planes *stoned*?" Mark asked, incredulous.

"Helicopters mostly. Usually we waited until after the day's missions were over before we smoked. But sometimes, you had to do a rescue after you had just smoked. Then it got interesting."

"And what was that like?"

The pilot looked at us big-eyed for a moment. "Colorful." We broke into laughs. A cloud of smoke spread across the table. "Flying this border is a piece of cake compared to Vietnam. At least they're not shooting at you."

Terry then gave us detailed directions about how to hike to the pickup point across the border in Mexico. When I asked for a map, Terry shook his head. "No evidence. If you can't remember it, you shouldn't be doing this to start with." He repeated the directions, and I wrote them down in my own private code.

I mounted a luggage rack on the roof of my Volkswagen. Then Mark and I packed up for a several day trip. I had just rebuilt the engine on my VW myself from the main bearings up. New rings, valves, pistons, and bushings. I had honed cylinders and ground the valve seats --- the whole works. It was practically a new engine. I could completely rebuild a VW engine in one day, from sunrise to sunset, including taking it out and putting it back in, with just a little bit of chemical help.

The entire population of the ghost town of Ruby, Arizona

# The Wild Years

Mark and I drove southward many miles on a winding gravel mountain trail, following Terry's verbal directions. Finally, next to the Mexican border, we came up to an immense tailings pile that blocked off the valley below us. On the hillside next to it, we saw a number of abandoned structures. Ruby, Arizona. I turned down the entrance road and began the slow descent on a rough trail. Littered all around were massive, rusted out pieces of mining equipment. Cranes, winches, dead trucks and ore lifts lay scattered about like toys in a giant's sandbox. I drove slowly past them and then up a steep hillside road. I saw what looked to be a general store. Three little boys were playing in front of it, next to a ratty pickup truck.

We walked into the store only to realize that we were now in someone's home. An older bald man stood up and introduced himself as Terry. *Another Terry.* He didn't seem too upset at our intrusion here. He had a protruding bump on the top of his head. I had trouble taking my eyes off it. Terry said he was the caretaker here. The absentee owners let him stay here for free as long as he did general maintenance and watched over the place.

"What you all do out here?" I asked.

He looked around. "Well, we cook food, then we eat it. We play music, hike around, look at the mountains, the plants, the animals. I guess that's enough."

I asked him if we could camp here a few days.

"Just keep the place clean," Terry said. "The national forest surrounds the mine and they can't keep you off that." He pointed off in the distance, beyond the tailings pile.

I drove past the pile and parked my car in the middle of a dense mesquite thicket. I studied the spot. We were well out of sight of everyone. Then Mark and I hiked away from our car and found a hidden spot above a stream wash. Our campsite.

Mark and I had done rough backpacking in the past. Across the Grand Canyon, through Bryce and Zion National parks, Death Valley, and Yosemite. We had hiked for over a week at a time. The rougher it was, the more we liked the challenge. On one trip, we ran out of water. When we finally found a trickle of a stream, we rushed it and drank on our knees like animals. We didn't get sick either. Rough journeys made my return to civilization just that much sweeter. While hiking in the wilderness, life just could not be any more real to me. I was reduced to being a simple monkey scrounging out a living on this spinning rock.

I was enchanted with the Sonoran Desert. I had lived on both sides of the border and my Spanish was beginning to flow. So Mark and I had talked

# Hippies with Guns
## (they are all dead now)

about combining our love of backpacking with our love of easy money by smuggling a load of marijuana across the border on our backs. This way we would be our own middle-men. I had never been paid five thousand dollars to backpack before, and those terms sounded good.

I had a bag of of peyote buttons that I had gotten from some Indian friends. These were completely dry, without a spine on them. They were covered only with small white tufts of fiber. I cleaned the fiber off and broke the buttons into small pieces. Mark and I tried chewing them, but they were just too dry and hard. So we washed them down with gulps of water. They tasted simply terrible. The older Indians had told me that I would get used to the taste of father peyote. But I never did. The more peyote I ate, the worse it tasted. I don't know if it was a brave man who ate the first oyster, but it sure was one crazy Indian who ate the first peyote. Peyote was the only cactus I ever saw in the desert that did not need spines for protection. It tasted so horrible that no sensible animal would eat it. Only humans like me. At the time, I was thinking that visions from father peyote would show us the passageway across the border for the smuggle. *Did I really believe that stuff back then?*

We wandered through the Sonoran Desert in high magic, under the organ pipe cacti, between the rough mesquite trees, around the ocotillo thorns, and the poisonous jumping cholla cactus. With my eyes wide open, I watched the desert pulse in waves of light.

I felt myself becoming sick from the peyote. It happened every time I ate it. I put my hand next to an overhanging rock ledge about chest high. Then I leaned forward and vomited. The peyote tasted even worse on the way out. I felt the blood pressure increase in my face as I gagged. Was this worth it? As I wiped my mouth, I saw a quick movement in the crevice under the ledge. Then I heard the distinctive rattle. I jerked my arms back and jumped backward. Mark came over and we looked under the rock ledge. There, coiled in the back, was a big black-tailed rattlesnake. I had just puked on its doorstep, and it had taken offense.

We carefully watched it, and it watched us. This snake stayed in a coiled position. It had no place else to go. A Mexican standoff. I had been close enough to it to have been bitten on the arm or face. This far from a hospital, that bite might have done its job. Finally, Mark and I called it a day and hiked back to our campsite. We built a fire at sunset and watched the flames dance in silence. Then we hit our sleeping bags early. We would have a busy day tomorrow.

We began hiking south before sunrise. We packed plenty of water, tortillas, beans, and cheese. Mark and I first followed the rough cattle trail. I scanned southward with my binoculars. Terry had told us to look all around for people. If we saw anyone, he said to hide, because anyone out there would be carrying a gun. And we were not. If a gringo got caught smuggling a gun into Mexico, it was an automatic ten years in prison. But if someone caught us *sneaking* into Mexico? We didn't know yet what would happen.

We passed through a dry gulch that descended into a flat wash. There we ran into a four-strand barbed wire cattle fence. That was the borderline. Beyond that was Mexico. I was expecting something much more substantial. Terry said that from here on there were only ranchers. He said he knew them all and that he had arranged for them to leave us alone today. I doubted if that were really possible, but it was still good to hear it from him.

Beyond the fence, we hiked hard and fast on a downhill slope into the desert. The land around us was now open desert, interrupted only with clumps of mesquite, ocotillo, and cholla cactus. I imagined that this was what the ancient Indians saw hundreds of years ago. There looked to be no good hiding places here. The sun rose higher and we lost our morning chill. We climbed out of an arroyo up a small hill. At the top, we spooked two

## Crossing the Border

horses. They ran from us in a panic. Wild horses, in a wild land.

From the hill, we saw the herder's shack. Behind the shack Terry said we would find a washed out arroyo. "You will find several gallons of water there for you under a tree. You cannot miss it," Terry had assured us. It was here that Terry would leave the fifty kilos of high-quality smoke. This all seemed so dubious to me now.

We sped down another cow trail that weaved to the shack. Then we

### Wild horses, in a wild land

approached it cautiously. The old door was open. We entered. There was an old cot to the side with a pile of cardboard on it that served as a mattress. Empty food cans littered the floor. A large can of lard and some jars of beans and cornmeal sat on a lone shelf. A few faded posters of half-naked *Mexicanas* were peeling from the walls. In one corner was a pile of fencing tools and a roll of barbed wire. In the other corner was a gnawed up old cotton blanket where rodents had made a nest.

Behind the shack was a small empty corral packed with manure. Not a plant grew inside of it. But deadly jimson weed grew in a ring around the corral. Fresh manure told me someone had been here very recently. The ground behind the corral sloped down to an arroyo. Mark and I nodded and followed the path. An old mesquite tree leaned into the gulch. There we saw two plastic one-gallon jugs. On the ground beneath the jugs was a piece of cardboard weighted down with a rock. "*Aqui esta!*" was written on it, with a smiley face. *A fucking smiley face, out here in no man's land?* Mark and I must have drunk half a jug of water. Next to the water was a pile of brush about three feet high. We pulled the branches off. There were four stuffed army duffel sacks.

"HEY!" we heard a shout from above us.

I froze in dread panic. Mark looked like he felt the same. There above us, on the edge of the arroyo, stood two men. With the sun to their backs we could only see their outlines. And one of them clearly held a rifle sideways. *Who were they? Was this a ripoff?* They could shoot us dead and no one would even hear the shots. What had we gotten ourselves into? Oh my god--

"Adam," one of them shouted. "It is me. Terry."

Adam was one of my aliases. The two men both began walking down the arroyo. Terry stopped in front of us. He was wearing cowboy hat and leg chaps, a vaquero shirt, and cowboy boots with spurs on them. The man next to Terry was tall, slender, and dark-skinned. He wore a beige cowboy shirt, western hat, levis, and cowboy boots also. He looked like he was pure Yaqui Indian. He slightly tilted his head to us, but his expression did not change. He did not put down the rifle.

"You look afraid," Terry smiled.

"You startled us."

"You should be afraid out here. You are late. I decided to stay here with the *mota* until you picked it up. I could not let some stray find it and steal from us."

Terry cleared the brush off the pile and revealed four large duffel sacks. He opened one and pulled out a large kilo brick. It was wrapped in green cellophane. He cut open the cellophane and it revealed brown wrapping paper. Terry tore open a corner and sat it on the ground. Mark and I got close to it and pulled some marijuana from it. It was dark brown-green in color and broke off in clumps of flowers. The flowers were gummy to the touch and smelled deeply of resin. *Colitas.* We searched through the kilo, In it, we found no large stems, no garbage, and not one seed. *Sin semina.* How rare this was.

"You want to smoke some?" Terry asked.

"No," I answered as Mark said, "Yes."

We laughed. Terry quickly rolled and lit a joint. It smelled rich. He and Mark smoked. After two tokes, Mark waved off a third. He looked at me and nodded his head.

"This is the best marijuana in Mexico," Terry stated. I believed him.

# Crossing the Border

"We had to pay more for it, so my friends, I am going to ask you to pay an additional twenty dollars a pound for it. Not now. But after you sell it."

I looked to Mark. We both knew we could sell this for double what people paid for standard Mexican commercial weed. This was the best weed we had ever seen come out of Mexico. Mark and I nodded.

"Can you wait two weeks until we sell it all?" I asked.

"*Seguro*. Also, I have another request," Terry continued. "You paid for one-hundred pounds. But here in Mexico we do everything in kilos. We brought four bags of fifteen kilos each. You can weigh them when you get back. That is over 130 pounds. Thirty pounds more. After you sell it, you pay me $4500 more."

Again, Mark and I nodded. Marijuana this good just sold itself.

"You call me from a pay phone at that number you have for me. Just say that you have tickets for the Tucson Gem and Mineral Show and I will know that it is you. Then I will come get the money and we will talk more business. We can all get rich."

I started to shake hands with Terry, but he reached with both arms and gave me an abrazo. He said we should get hurrying now, because we had a heavy load and a long way to walk before sunset. Then he and his companero walked over the ridge. A few minutes later they rode up to us on horseback with two mules tied together behind them. Terry waved his hat to us.

"Around here, this is better than any four-wheel-drive." They rode slowly to the south and disappeared into a gully.

Now I felt my adrenalin flowing. Suddenly my reality was the fear of being discovered, chased, arrested, robbed, or worse. We could not come close to fitting the sixty-five pounds each into our backpacks. So we wore our stuffed back packs and carried partially loaded duffel sacks in each arm. Going north now meant climbing hills with weight. A lot more work. We hiked as fast as we could, puffing all the way.

About an hour up the trail, we heard an airplane. In the distance to the west, I saw it flying toward us, along the border line. Was it US Customs? Probably. Mark and I looked around. There was not much cover around us other than a few mesquite trees about the height of bushes. We stuffed our bags beneath them and crawled under as best we could. We waited and listened. The plane continued eastward.

"You think they saw us?" Mark asked.

"No. If they saw us, they would fly back over us and make sure."

"What would you do if they saw us?"

# The Wild Years

I thought about that. "I'd smuggle it into the US anyhow. Then I'd stash it on the US side before we got to our car. Then, if they had a blockade on the road, they'd just find us driving a clean car. We would come back later to get it."

When we got to the four-strand cattle fence at the US border, I felt a strange relief. Now we might still get arrested, but we most likely would not get shot. We hiked fast through an open area until we got to a heavy cover of pinyon trees. There we stashed all our packs. Empty handed, we walked back to my car and our campsite. We looked about. Our gear was scattered about our campsite. Someone had been here! I looked closely and saw that our pack of food was torn open. But only our food had been bothered. A coatimundi had been here. Next time we would lock all our food in the car. We cleaned up the mess and salvaged what we could for dinner. We were tired and it was late. Tomorrow we would drive up to Tucson.

We were up well before sunrise next morning. I put on my cowboy clothes and we quickly packed the car and luggage carrier with our gear and the marijuana. Then I poured five gallons of extra gas into my gas tank and we began driving back to Tucson on isolated back roads. We finally had to get on to the main highway 19 about 30 miles north of the border. After this, I drove north to my ranch in the Coronado National Forest without incident. When I pulled in, Mark shouted "We did it! We did it!"

"Not so fast. We have to stash all of this first."

We reloaded our back packs and hiked a quarter mile to an abandoned mine shaft. I slid a rope ladder down its angled wall. Mark handed me the duffel sacks. I tied them to an old wooden beam, out of the light and anyone's eyes. This was finally good enough for me.

Next morning I double-wrapped all the marijuana in garbage bags, with moth balls between the bags. The luggage rack looked top heavy and unstable to me. All I needed was for it to blow off on the highway and cause an accident. Some evidence the police would find. So I drilled four holes into the roof of my car and bolted the mounts onto the roof. Now would the roof leak forever? I grimaced as I did it.

Mark and I decided to drive non-stop back to Indiana. When we needed to rest, we would camp out, away from motels and prying eyes. I loaded two five-gallon tanks of gasoline with us. I fit one under the hood and the other in the luggage rack. We loaded our camping gear in in the back seat and we were off at sunrise, heading north on highway 77. We figured the further from border, the safer.

## Crossing the Border

We spent all day lugging through the hills and mountains, through Globe, Show Low, and Springerville. Toward sunset we entered the Zuni Reservation in western New Mexico. We pulled off the gravel road onto a trail and set up camp. I passed out under another spectacular desert skyline.

We were breaking camp after sunrise when a car pulled off the main gravel road onto our trail. It was some kind of cop car!

"I'll do the talking, Mark. Just don't act like we're doing something wrong."

An Indian cop opened the door and stepped out. He was wearing a gun.

"What you fellows doing here?"

"Mornin' officer. We come up to buy some Zuni jewelry here. But we got in too late. All the trading posts were closed. So we thought to camp out, save ourselves some money, and go in tomorrow."

"You know you are on private land here?'

"Sorry about that officer. We'll be out in a few minutes. We never leave any trash laying around. You can see that."

He did look around. I looked at his police badge. It was made of thick silver, with inlays of turquoise, and red and black corals. I would never have thought that a police badge could be beautiful.

I turned to Mark. "Come look at his badge. You won't believe how incredible it is."

We stood there admiring it.

"You don't think I could buy one of those at the trading posts, do you?"

The Best looking
police badge, ever

# The Wild Years

He laughed and shook his head. I asked if I could take a picture of it. He said okay.

Then I asked the cop if he wanted to see the Zuni Jewelry I had already purchased for the lady-folk in my family. I opened the luggage carrier and got out a little suitcase. I pulled out a number of Zuni pieces. All of them had the red coral embedded deeply into silver. The policeman examined them closely.

"They're not bad, but ---"

"Do you know where we can get better items?"

"Ummm. Yes. You should visit my sister's store. She has some of the best pieces, and the best prices." He gave us directions to her place.

Just as we were ready to leave, I said, "Oh, one question officer. Just how did you know we were here?"

"Easy. I saw your tire tracks. They weren't but a half day old and there were only tracks going in. Nothing coming out. So you had to go up this rock trail."

"You saw all that, while you were driving?"

"We Indians are hunters and scouts. We see much that you do not."

We all shook hands and he left.

After he was gone, Mark implored "Why did you *open* the luggage rack?"

"So he wouldn't look inside."

Mark looked at me funny. He didn't get it. Then we drove to the cop's sister's trading post. They did have some great jewelry. I bought over a hundred dollars worth. We mentioned to the owner that we had met her brother this morning. "Oh, now I must fix him lunch," she laughed. As we were walking out, the cop pulled up in front. I showed him the necklaces I had just bought from his sister. She came out and invited Mark and me for lunch, but we politely declined.

While we were gassing up, Mark asked me to pay for it because he couldn't find his wallet. So I did. Then we pulled over to search for his wallet. We emptied the car, but could not find a thing. Only then did he say that he had probably left it in his day pack at my home.

"Goddamn," I moaned, sounding just like my father. "You have been driving all this time without any fucking ID? What if that cop had asked for it? He would have pulled us in. Then bye bye fucking freedom."

Mark just stood there with that perpetually stoned expression of his. And he wasn't even high on anything.

"So I have to drive all the way back by myself?" I asked him.

# Crossing the Border

"I can drive at night."

"We can't take that risk."

I knew you shouldn't smoke marijuana when you were transporting it. I wondered about what I could do better stoned on marijuana than straight. Eat food, listen to music, look at art, maybe love a woman, and not much else. Stoned, I sure could not do anything that demanded attention to detail, like mechanics, repairs, or long-distance planning. There was one other thing marijuana was good for. Making money. But you had better be straight when you were doing that. Maybe this marijuana run was taking on the characteristics of the marijuana itself; spacey, ill-planned, unfocused. Not smart.

We drove hard and non-stop across the back roads of New Mexico. I loved these open roads where one could see mountains, deserts, and plateaus all at once. Now my car radio only picked up AM stations. Most of them were the high wattage country-western stations blowing in from Texas or the Great Plains. I turned the radio up loud to cover the engine chatter and rush of wind around our open windows. By midnight, we were in isolated west-central Kansas. I saw a decrepit storage building alone in the distance. No lights came from it, no power lines went to it, and there were no other buildings nearby. I pulled up behind it and turned off the engine. Darkness and silence, after a day of noise. I could not see another human light from any direction. Wonderful stars all about us.

"And what do we do this time when a cop pulls up?" Mark asks.

"Well, you sure as fuck aren't going to give him your IDs," I snapped. Mark looked hurt. "But this time we will be *gone* on the road well before sunrise."

We crawled into our sleeping bags without setting up our tent. That way we could be packed to go in five minutes max.

Next morning I woke up wide awake when there was just the slightest hint of light in the East. It had  cooled off during the night. I shook Mark awake. He stayed in that dazed where-the-fuck-am-I phase for way too long for me. So I rolled up his sleeping bag while he pissed and then we were on our way again.

I drove non-stop across eastern Kansas and then Missouri, stopping only for gas and food to go. We camped out in a remote cornfield, and were gone again before sunrise. We did our bathroom stops outside on country roads, to keep our contact with the public to a minimum. I kept my hair bunned inside my cowboy hat. It was mid-afternoon when we got through the maze of St. Louis expressways. Now I was thinking that we were practically

# The Wild Years

home. I could get off Interstate 70 at Terre Haute, Indiana and take isolated back roads the rest of the way to my dear ole 'Bloom-Bloom' Bloomington, Indiana. Mark and I were congratulating ourselves for a successful run. Mark opened the dash of my VW and found two blue pills.

"What are these?" he asked.

"I don't know."

Mark handed one to me and smiled. "Let's try 'em."

"Naw man. They might be Mary's birth control pills," I said. "I don't wanna grow tits."

Mark swallowed his pill. "I dare you," he said. Then he made chicken clucking sounds. We laughed. So I swallowed the unknown pill. And we were off driving east on Interstate 70 at 65 mph. Full cruising speed for that bug.

In a bit, neither of us could read the highway signs. It seemed like we were making no progress at all. The signs said Indianapolis 110 miles, then 106 miles, and then hours later, 101 miles.

"Are we still going east?" Mark asked.

I wasn't sure. We saw a sign that said SAFETY REST AREA and pulled over.

"I can't drive anymore, Mark." I walked over to an isolated picnic bench and laid down on the table.

*"Those pills. They were LSD."*

Mark nodded. We were someplace in eastern Illinois. I noticed flies buzzing all around us. Then I realized that the table I was lying on was covered with watermelon juice and seeds. The back of my clothes were soaked. We watched a man wearing a Department of Natural Resources uniform approach us.

"May I help you?" he said.

Mark and I looked at him, and then each other, with our monstrously dilated eyes. Mark or I were having difficulty talking. Somehow, some way, he finally left. We still knew enough to scurry to the car and take off.

A week later, I headed back to Tucson from Bloomington by myself in my VW bug. Mark had decided to stay in Bloomington. When I cleaned out my car after we delivered the marijuana, I found all of Mark's identification and his money in a bag hidden under the hood. So we had been carrying his ID's with us the whole time. But Mark had been unable to remember it. I returned them to Mark with irritation. This was just like Mark now. He was unable to focus on anything. Whether he was straight or stoned, he was getting less and less coherent. When he spoke, his comments did not connect with what others were talking about. They were soliloquies that only he understood. He wore the same clothes for a week on end, and was unable to help me with any work we had to do. I grew tired of taking care of him. 'What had caused this?' I wondered. But I would not dare ask myself whether I had I helped cause Mark's state of mind with all these drugs.

I stashed a large stack of dollars into a secret compartment that I had made myself in my VW bug. This money included the six thousand dollars I owed Terry. Then I drove 500 miles a day. In the evening, at the end of each day, I found a deserted area to camp. First by a cornfield, then in a wheat field, then the high desert, and then onward to my little ranch, south of Tucson. Each night I had the stars overhead for myself. There wasn't a night when I did not see a few shooting stars streak overhead. Oh, lucky me to live wild and free and outside. Lying in my sleeping bag in the high desert one night, I got out my high-powered binoculars and found the Horsehead Nebula in the sword of Orion. Oh, the beauty of living outside. That people would pay for a motel when they could have all this for free seemed incredible to me. I did not understand them, and surely they would not have come close to understanding me either.

I rolled into Tucson in the high desert heat, well over 100 F. I liked the desert more in the winter. I called Terry's phone number from a pay phone. Someone else answered.

"May I speak to Terry?"

"He not here. Who call?" I heard a Spanish accent. Terry had told me that only he would ever answer this phone. No one else. "Who call?" the voice repeated. "You leave message for Terry." I told him I had the tickets to the Tucson Gem and Mineral Show. "Where you are?" the man demanded.

I hung up and called back later. The same voice answered. Again I refused to identify myself. "Terry say leave message for him," the voice commanded. I paused, and hung up again. I tried one last time, but I got the same thing.

I had to get back to Terry, if not for future business, then to at least give him his money. But without him answering his phone, I had no way to find him. Terry had made a point of always controlling where and when we met. I guess if you were a smuggler, that would be a best practice.

I drove back to my desert home. When I came to my front door, it was smashed open. Panic. *What if whoever did it was still here, waiting for me?*

# The Wild Years

I ran from my home and climbed a small hill nearby. I saw no other cars parked nearby. Then I crept back.

Inside, my place was a complete mess. Every shelf, drawer and closet had been ransacked. But it appeared they did not take anything. Whoever did it was looking in detail for something small, something hidden, like *money or drugs.* Someone knew what I was doing here.

I never kept my money or drugs in my home. The only gun I kept inside was the one I was carrying. Since I lived a half mile from my nearest neighbor, I had plenty of space in the desert to bury things. But living so far from others also gave me less protection in case of attack. I went outside and dug up my 22 LR pistol. It was cheap and weak, but it was something.

Hardly anyone knew I lived here. Who could have tried to rob me? I drew up a list of everyone who knew my home. Then I went through the process of elimination. I sat there, shaking my head. None of them would have robbed me. *None of them.* But one of them had.

Could it be Terry and the pilot? I owed *them* over $6000. Why would they rob me when I was going to pay them back anyhow? They had fronted me a lot of marijuana. You don't rob the people you are trusting with your marijuana and money, do you? As the sun set, I felt very vulnerable. Where was I now safe? Not in this home. Anyone looking for me would expect me inside. I moved my vehicle to a dry wash, well out of sight of my home.

I got my bedroll and set up a little campsite on a rise about 75 yards from my front door. With my binoculars, I had a good view of my home and the long driveway. I laid there in my sleeping bag and tried to sleep. Oh, I guess the stars were still wonderful, but I was too agitated to pay them any attention.

Much later that night, I awoke with a jolt. I heard a vehicle and saw its headlights coming down my long driveway. I groped around for my glasses. Then I grabbed my binoculars. Through them I saw the lights of a car stop in front of my home. I heard a car door open. Then I saw two men run into my home. The inside lights of my home went on as my binoculars steamed up. As I cleaned the lens, I remembered I was barefoot. A good way to run through the cactus desert at night. Just as I got my shoes on, I heard the car door slam shut. The car spun around and took off in a roar down my driveway. After it was gone, I watched my front door and the driveway. I did not sleep anymore that night.

At sunrise the next morning, I was up. I walked to my VW and drove to town for food, supplies, and batteries. From a pay phone, I called a mutual friend of Mark Watson and myself. Our mutual friend had not heard from

Mark since I had been in Indiana. Strange. Mark and I had agreed to leave messages for each other with him if we did not speak directly on the phone. Then I called Terry again. This time I got a message that his phone had been disconnected. *More strange.*

As I was paying for my things at the general store, I looked at the morning copy of the Arizona Daily Star. On the front page was a picture of a small airplane with shattered glass. The headline read:

TWO MEN KILLED AT AGUA PRIETA AIRPORT

I picked up the paper. Agua Prieta was a Mexican border city southeast of Tucson. Below that picture was a photo of two men lying in pools of blood. I glanced over the article. Then I saw the name *Terry Madera.*

I took my purchases from the country store, sat on the bench out front. I read the article, then re-read it. Terry and the unidentified pilot had been ambushed by multiple assailants after they landed their plane on the Agua Prieta runway. The plane was found to be empty and they were *shot point blank multiple times.*

It began to sink into me that the peace-and-love times of the marijuana business were gone, gone, gone forever. It was no longer about non-violent hippies spreading an evangelical message.

It was time for me to move. I drove home and mailed my landlord another month's rent with a note telling him about the break in. I said he could keep the security deposit for repairs. I went inside and packed up quickly. I never returned to that home again. I resolved to quit my border business and get a real job. And I did, for two years...

Mark Watson never called me back. In the coming months, I asked mutual friends if they had heard from Mark. But no one had. Then one day, I got a phone call from Mark Watson's father. He asked me when was the last time I had seen or heard from Mark. I told him when I last saw him in Bloomington. Mark's father said that the last known sighting of his son was when he began hitchhiking northeast out of Bloomington on Highway 37. That was a few days after I had last seen Mark. His father asked me to please call him collect if I got any news about Mark. I promised him I would. I figured that in a few months Mark would pop up, probably at some spiritual ashram, spouting a healthy, drug-free lifestyle with the enthusiasm of a door-banging Christian. I thought that could be good for him.

In the coming months, I also spoke with Mark's brother and sister. Almost simultaneously, we asked each other if the other had any news on Mark. No one did. Then there were long silences. Mark's friends and I

## The Wild Years

began to speculate, but never in front of Mark's relatives.

No one ever heard from or saw Mark Watson again. Ever. He disappeared completely off the face of the planet. When Mark left Bloomington hitchhiking east, he left his wallet and all of his identification at a friend's home. So Mark was traveling broke and without ID's. Whatever happened to him, we can only imagine.

Back out West, I thought of that day when Mark, Terry, Billy the Pilot, and I all sat in my living room together. We were making big plans. *We were all gonna get rich.* And then shortly after that, I was the only one left alive of us. No longer was marijuana about peace and love hippies. That was gone forever. There must have been some message here for me. But whatever the message was, I surely did not get it.

## Mark Watson on the right.
## He disappeared from the planet, without a trace

# 25

## Crying at the Free Clinic

I limped into the free medical clinic in Taos, New Mexico, with a bad staph infection on my knee. Pus was oozing out of it and running down the front of my leg. The herbal compresses that my friends put on it seemed only to feed its growth.

The doctor called me inside. She was freshly minted from UC Berkeley and was enjoying living in the New Mexico mountains for the summer. She was smart, attractive, and all business. I told her about falling down a slope and skinning my knee. When I told her about the herbal compresses, she grimaced. I felt embarrassed at my new-found ignorance.

"I'll have to clean it and put you on a regimen of antibiotics and anti-bacterial salve."

I thanked her and took the pills. As I was walking through the lobby, a young woman waved to me. It was White Cloud. She gestured for me to come over. Then she took my hand. She was wearing a Mexican wool blanket that she had hand-fashioned into a tunic. She had beaded it elaborately with pieces of turquoise and malachite, and polished beads of catlinite. Catlinite was the orange-red stone from Minnesota also known as pipe stone. Every time I saw White Cloud's tunic, it was more decorated than the time before.

A buck knife hung from her hip. She had feathers and beads woven into her braids. A beaded leather headband corralled whatever hair the braids had missed. Here was hippie earth mother meeting Annie Oakley and Indian princess. White Cloud would have gotten lots of attention any other place, but here is Taos in 1970, she was just ordinary folk.

White Cloud's face was already weathered like a lifeguard's from spending so much time outside. She was of tough stock, stout and strong, maybe even handsome, but definitely not pretty. She had gone straight from the streets of New York city to the bandito encampment in the New Mexico mountains.

In these mountains, White Cloud thrived on the rugged living. The cold seemed not to bother her at all. She rejoiced in surviving with privations and solving the day-to-day problems of food, shelter, and warmth. Whenever I saw her, she was building a fire, cooking, doing bead work, or on her horse.

White Cloud's big mare, Cadillac, was her one steady love through all these times. She had arrived in New Mexico knowing nothing about horses. But within a year, Cloud had become an excellent rider. She groomed and massaged Cadillac daily. In the summer, she found pasture and gathered grass for Cadillac, and in the winter she bought hay. In turn, Cadillac always came whenever White Cloud let out her shrill whistle. Cadillac often followed White Cloud around like a dog. Men came and went in White Cloud's life, but she and Cadillac were inseparable.

When Cadillac went into heat, my stud horse Pharaoh mounted her repeatedly and violently. White Cloud watched in awe. Later, when Cadillac began to swell, White Cloud flushed with joy.

We were sitting around a campfire drinking one cold spring night on a mountain slope above Mora, New Mexico, when White Cloud shouted that she had an announcement to make. In a burst of drunken laughter, White Cloud yelled that she wanted to have a baby to go along with Cadillac's. The only question for her was, who would be the lucky father? She looked around at the guys in the firelight. A silence descended, along with some nervous twitching. White Cloud was now in charge here.

That was a year ago. This was the first time I had seen White Cloud since then. But this time, White Cloud looked different.

"Are you in a hurry?" She asked, and gestured for me to sit next to her.

"No. I guess not." I sat down. "What's the matter?"

"Will you stay here with me for my appointment?" She pleaded.

"Yeah---Sure. What's up?"

"I have---I have—some woman problems." She paused. Then she added "It really hurts. I've been comin' here for a while."

White Cloud told me she had hitchhiked over the mountains from Mora and slept outside, behind the clinic last night. She didn't want to be late for this appointment. She had bathed up as best she could in the bathroom here.

Then White Cloud's face lit up. "Guess what? Cadillac had a beautiful little colt. I named him Wild Wind, 'cause it was really blowing when he was born. He's a little gray stud. Looks just like your stud horse, Pharaoh, too. I ain't cuttin' him either." I watched her face slowly change to serious again. "Could you come in with me for my appointment? I don't want to be alone."

"I—I don't think the doctor would allow that. But I'll stay out here."

White Cloud bit her lip.

# Crying at the Free Clinic

The same doctor who had treated my knee called for 'Mrs. Cloud'. White Cloud asked the doctor if I could come in with her. The doctor asked if I were her husband. *What?* No. Then I would sit here.

I waited a long time. I saw the doctor come out of the examination room and call another doctor. A while later, White Cloud came out. Tears were running down her cheeks. She surprised me by throwing her arms around me. She smelled of horses.

Finally, she leaned back. "Could you give me a ride to the hospital?"

"Sure."

We drove off together. White Cloud sat silently on the far side of my truck. When we got to the hospital, White Cloud asked me to come in with her. I did.

At the intake desk, White Cloud handed the nurse some papers. Then White Cloud turned to me. "The doctor told me the infection is way up inside me. The pills can't seem to get at it."

I did not ask anything more.

The intake nurse returned with some papers. "Mrs. Cloud. Can I talk with you alone?"

White Cloud told her she wanted me to stay with her.

The nurse looked at me. "Okay, uh, Mr. Cloud. Your doctor feels your situation is quite serious, and that we should schedule an appointment for surgery soon. As you know, this is a serious surgery. Do you have any insurance?"

White Cloud looked at me, and then shook her head.

"Well, that's all right. The state does have a program for indigent people, and I am quite confident that it covers hysterectomies."

White Cloud clung to me, and cried and cried and cried.

Somewhere up on those mountain meadows above Mora, a gray stud pony was romping along side a large white mare. But nowhere on that meadow would a young woman with her baby be seen.

# 26

# Richie's Last Party

My isolated cabin in the Sangre de Cristo Mountains

"Jimmy. Jimmy. Are you there?" I heard someone yelling in the darkness from outside my door. I was startled. Rarely did I get any visitors at night. I was living at the end of the trail in my cabin at 8800 feet in altitude in the Sangre de Cristo Mountains of New Mexico in the middle of winter. But whoever it was outside now, they knew me. I turned up the Alladin kerosene lamp and opened the door. A gust of cold air rushed in. I saw three bearded men standing out front. I only recognized Packrat among them. He was one of the Banditos who who were camping out on the other side of the mountain range this winter. He and his gang had come over to my small ranch in the past, always unannounced. They only came when they needed something from me.

"Jimmy, we need your help. Lobo's been hurt."

I motioned them all in. Packrat and the other man held a wiry, bronze-faced man between them. He had long black curls that fell to his shoulders, almost covering his violently pierced ears. So this was Lobo, the leader of the Banditos. I had heard much about his exploits, and the troubles he had made for everyone else. I was expecting someone bigger, to match the stories. But now he only looked weary.

Packrat pointed to the other man. "This is Richie. He's been helping us." We looked each other over. Richie was burly and muscular, like a wrestler. He wore raw buckskins and a heavy beard. We nodded to each other but did not shake. The Banditos were not into shaking hands.

Packrat motioned to Lobo's left side. I saw a bloody shirt.

"Let's get him on my bed." We moved him from the kitchen through the living room to my bedroom and laid him out. Why did the Banditos come to me when they needed help? Because I was a certified Emergency Medical Technician in the state of New Mexico, because I was their age, because I did not refuse when they smoked, and because I didn't rat on them. In their own way, they sort of trusted me, and they did not have anyone else to turn to when they were hurt.

I lit up another Alladin lamp and began removing Lobo's winter clothing.

"Got stabbed in Santa Fe," Lobo finally spoke. "Can you fix it up? And don't tell no one."

I told him I didn't have any painkillers. I did have some, but I knew never to mention it around these guys.

"I don't care. Just sew me up. I can't go to no doctors," Lobo said. I caught his accent and we began speaking in Spanish. He was fluent.

The left side of his cotton shirt was soaked with blood. I cut the shirt from him. Lobo had a slashing wound from his hip bone toward his navel. Nasty, but not lethal. First I washed the cut clean with alcohol. Lobo did not flinch. This wound cut through his skin, what little fat he had, and some abdominal muscle. But I did not see any cuts into his intestines. Good for him, because cut intestines went way beyond my limited skill set. I feared ruptured abdominal muscles, staph infections, even gangrene. But I also feared all of the Banditos' guns. I boiled some water first and sterilized my stitch kit. Then I cleaned and slowly sewed up the cut to the abdominal muscles with dissolvable stitches. The other Banditos stared intently as I ran the sterilized stitch needle through his flesh. Again, Lobo did not flinch. I finished by closing up the skin with another row of stitches. I washed it again with alcohol and covered it with antibiotic ointment, gauze and tape. As dirty as Lobo was, he would likely get a staph infection. So I gave him a small bag of ampicillin and told him he couldn't do anything strenuous for two weeks. Come back in a week and let me look at it. I sounded just like a doctor.

He got up and squeezed my hand. "*Gracias, mano*. Anything I can do

Pharaoh, and his harem

for you, I will."

I told him I wanted to talk with him alone. He waved the other Banditos out of the room.

"There is something you can do for me. Tell the other Banditos to stop taking my horse feed and gear. When they don't replace it like they promise, it becomes stealing."

"*They do*? I am sorry, man. I did not know," he spoke softly. "They won't do that no more." He squeezed my hand.

Lobo walked outside. He started to hop up on his horse, but I stopped him.

"Wait a minute. Lobo, you're going to have to stay here a few days, or you're going to tear those stitches straight out."

"You sure?"

"I know so. I can fix up a bed for you here. But you shouldn't be on horseback any time soon."

The Banditos conferred among themselves.

"You ain't gonna go to the law are you?" Packrat asked me.

"Fuck no. I'm not that stupid."

They liked my answer. All three stayed the night. Richie rode off alone in the morning. Packrat stayed with me three days while Lobo recovered.

While they were with me, I gave Packrat a basic hygiene class on how to clean and change Lobo's dressings. He struggled with it. He thought it was just too much fuss.

While Lobo recovered, he told me he was born in Sicily during World War II. His mother never married his father, and Lobo never knew him. His mother told him nothing about his father. But the local villagers sure did. They hounded his mother about being an unmarried mother until she fled to Rome. After the war, she somehow managed to emigrate to New York City. There, Lobo said he grew up mostly on the streets. He laughed and shook his head at how wild his life had been. He ended his story by stating that he could never go back to NYC.

On the last day, I ran out of fresh bandages for Lobo, I told Packrat I would have to go to the pharmacy in Mora to buy more.

Packrat looked at me darkly. "You come back by yourself."

When I got back, I re-dressed the gash. The edges were pink and rosy, with no obvious drainage. It looked like he was healing well. I gave Lobo a bag of dressings and a vial of antibiotics. He nodded as Packrat helped him into his saddle. Then he leaned forward and handed me a purple cloth tobacco bag. It was filled with something heavy.

"Thanks," Lobo tilted his moppy hat to me. "If we ever need doctor help again, you be there. We'll get you more feed too." I told him to come back if he thought it wasn't healing right. Then they rode up the trail over the Sangre de Cristos. Was I relieved that they were finally out of my place.

I went back in and poured the contents of the tobacco bag on my table. There was a stack of ancient silver dollars and one five-dollar Liberty Gold Piece. I felt its density as I held it. I looked at it closely. 1902. Real doctors didn't even earn this much. I knew not to ask where they got this silver and gold. Then I carefully hid the bag outside, underground. Gold and silver don't rot.

One afternoon, about a month later, I saw the blue-black clouds of a storm blowing over a mountain. I went outside to finish up my work when, in the distance, I saw a solitary woman riding toward my place on a horse. She had a pack horse tied behind her. And behind that horse a big red truck was following her. The woman was dressed in leathers and beaded buckskins. She rode up to me and smoothly slid off her horse.

"Your name Jimmy?" She asked. I nodded. Jimmy was my alias here. "Good. I thought I was lost. I'm Springflower." She looked me over. Underneath the grit on her, there was a pretty woman. A very pretty woman.

# Richie's Last Party

"Lobo sent me to give this to you." I couldn't place the accent, but I thought it could be Appalachian. She pointed to the pack horse. I walked over to it. It was a gray speckled gelding. I checked its teeth. It looked to be about seven years old. A gift horse in the springtime is good news. But not so in the winter. I took the horse bridle and the gelding to my pasture. My stud horse Pharaoh came running up. Soon he would be kicking it into submission. I told Springflower to tell Lobo thanks. She gestured to the truck waiting at my barn. "Lobo paid that guy to deliver a load of hay and grain too."

She waved the driver forward. He was a middle-aged cowboy. He drove the old twin axle International flatbed truck up to my hayloft and hopped out. Springflower and I helped him unload the square bales and bags of corn into my barn loft.

"I'm just doing what they paid me to do," was about all the cowboy ever said to me. "Looks like there's a big storm coming in. I got to hurry down the mountain and beat it." He drove off.

Springflower and I went inside my cabin. I asked her if she was hungry and she nodded. I began frying potatoes and heating up some beans. I put a tub of water on the wood stove. She looked at the water.

"Hot water for your bath," I said. I handed her a cup of hot tea.

"*A real hot bath*," she said, and smiled for the first time. "Wow. Has that been a long time."

"If you want, after you're done bathing, you can wash your clothes in the water and hang them above the stove. They'll be dry by morning."

We ate in silence as the storm sat in. Then I left her alone to bathe. I watched the fire in the wood stove burn. My television. After Springflower finished her bath, she sat next to the wood stove with me. I stoked the stove and gave her a sleeping bag and a pad. She unrolled the sleeping bag and wrapped it around her. Then I went to my bedroom and climbed into my bed.

Later in the night, I heard a rustling. I felt Springflower crawl under the covers on my bed without saying a word. She pulled me to her. I felt her nakedness and warmth. We loved, and then slept wrapped around each other. Springflower was a good name for her.

In the morning, Springflower told me of her dreams the night before. They were vivid and true for her. She believed they had meaning and sent messages to her. She told me of her recurring dreams that she had had since she had left home. These were not pleasant stories. She asked me what I thought these dreams  meant. I did my best to interpret them. Then she asked me of my dreams. When I told her that I could not remember them,

## The Wild Years

she was disappointed. She told me that I could remember them, only if I would pay more attention to them.

Then we got up and rode our horses into the new snow. Low clouds curled over the mountains, throwing snow at us in blasts. Springflower raced ahead into it, shouting screams of pure joy and excitement. She galloped her horse straight into the high snowdrifts until her horse stopped with a jolt. She flew off into a snowdrift. But she bounced up out of the snow laughing and hopped right back on to ride again. With a yell, she took off riding with the mountain wind, riding like the mountain wind.

When we got back, I began heating more bath water for her. I studied her. Her eyes were aglow, her cheeks flushed red, her face an irrepressible smile, her body bouncing with energy. She grabbed my hand and led me to my bed. "I just can't wait," she laughed. We quickly stripped and got under covers. I reached for her. Her garden was juicy matted wet. "This happens every time I ride," she giggled. Then she sort of turned away. *Was she embarrassed?* I loved it.

I thought of my stud horse Pharaoh. When he caught the scent of a mare in heat, there was no stopping him. He rolled his front lips back, laid down his ears and whinnied. His massive cock came out and he slapped it against his belly. He whinnied again and then took off after the mare. *Nothing got in his way.* Not fences, not other horses, not ranchers, and as I had learned painfully, not me either. It would take a bullet to stop Pharaoh from going after a mare in heat. He was going to spread his seed.

# Richie's Last Party

In bed, I grabbed Springflower's hands and held them over her head. Then I quickly straddled her, threw my head back, and snorted and whinnied like my stud horse. Springflower whinnied back and kicked at me like a mare. We laughed hysterically, until we were completely out of breath. Only now did I think that I might be able to know this wild woman. We loved violently, she taunting me, me mounting her, animal sounds, loving all night long. The sounds she made while galloping on a horse and while loving me were the same. I held onto her for my dear life. *Just who was this woman?*

The next day it snowed again and the wind blew high drifts. Now we were truly snowed in. I had plenty of firewood and food, and kerosene enough to read a stack of good books I had collected for the winter. I had thought I was all set for winter. But then this Springflower came along. Now I wanted nothing more than to be snowed in with her for the whole winter.

*Who was this person?* She didn't talk much. She didn't read much either. When she wasn't helping me work, she played soft songs on her bamboo flute, or just sang to herself. She did bead work and embroidery on some buckskins she had brought with her. She never missed a day on the saddle. Life was clear and simple to her: Fire, food, water, horse-riding riding riding, playing music, making beautiful things, *loving me*, and sleeping.

I asked her questions. She didn't answer at first. Then reluctantly, she told me she had run off from home in West Virginia to New York City when she was very young. She said she never had much of a family and would *never* ever go back to West Virginia, after what happened there. "Well, what happened?' I asked, but she ignored me. She said she lived on the streets in New York City for a while. She would not tell me any more about that. Then she met up with a street gang called The Motherfuckers. They took her in and gave her a place to crash. She said that, for the first time, she had people and felt safe.

Springflower stayed with me through the storm. She said that sometime she had to get back to the bandito camp on Jack Nicholson's land, but she wasn't in any hurry. Every day, she found a reason to linger on. When the trails were clear enough, we took long horse rides up the mountainside. One day, she wanted to camp outside overnight, atop the mountain behind my cabin. "Just like the Indians," she said. So we packed plenty of feed for our horses in large saddlebags. We rode a half day through the snow, climbing to the shoulder of the peak. We set camp just before sunset at the frozen pond. The wind was picking up and the temperature was dropping to zero. I anchored my tent while Springflower watched. She said she knew tepees, but not tents. With her help, I managed to get the rain fly on. Inside the tent,

# The Wild Years

I put two pads on the floor. Then I zipped my two down sleeping bags together into one big bag. My teeth were chattering as I got into the bags and took my clothes off. I left my socks on. My body shivered. I handed Springflower the flashlight and she undid her clothes inside the bags too.

When she turned on the flashlight, she said, "You sure have a white ass."

We laughed.

From the one big sleeping bag we gnawed on frozen bread and goat cheese. Eventually we sated our hunger. Outside the tent the wind blew strong. The rain fly snapped against the tent like a wet towel. Darkness set in.

"Well, what's on TV tonight, dearie?" Springflower said, and we laughed some more.

We held each other for warmth. We breathed on our fingertips and kept our heads within the bags to save the warmth in our breath. And when our hands were finally warm enough, our fingertips wandered over each other in the darkness. We felt ourselves fit together as man and woman naturally do, and that kept the hostile world outside at bay.

When we were not holding each other that night, we were talking about life. Springflower spoke of horses and riding and the joy and freedom of the mountains. She seemed unfazed by the winter. Everything wild and free was good for her.

In the morning, we lay holding each other in the sleeping bag. The inside of the tent was covered with frost and crystals from our breath. Neither of us was eager to be the first out. I asked her again to stay and live with me.

She squeezed me. "Thank you. That is so kind of you." She paused. "But that would mean my horses too. Love me, love my horses."

"It's a deal."

"But I still have to think about it. I have to tell you my dream first. It is telling me what I should do. What I want to do. I want to leave on horseback next spring and ride all the way to Canada. All the way."

"Am I in your dream?"

"You weren't last night. But you could be. We could take a pack horse too, maybe a nanny goat, and fishing stuff. You could bring your shot gun. We could live off the land, just like Indians."

"You think it could be done?"

"Sure. My only worry would be roads – and people. Stay in the national forests, along streams and rivers. Buy supplies when we have to. But live

## Richie's Last Party

outside wild and free, on horses. Like it used to be. We could get there. I don't want to go alone. Would you come with me?"

"Yes," I said to her, before I ever thought of what this meant. To live wild and free with this woman. To cross state and national borders like they weren't there, to move with the wind and live off the land. To be as wild as the first humans. So wild that we didn't even know we were wild. *Just who was this woman?*

We played in our sleeping bags as long as we could. Then we quickly dressed in the cold. We fed the horses and unshackled them. They hoofed through the snow for more grass. Around us on this gray, windy morning at 10,000 feet was over a foot of new snow. The trail we had come up on was completely covered. We let our horses pick their way down the slope to my cabin. It was sunset by the time we got back.

We fed the horses again and led them into the pasture. The cabin was ice cold. Water had frozen in its containers. I quickly built fires in both the wood stove fire and the cooking stove. I went to the stream and broke through the surface ice. I lugged back a metal container of five gallons of water and put it on the stove.

"What is that for?" Springflower asked.

"Your nightly bath, sweetness."

"You're just trying to spoil me into staying here," she poked me in the ribs and laughed.

"Whatever works."

We played house for another week. Springflower rode the fences with me and helped restring barbed wire. She said she didn't believe in fences, but would do it for me. We spent a day riding to Mora for more supplies. When I caught her looking at chocolate bars, I bought her a handful. She was embarrassed about it, but then took them greedily. Of course she had no money. None at all, and no people to help her either. She was as on her own as anyone I had ever met. I wanted to protect and help her. I was already thinking of she and I as 'us'.

She never directly answered me when I asked her to just stay stay stay with me. So I behaved as if she would be here always. I thought that maybe if I acted like that, it would cause her to stay. Think and act positive and it will happen. I assured her there would always be food and heat and love in my home. She said that she loved a hot bath after horse riding-- and the warmth of my bed. Coming from her lips, those words were so sweet. So here she and I were, in the winter, snowed in high in the New Mexico mountains, incredibly alone except for just each other, just staying alive. The only man and the only woman. I could do this with her...

# The Wild Years

Then one day she got up early. Her face was disturbed.

"I am leaving today," she said.

*"Why?"*

"Because Lobo told me I had to come back."

"You can stay with me."

"Lobo said I could stay a while, but that I had to come back."

*"Stay with me."*

"I must get ready for my ride to Canada." She held out the buckskin jacket she had been working on. It had a large eagle on its back, and a rocky Mountain columbine on the front. *A Springflower.*

"This is yours."

I held it to the morning light. It was stunningly beautiful.

"Please stay. Please." I reached to her.

She climbed onto her horse.

"You can come back whenever you want."

"You can come with me, too," she said.

Then she rode off. I had never felt lonely here, until Springflower left. Now I thought of her every day. I missed her dearly. I needed to ride over the mountains and see her. But I needed to find someone to watch my animals and home too. And I needed to start work as soon as our county had medical funding approved. But now my home and bed was empty and cold.

About a month later, Richie and his woman, Melody, came riding up on their horses to my ranch. Their daughter, Rain, trailed them on her pony. Lyric had her new baby strapped to her chest. And behind all of them, Richie's buddy, Packrat, rode on his pinto mount while leading an overloaded pack horse. Their horses were gaunt and bony. Richard and Melody were wearing the same buckskins that I saw them wearing last fall. But now their buckskins were gray-black. *What did they want from me this time?*

It was early springtime in 1971. Despite the sun, the wind still blew cold over the remaining snow drifts around my cabin. From the saddle, Richie leaned over his leather rifle holster. "Hey Jimmy. I'm *really* sick. Can you do something?"

He looked sick. His voice was weak and raspy. Without waiting for my reply, he slid off his horse and stumbled into my cabin. He went straight into my bedroom and lay on my bed. We followed him in. Richie looked up at me. "I gotta sleep in some place warm, man. You gotta help me. But I don't want no white man's medicine from you."

# Richie's Last Party

I looked at him for a moment. "Last I checked, Richie, we were still white men." Richie didn't answer me.

Richie was wearing a long barrel single-action Colt 44-magnum revolver. That was the preferred handgun of the Banditos. He and Melody had been living outside at over 9000 feet all winter. They had dug out a shallow hole and then covered with logs and a tepee canvas. They had held up like that all winter, living with their horses and goats in below-zero temperatures, with three feet of snow. Twice, Richie had ridden down to my cabin to 'borrow' bags of cornmeal and beans from me. On the second trip he told me that they had eaten their goats because they weren't giving anymore milk and were going to die anyhow. Richie also fed my hay to his horse whenever he came. I could have resisted him, but it might have ended up with more Banditos coming by with guns. Richie had a loyal tribe of co-Banditos who stuck together when it mattered.

Melody carried her newborn baby into my home while her daughter Rain trailed her. Rain looked to be around four years old. Melody held the new baby up to me. "We named him Cold Winter." The name was appropriate for this winter. Little Rain was bundled up like an Eskimo child, with layers of wool and a crude sheepskin coat made directly from a sheep, without the benefit of tanning the hide first. However they got that sheep, I knew they did not pay for it. Rain had knotty blond hair like her mother, and the rosiest cheeks I have ever seen on a child. I had seen Rain a few other times this winter, and that little girl never seemed bothered at all by the cold. Whenever she was around my cabin, she played in the snow.

Richie and Melody never complained about the rough conditions they lived in. Instead, they seemed to revel in their hardships. The last time I saw them, they talked about the three day blizzard we had. They only went outside their hogan to relieve themselves or bring in more firewood. Both of them were zero on the wimp scale. I respected their toughness.

In his better moods, Richie teased me about living inside four corners. He said that square houses made for square minds and square people. But today, Richie had no energy for words. My home did not have electricity, running water or a telephone, and I was snowed in for the winter too. But I did have something Richie needed now; *warmth*. Richie and Melody smelled of no baths and wearing the same clothes all winter. Their newborn kid reeked of shit and piss. Their odors spread through my cabin.

While they rested in my bedroom, I heated up a wash pan of water on the wood stove. I told Melody she would have to undress Richie and bathe him first before he could sleep here. But Richie had already passed out. He looked like he had pneumonia. He needed rest, warmth, humidity, and antibiotics. Just what did he mean by "no white man's medicine" anyhow?

# The Wild Years

While Melody was undressing Richie to wash him, I saw the wound. It was a long, deep cut on his side. It swelled out along its edges, with a greenish-yellow puss oozing from it, *onto my blankets and bed.* Parts of the center of the cut were blackish. It smelled putrid.

"He fell off his horse tryin' to get it to jump over a barbed wire fence. Cut himself on the fence," Melody said.

"When?"

"Oh, sometime last week, I guess."

I told Melody that we should get Richie down to the clinic in Mora right now. Only then did Richie open his eyes. "No way," he muttered.

Melody pulled me off to the side. She was blond and blue-eyed, petite and, somewhere under all that filth and grime, a very pretty girl used to live. She'd gone from Texas high school cheerleader to Richie's bandito moll in only a few years. Melody led me out of the room. "Richie's wanted---for armed robbery. He's 'fraid to go to town."

Well, well, well. I thought there might be a warrant for my arrest out there someplace, too. Maybe for selling marijuana, I didn't know. I did know that they would arrest me first, before they told me about the warrant, so I wasn't taking any chances. So I used different identification, and I never told anyone about my past.

When the Banditos rode into to my ranch earlier this winter, they took a lot of my horse feed, food, and tack gear. They said that they were just 'borrowing it.' I did not go to the police afterward because I did not want to identify myself. But worse yet, if the Banditos ever found out that I had gone to the cops, they take revenge for sure. Just last month I had seen a bumper sticker in town that said:

IF YOU THINK ALL COPS ARE PIGS,
NEXT TIME YOU NEED HELP, CALL A HIPPIE!

Ha ha ha. The joke was now on me.

I told Melody that they could stay here while I went to the clinic to get antibiotics. Just don't tell Richie that it's White Man antibiotics. My truck was still stuck in the snow-melt mud, so I saddled up Pharaoh, my Spanish mustang. Under the best of conditions, he was not an easy ride. But on his first ride in a week, he fought me much of the way to Mora.

I did not get back from the emergency medical clinic until nightfall. When I entered my bedroom, I found Richie lying in my bed with Melody next to him. Her new-born baby, Cold Winter, was suckling, and their daughter Rain was asleep next to her.

"How's Richie doing?"

"He's asleep. Out cold."

"We should wake him, get him to take these antibiotics."

Melody thought about it. "He said he didn't want those."

"He'll never know – unless you tell him."

She paused again. "Okay. But let's wait till he wakes up. He needs to rest."

I stepped out of my bedroom and shut the door on them. I would be sleeping on the floor in my own home. I added wood to the stove and unrolled my sleeping bag in front of it. Under the orange flicker of the flames through the Pyrex stove glass, I fell asleep. I got up once that night to feed the fire. I went outside to piss and saw the glory of the mountain stars.

Just before dawn I heard my bedroom door open.

"Jimmy? You there?" I heard Melody call. "Could you come here?"

I got up and went into my bedroom. There was a candle going.

"It's Richie---"

I sat on the edge of the bed and put my hand on his head. He was no longer hot. I felt for pulse on his neck. Nothing. I had done this before in the ambulance.

"I think --- he's dead."

I lit my Alladin lamp and waited as it filled the room with light. There Richie was, lying across a Mexican blanket on my bed. Long greasy black hair and beard matted together, dirty red bandanna around his neck, stained leather buckskins, several ear rings on both ears, a small cross tattoo on his cheek. He looked like a rugged mountain man—and now a dead one. No breath, no pulse. I unbuttoned his shirt. He was all blue on the side he was lying on. His wound now stuck to my blanket.

"Shit. What am I gonna do now?" Melody asked. Cold Winter began to cry. Lyric opened her blouse and put him to her floppy breast. I looked at Richie's body again. *How did this guy ever make the jump from being assistant college professor of English at Cleveland State to armed robber bandito?* And now he was lying dead in my bed.

"Well --- you can't leave him here."

I heard Packrat walking on the porch. He had been sleeping in the hayloft of the barn. Melody called him in and told him Richie was dead.

"Wow. Another one," Packrat said.

"But what am I going to do with him?" Melody started putting Richie's clothes back on. "I guess we could bury him up in the national forest – 'cept the ground's all frozen."

"Naw. Richie wouldn't wanna be buried," Packrat said. "He'd wanna fly. Not be in the ground like some piss-ant worm."

"Well, first we should get a death certificate for him," I said. "I can get that started---"

"*He's dead all right,*" Packrat glared. "Don't need no fuckin' doctor tell you that. Fuck death certificates. Fuck birth certificates. Fuck all certificates. Let's just take his body an' care of him ourselves. We put Roger in the ground and Richie didn't like that." He and Melody mumbled something to each other.

We bundled Richie up in a Mexican blanket I had bought in Sonora last year. It was already covered in ooze and puss. Looked like I wouldn't be using it anymore. Packrat went down to the stream. He returned a bit later with two cut aspen trees. They were about fifteen feet long and maybe four inches wide at the thick end, with all the branches stripped from them. He took a heavy blanket and tied it between the two poles. Then he tied the two ends of the pole to the saddle on the pack horse. And there it was, a travois.

We carried Richie's body out from my bedroom and put it in the center of the travois. The sun was getting higher now and it looked like we were going to have our first warm day of this early spring. I looked at Richie's face. Black vacant eyes stared back at me. Not so different than when he was alive. I cut some cord and we tied the blanket over Richie's face. We covered his hands and feet with the blanket and roped him in tight. No one could see his body now. Melody and Packrat stepped to the side and talked between themselves. Then they came back to me.

"We're taking them over to Nicholson's land above Le Doux," Packrat said. "The party will be in a few days. We'll let everyone know when."

"Shit," Melody said. "This is really gonna be a hassle." She began repacking her horse and dressing up her kids.

I heard a car coming down the road. I lived at the end of a five-mile mountain trail, so whenever anyone got this far on the road, they were coming to visit me. Since there were no phone lines, mail boxes, or electricity up here, people just arrived when they arrived. I went outside and saw my old friend Damien pull up in his four-wheel drive truck. With him was his girlfriend Christina. We hadn't seen each other in over a year. I knew that he had been supporting himself with the risky business of running marijuana across the Mexican border. Damien loved doing it. He liked his life as a smuggler and saw himself as a Robin Hood, making marijuana available to the masses until its inevitable legalization. He considered his smuggling a political act against the empire. The truck stopped, they got out, and we hugged.

"Who's that guy over there with the gun?" Damien tugged on me while pointing at Packrat in the distance. "In my business, I always watch for men with guns."

"Let's go for a walk." I led them up the hill. When we were away from Melody and Packrat, I said "Just call me Jimmy here. That's the alias I'm using here. Now listen. Those people are Banditos. Don't say anything in front of them about what you do, or they might rob you. So be careful."

"Like in real, live bandits? Why do you let them in your home?"

"I haven't found an easy way to throw them out when they come riding in with their guns and I'm way up here alone. They usually come here to get something from me. Stitches, antibiotics, horse feed, even ammo. You name it. Sometimes they pay me back, sometimes they don't. There's a bunch of them in these hills now. So be careful. They rip off dope dealers for both the dope and the money. So you stay low and don't say anything. These Banditos here, they just came yesterday. One of them was sick---"

Just then Packrat and Melody come walking up the hill to us. He eyed Damien and Christina over and then looked to me.

"Friends a yours?" Packrat looked them over. ?Can they be trusted?"

*Who the fuck is this guy asking me about who my visitors are at my own home?*

"Well, Melody and me, we decided we're gonna burn Richie. Send him to the sky and the spirits. We're gonna get all the family together. I'm gonna take the travois with Richie over the mountain to Nicholson's land. We'll have the cremation there. You welcome to come if you want. Melody's gonna be contactin' all a Richie's friends best she can. I gotta get started riding now." Packrat strode down hill in big lopes while we walked behind him.

Damien stopped me behind the tack room. "Just what the *fuck* was that all of that about?"

"Well, you see, I was just telling you, this Richie bandito, he comes to my home yesterday to rest because he's sick---" We stepped around the horse shed and we can see the travois attached to the horse. Richie's arm had come loose. Packrat was working on tying it back in. I point to Richie. "---and he up and dies in my bed last night."

Damien and Christina stared at me. Then they walked over to Richie and stared a while. Christina slowly touched Richie's arm with her finger.

"Hey!" Packrat shouted. Christina quickly pulled her hand back. "He's dead all right." We watched Packrat mount up and ride off, leading the pack horse that was dragging Richie's travois.

When they were out of site, Damien said "This happen all the time up here? I mean, I drive up here and find a dead fucking body."

"It's a first for me too. I'm glad they're outta here."

Christina wrinkled her nose and said nothing. Then she leaned over to a small mountain stream that flowed by my home and washed her hands in it.

I went inside and started a wood fire to heat up water to fix breakfast for

Damien and Christina. Then I washed my clothes and the bed sheets and everything that they had lain on or touched. Christina helped me do the wash. She mentioned that she had never done laundry over a fire. "Sure is a beautiful place you have here. Too bad he had to die on you."

"You mean like in one less bandito?'"

For the remainder of that day Damien, Christina and I hiked. First up the mountain, then along a trail to a waterfall near my home for an ice-cold quick dip. We shrieked in pain and laughter when we hit the water. Then we rushed to dress and get back to my wood stove. We cooked a simple meal over my stove and ate silently on the porch, while watching the sun go down.

I told them I would be going to the cremation and that they should come along with me. Both of them hesitated. They wanted to know just exactly what went on with cremations in the mountains. I told them I had no idea either, but I wanted to see it for myself. Damien thought it was just too creepy to consider.

"So this big-time marijuana smuggler is afraid to go to a little ole cremation?"

Damien looked at me funny. "Fuck you," he laughed, and then agreed to go with me.

Next morning I started rounding up my three horses to pack up for our ride to the bandito campsite. Damien stopped me with an emphatic "No!" He said there was no way he was going to get stranded someplace with a bunch of banditos and no other transportation except horses. He and Christina would drive their truck over instead. I told him that he could not get his truck closer than a mile to the Banditos' main campsite. Damien said that he and Christina would backpack the remaining distance. I told them the Banditos wouldn't let strangers ever come into camp. They would need my presence to enter their campsite. So I would ride with them in their truck.

I had one problem with that. Packrat said they would pay me for a billy goat. So I had to deliver it. Damien objected to putting such a dirty, stinky, piss-smelling beast into their camper truck. "No choice," I said. We bound up his feet and laid his struggling body onto a tarp inside the camper. I had named this goat Dirty Ole Man. He was an aggressive old Nubian billy goat, the meanest one I had ever had. More than once, he had butted me over and then trampled me. But now that I had a younger, tamer billy goat, Dirty Ole Man could go.

We packed three backpacks with sleeping bags and a tent. I put on the new, beaded buckskin jacket that Springflower had made for me. Christina admired the bead work. Damien brought along three bottles of good tequila

Richie's Last Party

and a load of smoke. Then we set off down the hill in his truck.

We drove down winding dirt roads until we got to the little village of Le Doux. Dana asked a Chicano farmer there if we could park on his land. I intervened in Spanish and offered the man five dollars to guard our truck for a few days. We shook on it. I tied a leash onto the billy goat and then undid its legs. We grabbed our packs and began hiking up a washed out wagon road, leading a reluctant goat all the way.

The road quickly turned into a muddy horse trail. Strong cold winds blew down off the mountains. We passed a few remnant snowdrifts. As we approached the bandito camp, I saw an increasing number of wet white clumps. They were wads of used toilet paper next to thawing human excrement. I told Damien and Christina to watch their step. In a few weeks, this place would be stinking. What would it do to the runoff water below?

We hiked around a clump of pine trees and saw a cluster of guys standing around a fire, smoking. Packrat was among them. All around us were tepees, tarps, tents, and piles of gear. Empty beer cans, wine bottles, and food containers covered the ground. A young woman stirred up a fire while another woman dragged in firewood. Other young women were mixing pots of food. A bearded man was working on horse gear.

In the field I saw a small herd of skinny, starving horses; geldings, old mares, and at least one stud horse. We walked to the center of the camp where a large fire was burning. Over it were two large kettles with food boiling in them. Two women looked up at us from the fire. Their faces were smudged with ash and smoke. They said nothing to us. I tied my billy goat

# The Wild Years

to a small gambel oak near the fire. Then I walked up to the main tepee in the center.

"Lobo. You in there? It's Jimmy."

Someone yelled from inside. Then a wiry man came out of the tent. Lobo. Clumps of his hair were matted together into forever balls of tangles. Bright beads and feathers were permanently woven into it in an intricate pattern. His hair had become a one-piece, inseparable mat. A bear claw necklace hung over his soiled buckskin jacket. Lobo threw his arms around me.

"Hey, Jimmy. Goooood to see you." Lobo spoke slowly with an accented English. "You could not help Richie, no?"

"He was gone before I could give him some medicine."

"Too bad. I really dug Richie. Good man to have at your back. This time we send him to the sky. That's where Richie would want to be."

We stood silent for a bit. Then Lobo pointed to a kettle. "It's just beans man, but it's food. Eat."

"I brought a goat for you all."

"*A whole goat?* What a brother you are. We're starving for meat here. We shot all the deer around here. And our neighbors---they don't like when we *borrow* their cattle." Lobo grinned darkly. "I'm so sick of these fuckin' beans, I was thinkin' on killin' another horse. 'Cept we need the rest. Where's this goat anyhow?"

We walked to the tree where I had tied it. And there was Dirty Ole Man, stripping away bark from the tree, just like he had done to my fruit trees.

"We're hungry now," Lobo announced. He walked back to his tepee and came back with a old lever-action rifle.

"Everybody back!" He lever-actioned the 44-40 and aimed at Dirty Ole Man.

BOOM! Dirty Ole Man's head blew apart. Lobo did not waste any time.

"You didn't tell me you were going to do that to Dirty Ole Man!" Christina shouted at me. I had no idea that Lobo was going to do that. But Lobo probably didn't know either, until he did it.

"You eat meat? Because we sure as hell don't milk billie goats here," I answered.

"That has *nothing* to do with it."

Lobo shouted to his guys to butcher this goat right now, if they wanted meat tonight. From out of lean-to's and tepees came a few grizzled guys. They pulled out their buck knives and went at Dirty Ole Man. They quickly had him gutted. The skinning took a bit longer. Then they rammed a long, sharp metal spit through the body. Together, two guys put the spit on two Y-shaped pieces of metal on opposite sides of the fire. Then they built up the flames beneath it. Damien and Christina watched it all. I motioned for them to come over to Lobo and me. "Friends of mine," I introduced them to Lobo. Damien stuck out his hand. Lobo just nodded.

"They're cool," I said.

He looked them over with his dark eyes. "You don't tell nobody nothing. Any cameras and they go straight into the fire. Okay?" Lobo smiled darkly through his broken teeth.

We stood around the open spit and warmed ourselves up as the flames rose. Lobo drew his buck knife and cut off a thin slab of goat meat. It was charred on one side and raw on the other. I smeared salt all over it and went at it. It was either too hot, too cold, too charred, too raw, too bloody, too salty, too greasy, or too grisly. But mixed all together on this cold windy day on the side of the mountain, it was almost delicious. Around the smoking fire I turned to Lobo with a slab of goat and shouted, "CARNE!"

Lobo smiled and shouted back, "CARNE!"

In a moment we were all chanting, "CARNE CARNE CARNE!"

I grabbed a slab of goat meat and handed it to Damien and Christina. They looked at it, but didn't take it.

"What's up?"

"I don't know that I eat like this." Damien gestured to the goat carcass over the spit. Banditos had surrounded it with knives. The meat was going fast.

"Your ancestors did."

Christina pushed the goat meat away.

In the open field, the some Banditos were whooping it up. They were drinking fire water and racing on their horses. Five of them managed to stop their horses in a clump for a moment. Lobo shouted for them to race to the lone pine tree at the end of the meadow and back. Then he shot his rifle and they took off galloping through the snow and mud. They were all riding bareback. A woman was the first to get to the tree. As the horse turned to come back, she flew off and hit the ground hard. Another rider's horse jumped over her. In the distance I heard her cuss. She got up and started chasing her horse. The Banditos cheered when the riders raced past us. A different bandito woman won the race. She came trotting up to the fire. I looked at her.

*It was Springflower.* She let out a victory cry. Her long hair had been blown back into a tangled mane behind her. A proud smile covered her face. She looked more wild and beautiful than I had ever seen her. She rode her horse up to me and gave me a kick with her moccasin boot. "Hey dude. Where'd you get that beautiful jacket?"

We looked into each other's eyes. Her face was aglow again, her cheeks flushed red. "Some angel gave it to me. I've been looking for her ever since."

She stopped her horse and smiled at me. From the horse she gave me another kick and then she trotted her horse across the meadow.

The woman who fell off the horse came striding up to the fire with her horse trailing on an Indian bridle. Her mouth was bleeding. She was stocky and looked tough and strong.

"*Goddamn!*" she shouted. "I lost it on the curve." She tied her horse up. A guy looked at her face. "I'm all right," she yelled. "I just chipped a tooth." He brought her over to me. Everyone knew I was the local 'doc'. One of her front teeth was chipped half off. "*I'm okay,*" she shouted to the guy and shook loose of him. She wiped off her face and walked back to the fire.

I went into Lobo's tepee and waved for Damien to follow me. It was dry and surprisingly neat inside. There was a small smoky fire in the middle. They had covered the ground with grass and laid some deer and cow skins over it. Lobo was lying there, with two rifles next to him. A woman was heating something over the fire while another slept next to him. Damien handed Lobo a bag of good Mexican marijuana. Lobo's face lit up.

"I'll have to share this with everyone here. It's how we do it here," Lobo said.

Damien nodded.

"Hey Jimmy," Lobo waved me over and handed me a peace pipe. I passed it to Damien. He inhaled, then handed Lobo a bottle of tequila gold. "For you."

Lobo held the bottle like a baby. "Far out, man. Tonight we send Richie off to the sky. All his brothers will be here. It'll be good."

The smoke came in waves of color over me. Time shifted its gears down to granny. I slowly looked around. A 44-magnum single-action pistol hung from a tepee pole next to me. A pair of golden eagle wings were drying above, along with the hide of a small black bear. Carrion smells came from the untanned deerskins. Lobo swigged the tequila. Bleeding cracks on the corners of Lobo's mouth. I thought scurvy --- or cold sores.

Then I saw it, next to Lobo's bed. *Springflower's Indian blanket and bed roll.*

Lobo took the pipe. "I think we start getting a pile of wood right now, before it's dark. A big pile, 'cause we don't want anything left of Richie when the fire's over."

Lobo lifted up his buckskin jacket and showed me the scar on his left side where he'd been stabbed. "No problems with it. *Nada.* How it look?" I examined it. "It healed well. No signs of any skin infection." "Last time I got stabbed, it got infected bad. You better than a doctor. You like the horse?" I nodded. *"And the girl too?"* He laughed darkly, to himself.

We went outside his tepee. Lobo yelled for everyone to gather around. He told them to get as much firewood as they could for the fire. We walked to the nearby woods and helped the others drag in every dead branch, snag, and tree that we could find. Before darkness, we had a pile higher than we could reach. We threw the last pieces on top. Pipes and tequila went around the fire. Some people began beating on drums around a small fire to the side of the wood pyre. Others started dancing slowly around the fire. Elbows, knees, legs kicking, hair tossing back and forth. Melody led them with yells. She began trilling "RICHIE RICHIE RICHIEEEEEE!" as she danced. Others joined with her. Melody waved Richie's rifle in one hand and his eagle feathers in the other. The fervor rose. Everyone was shouting and chanting and dancing, except for Damien and Christina. They stood apart, at the edge of the firelight. From the mountains, I heard the drum beats echo back to us.

I walked over to Christina. She tugged on my sleeve. "What's that Melody dancing about? I mean, her old man just died and she's having a good time."

Damien handed me a bottle of tequila. I swigged. It was good. Packrat walked up to us. I handed him the bottle. He swigged it hard a few times. Melody came bounding up to Packrat and grabbed Packrat. "HEY, LET'S DANCE!" She saw the tequila and took a big gulp. Packrat took the tequila back from her and walked off with it.

"Hey, that fucker just ripped off my tequila. Who the fuck does he think he is?" Damien snapped.

"Just a bandito with a gun," I said. "They'll give it back to you – when it's empty." I handed Damien a drum. He stood there holding it.

In the firelight, I saw some Banditos walking up to the pyre carrying a bundle overhead. Lobo was leading them. Richie's body was wrapped tight with a blanket, but his face was exposed.

"HEY HEY EVERYBODY!" Lobo shouted. "LET'S SEND RICHIE OFF TO THE SKY!" The men all took Richie, then flung and pushed his body onto the highest part of the wood pile.

Lobo said something to Melody. She took a large burning stick from the small fire and lit the base of the pyre. "AYEE YIII YIII YIII YIII!" Melody was shrieking. Other women trilled in with her. High-pitched wails into the cold mountain night, so far far away from the power and the lights and the telephones and televisions of the cozy warm houses...

The flames rose to Richie. I danced around the fire in the crowd. The voices rose with the flames. Damien stayed to the side with Christina, beating the drum. I grabbed Christina pulled her into the dancing bodies. She pushed me away and went back to Damien.

The flames were now burning at the blanket that covered Richie. The blanket began to shred off. Soon the flames towered over Richie, glowing brightly on all the screaming dancers. The dancers picked up their pace with the flames. Richie's hair disappeared in a flash. Melody stood screaming in front of Richie's burning body. His clothes burned away from him and his body now stood out all black in the middle of the flames and coals. Christina walked to the edge of the pyre and stared. The wind blew our way, and everyone smelled the sickly sweet scent of Richie's charring flesh. *Human barbecue.* Christina covered her face and ran off. Springflower came dancing past me.

"LOOK! LOOK!" Melody shouted. "LOOK AT RICHIE'S HAND! RICHIE'S SENDING US A MESSAGE. HE'S SAYING 'PEACE.' SEE IT? HE'S SAYING `PEACE!'"

Richie's body had shifted on the burning wood and his left arm had lifted with his hand pointing up. I saw only two remaining fingers on it, both pointing up and apart in a "V" position.

*But Richie saying "peace?" Richie, the strong-arm robber who shot up people in Albuquerque for money and dope? Richie, who took whatever he needed? And now Richie is telling us "peace?" No no no. Too late for that, Richie.*

The fire roared so hot we all had to step back. I stared as Richie's legs and arms fell off. The flames snapped and the wood exploded. Richie's eyes looked to be glowing red. For a moment there was a large red coal on his forehead. *A third eye.* Then Richie's head tilted backward and slowly, *it fell off.*

The dancing was now frantic. Melody swang around the fire in everyone's arms. Drums and shrieking and dancing. The flames rolled higher and hotter. Waves of smoke swirled into the clear mountain sky, under ten thousand stars. The heat pushed us back further and further.

I danced and danced until the flames settled onto a knee-high bed of coals. I no longer saw any trace of Richie. Some Banditos began to drift off. I watched Melody lay out her bed roll next to the fire along with the others. She tucked her kids in. Two horses were shackled not ten feet away from the kids. Any one of the horses could step on her kids and crush them dead. Would that mean another cremation?

Damien got out our sleeping bags and spread them out on a tarp. Then he handed me a bottle of tequila. "This is the last one I have. Don't let any of them see it." We sipped in silence. Christina lay between us. I looked up at the constellation Orion.

"Just think, Jimmy," Damien said. "If you hadn't deserted the army, you'd just be laying out under the stars in Vietnam right now."

"Yeah, and you'd probably be a lot safer," Christina added.

We drank under the stars in the orange glow of the embers. I felt warm and good inside my bag.

"Jimmy," Damien called for me from his sleeping bag. "Jimmy. This is all crazy. You know that, right?"

"How so?" I asked.

"We're worried about you, Jimmy," Christina said.

I looked at Andromeda in Orion's sword.

"Damien, you just smuggled 200 kilos of marijuana from Mexico and you are *worried about me?*"

"That's different, Jimmy, and you know it. That's about getting high. That's about business. But these people--"

"They're just wild animals! Jimmy, you've got to leave here," Christina shouted.

I reached over and swigged another hit of tequila. Then I lay back and looked at the stars. To my side I saw the dwindling pyre fire. Smoke drifted toward us.

A bit later we heard some commotion to our side. It was coming from where we had seen Melody lay her sleeping roll.

"What's that?" Christina asked. We listened some more. "It sounds like --- like someone's *doing it,*" she finished.

Damien sat up. "That it is," he whispered. "I'd recognize that sound anyplace."

"But right outside, here, in the cold mud – in front of strangers – I mean-- who could?" Christina said.

Damien leaned over me and gawked. "It's coming from where-- what's her name – the widow – she laid her sleeping roll. Yeah, I think she's banging – what's his name? You know, Mr. Bad Ass."

"You mean Melody and Packrat? No," Christina said. "*No.* Not at your husband's funeral. *That's not right.*"

They were huffing up a storm all right, right next to us.

"Well, you know, just like Melody said. Richie was sending a `peace' message," Damien said. I laughed.

"*I want to leave*," Christina insisted.

"Sure. First thing tomorrow morning."

"*Now.*"

"We can't go now," Damien whispered. "We don't know where we are. We'd get lost in a minute in the dark. And besides, we might step on some bandito – fucking a goat – and he'd shoot us for sure. I'm going to sleep now."

I laughed. Damien was reminding me why I liked being around him. I didn't hear much more from him or Christina after that.

*I stared at the stars. Oh the wildness of it all. The wilderness around me. The big wild. My only true home. Man must have felt like this a hundred thousand years ago. Complete awe. I felt divine and magical with the world.*

Then I heard a rustle next to me.

"*Jimmy,*" a voice whispered. *It was Springflower.* "I thought I'd *never* find you," she whispered. She bent down and squeezed my hand. "Let's go sleep next to the fire." She pulled me.

I got up and gathered my sleeping gear. I followed her to the edge of the fire where she had spread her sleeping roll. I laid my sleeping bag next to her and lay on it. She reached over and pulled me to her and kissed me. She lifted her bed roll over me and unzipped my sleeping bag. She helped me out of my clothes, and then she slipped out of hers. Then she pulled me into her and moaned and moaned to the stars above, smelling of horses and smoke, tasting of sweat and musk.

Maybe it was in a dream later that night, that I asked her to please come live with me. I pleaded with her again and again. But she just held me close and shushed me. But I do know that I saw her smile in the starlight.

When I awoke in the morning, Springflower was gone. I wanted to tell her of my dream, and listen to hers. But the sun was up and I was alone. I looked around. Very few people were stirring. Damien and Christina and all their gear were gone.

I saw Melody sifting through the ashes of the fire. I walked over to her. She was filling up a hand-made buckskin bag with Richie's bones. "I'm gonna make a necklace, some jewelry, maybe a pipe out of these," she said to me. I watched her for a while more. Then she left to tend to her kids. I turned the ashes over with a stick. They were still hot. I found parts of Richie's skull and hands.

# Richie's Last Party

"*What are you doing?*" Christina was standing behind me.
I held the bones out to her. "I'm taking these with me, to make something. You want some?"
"NO!"
Damien came up with our back packs. "Jimmy, let's go." Christina pointed to the bones I was holding. I held up the bones for Damien to see. Then I stuck them in my medicine bag.
I stood up. "You go ahead down to the truck. I'll be following you in a little bit. I got to repack my backpack."
Christina took off first, taking big strides down the hill to the trail.
I walked around and searched. *Where could Springflower be?* I could not go into their tents or tepees. I looked for her horse but I could not find it. After I had covered the camp, I double-checked and searched again. I looked for any fresh hoof prints leading away from the camp. But I would not be able to recognize them anyhow.
*Springflower was gone again – like the smoke and the fire.*
I quickly gathered up my gear and began hiking down to Damien's truck, before Christina convinced him. When I got to the truck, they had the engine running and the heater on. As soon as I tossed my backpack into the truck, Damien took off driving without saying a word. Damien and Christina dropped me off at my cabin and left in a hurry. We did not even make plans to meet again.

Whenever I met someone who was going to the bandito's camp, I sent a note to Springflower. I did not receive anything back from her. I began my paying job at the clinic in Mora as an EMT. Whenever I had extra time, I worked hard on my ranch. Fences and buildings, irrigation and fruit trees, horses and goats, a hive of honey bees and berries. My daily work as an EMT consisted mostly of dealing with the results of drunken car accidents, violent husbands, and bar fights. It was just another typical summer in the New Mexico mountains.

It was on a bright sunny day when I saw four riders approaching from the mountainside, in the distance. I stood with my 38-40 Winchester nearby, just in case. As they approached, I saw Melody and Packrat in front. Behind them rode her daughter, Rain, all by herself on a pony. Riding last was Texas John. He was also leading a pack horse. Melody had her new baby, Cold Winter, wrapped up in a baby blanket in front of her. I put the gun away. They dismounted in front of my barn. I watched the little girl Rain expertly swing herself off her pony and tie it up to a fencepost. That kid was literally growing up on a horse.

"Is the date May 15th?" Packrat asked. I nodded. I gathered that was as close as he ever got to keeping time. "We supposed to meet Richie's parents here today. Hope you don't mind, but this was the only place we could give them directions to from the road that they could find. They're driving all the way out from Cleveland, Ohio."

"Yeah," Melody said. "They want to meet their grandkids for the first time. I never met them yet either."

Well, of course it would have to be okay for them to hang around here all day and meet Melody's would-have-been-in-laws. I'd just go back to working and let them wait.

"Mind if I clean up some before they get here?" Melody asked. She was already taking the kids into my kitchen. I looked at the kids. Melody had a lot of work to do.

"Maybe it's best you don't talk to Richie's parents," Packrat addressed me. "You see--" Packrat turned his head to Melody's two kids. "They want to support their grandkids. And we don't wanna mess this up."

"I'll just tell them I own this place and live here. Nothing more."

I went down to the fence line of my pasture where my stud horse Pharaoh had broken out again. He had caught a whiff of a mare in heat again and he was *gone*. Having waited so long for Springflower to return, I felt like doing the same.

I continued with my tamping rod, lifting it up and pounding it down onto the soft dirt next to my freshly cut fence posts. The tamping rod was eight feet long and weighed maybe twenty pounds. One end was sharp, the other flat. I alternated it with my post hole digger. Once I had a hole two feet deep, I stuck a seven foot long gambel oak post into it. Then I packed dirt and rocks around the edges and tamped it down hard with the flat end of the tamping bar. One post hole done. On this sloping, hard scrabble rocky soil, getting ten of them into the ground was one good day's work.

Up above, I heard a vehicle pull into my home. I thought to leave them alone and keep working. But five more fence posts later and I was hungry and thirsty. I walked up to my home. *It was my home anyhow.* I saw a new Volvo parked in front of my cabin. Maybe the first new car I'd ever seen parked here. Melody and Packrat were tending to their horses while they grazed in my pasture. Little Rain was sitting on my porch with an elderly couple. I walked up to them and introduced myself. We shook hands. He was a smaller man, almost bald, with a neatly trimmed white mustache. He wore an old brown sports jacket with a matching vest, a clean white shirt,

## Richie's Last Party

and pressed dark pants held up with suspenders. His wife was wearing a conservative blue dress with a gray sweater. Their matching wedding rings looked worn with age. She was holding her new grandson, staring into his face, with Rain to her side. The woman barely looked at me.

"You knew my son Richie?" Richie's father asked. His voice had a thick central European accent. His hands seemed to tremble in unison with his voice.

"Yes --- sir."

"You live up in the mountains with them?" Then he pointed to Packrat and Melody. *"Like them?"*

"No sir. I live here. In this building. This is my home. I work part-time at the medical clinic in Mora."

"You work, huh?" He looked up at me. "That is good." I nodded to him. "Now tell me. Is it true that Richie died here --- in your home?" The man was now visibly shaking.

"Yes. Yes sir it is."

"And--- and were you here at the time?"

"Uhh, yes. Yes, I was --- in the next room."

"And you did not take him to the hospital?"

"My truck was stuck in the mud at the time. So I rode my horse to our Mora clinic to get antibiotics for him."

Richie's father paused and took a few deep breaths.

"Now tell me true. What happened with my son? They--" he gestured to Melody, Packrat, and Texas John in the pasture. "They tell me hardly nothing. What he die of? How did he die?"

I whispered that I really couldn't talk much while Packrat and Melody were here. Then I said softly that Richie had a very bad cut from barbed wire, and it looked to me that Richie got tetanus from it. I treated the cut as best I could. But Richie did not come to me for help in time.

The old man slowly shook his head, and then drooped forward. "But tetanus? With medicine, you can treat."

I watched Richie's mother holding her grandson. She had taken off his little shirt and was slowly examining him. Hands, fingers, nails. Then she took his pants down. Cold Winter needed a serious change and cleaning. She got up and went into my kitchen. She came out a moment later.

"Where is your faucet?" were the first words she said to me. I explained that there was no running water here. I had a good well and there should be ten gallons of water on the stand in the corner of the kitchen. She looked at me disturbed.

"But hot water?"

# The Wild Years

"I can heat some up."

"Never mind." she went back into the kitchen with the baby.

"Richie – Melody, they live like you?" the man said.

"No. They didn't have a home. A tepee, but no home."

"*A tepee?*" he repeated.

"A hogan, actually."

"A hogan? What is a hogan?"

I started to explain what it looked like. After he got the idea, he shook his head and told me to stop.

"Did my son ever talk about his religion?" the man asked.

"I remember him saying something about the Great Spirit or something but---"

"The Great Spirit? No. I mean his religion. Richie is Jewish, you know."

I shook my head.

Melody and Packrat returned from the horses.

"You want to show this man the toys we brought the children?" Richie's father said.

Melody and Packrat exchanged private glances. Melody walked over to a large outdoor table against the side of my home. Just now I noticed that it was covered with toys and opened boxes. I saw several dolls, teddy bears, a race car, a Mister Potato Head, tinker toys, Lincoln Logs. Toys that I had had as a kid. Melody held a few of them up to me, with a smile of sorts.

"Show them that doll with the string in back," Richie's father said to Melody.

"Naw," she said.

"Go ahead. Show it. I never see a doll like that."

Melody looked to Packrat. Then she lifted the doll and pulled out the string.

HEL-LO MOM-MY!

Melody pulled the string again.

HEL-LO DAD-DY!

Melody quickly put the doll down. Richie's father nudged me. "It says both 'mommy' and 'daddy'. Isn't that something? Amazing. I tell you, they never had dolls like that when we were children in Germany."

Richie's mother came out of my kitchen. "Where is your bathroom?"

I explained to her that all I had here was an outhouse. It was a sanitary one, but still an outhouse. I showed her where it was located, in the middle of my fruit orchard. She looked at it for a moment, and then walked back to my home. She talked with her husband.

"We are going to the gas station we saw in Mora. We will not be gone long. We come right back." Richie's father said to all of us. He repeated himself to Melody and Packrat.

"We will have to be going soon," Packrat said. "We don't want to ride the trails at night. We might get lost, or a horse could slide off the trail. Plus, we got no place to stay here tonight."

*No place to stay here? What? You Banditos had come down to my home and stayed here any fucking time you wanted, and you never asked me once then. But then, you had a few more rifles with you.*

"Can you not stay for another day?" Richie's father asked.

Silence.

"Okay then. We hurry back."

They walked slowly to their car and drove off.

Texas John walked up. He was long and skinny. Excellent with horses and a rifle. They said Tex was the only bandito who had ever stood up to Lobo. I wasn't sure what that meant, or whether it was over with yet.

"Well, let's git packin' 'for they git back."

Melody sort of wrinkled her face. "You think we should?"

"You got your money, right? They know where to send more. What more you need?"

"Uhh, I dunno." Melody began gathering up her things.

Texas John grabbed the doll, pulled the string out, and let it go.

"HEL-LO MOM-MY!" he screeched in disharmony with the doll. The little girl Rain said, "Hello mommy," softly. Tex pulled it again. "HEL-LO DAD-DY!" He and Packrat chorused in. He pulled the string again and again, faster and faster, He and Packrat mimicking in falsetto as the doll did her two tricks. They laughed hard between pulls. Finally Texas John yanked the string too hard and broke it. The doll had just said its last "Hel-lo mom-my."

"Goddamn, will you look at all this shit," Texas John's arm swept across all of the toys on the table. They went clattering on my stone walk. Little Rain ran over and began picking them up. "Sona-abitch what shit! It's what's wrong with this fuckin' country. All it makes is shit!" Texas John stood there shaking the newly mute doll. "Hey Packrat, come with me," he said with a smirk. They walked off with the now mute doll, down the path that led to the outhouse and the wood pile.

I watched Melody slowly pack up. She would never be ready before Richie's parents got back. She seemed slow to me in every way possible. Her daughter Rain sat on the stone slabs, playing contentedly with the dolls now lying about on the ground.

Packrat and Texas John came back from the path, laughing. Tex turned to Melody. "You ready to go?"

"In a little bit," Melody shouted back from behind her horse.

"Bulllllllll-shit," Tex grumbled to Packrat. "She'll be here all day. She always is. I'm riding back to Le Doux now. You can catch up with me if you want. But I'll get there before you leave here, most likely."

Packrat took a smoke from Tex and nodded. Tex checked his gear and then started riding up the trail to the Sangre de Cristos.

I ate some food and filled up my canteens. Just as I started hiking down to finish today's fence line, I heard a car coming. Down the road I saw Richie's parents returning.

"Here we go again," Packrat mumbled.

They got out and slowly walked up to my front porch. They said hello to Melody. She answered back, but continued packing her horse. Then they sat next to me. The old man took my hand and squeezed it. He did not let go.

*"Why?"* he looked at me. There were tears in his eyes. "Why? We ask Melody to come stay with us for a while. We want to know our grandchildren. They are all we have left of our son now. But she say 'No. Not now,' and nothing more. She say she cannot come out to Cleveland. Of course we pay for everything. We have room, food, money. We can send the children to good schools. But she just say 'No' and nothing more. Why? *Why?"*

I saw his wife listening. She too was crying, nodding as her husband spoke to me. "We have nothing else of our son. They burn him. That is true?" He paused, and then I nodded. "We-- we do not even have his ashes. But now we cannot even have our grandchildren. Oh this Melody say maybe later. But give me address in Mora, *general delivery.* What kind of address is that? She say we can send money there. And this 'Packrat' man. What kind of name is that? What kind of work he can do? Live on mountain? Where is the work here? Where is the life here?"

I thought about the few bones I had of Richie. Some finger bones, part of an ulna, and his sagittal crest. These bones were less than fifteen feet from where Richie's parents now sat. Did they know that Melody now wore Richie's bones on her necklaces? Did she tell them? Suddenly I felt creepy.

"You think – you think she come back to Cleveland sometime and stay with us? We can help her, you know."

I wanted to tell the man yes, of course she would, but I had no idea what she would do. Maybe, when she was totally against the wall, homeless with the kids, hungry and desperate, abandoned by all the Banditos, maybe then she would visit them. How could I explain to them how their college professor son became an armed robber and a bandito? I couldn't even explain myself to my parents. What would Melody do now? Well, there she was, packing up her horse, getting ready to ride off after meeting her children's grandparents for the first time, after one visit of only a few hours. The grandparents had spent a week just getting here, and now Melody and her children were leaving. I wanted to lie to Richie's parents and say that yes, Melody and the kids would be coming. But I just sat silent.

Richie's mother abruptly stood up. "I want to play with Rain while I can." She walked over to Rain and sat next to her. They began playing with the dolls.

The old man breathed deeply next to me. "You have children?" he abruptly asked.

"No. No I don't."

"Well then, you cannot understand how we feel. You can never understand until you have children. We are from different worlds. That I know is true." He squeezed my hand again.

We watched Richie's mother take Rain by the hand and go walking down the path. There was a bit of a girlish hop in her step. The presence of their grandchildren seemed to diminish some of the pain from the loss of their son.

"Well, I think---I must believe---that Melody will come and stay with us sometime. Soon I hope, because this pain is too much. You see, Richie, he was our only child. And what is life for us now?" Richie's father gestured toward Melody and Packrat with their horses, now almost packed full. "What did we do for Richie to go this way? *What?* We do not know."

Then we heard a scream from down the path. There was another scream. I heard a wail. It could only have come from Richie's mother. I jumped up and ran down the path. I saw Richie's mother crying, clutching her granddaughter. I asked her what was wrong, but she just continued sobbing. Richie's father came down the path to us. The granddaughter was crying too. I asked again. She said nothing, but gestured with her arm.

I turned and looked at my chopping block. On it lay the talking doll. It had been chopped into pieces, doll-dismembered, with my ax. Both legs lay separately, the body chopped in two in the mid-section. Pieces of spring and recording tape hung from the mashed stomach. The head was shattered, severed off at the neck. One eye was missing. The eyelash hung over the

## The Wild Years

plastic eye socket.

Richie's father stared at doll remnants with me. He squeezed my hand again. His lips voiced "WHY?" but no sounds came out. He did not let go of my hand.

We heard a horse whinny. Melody rode over with Cold Winter tied to her chest in a sling.

"Rain, you've got to get on your pony now. We've got to go." Melody dismounted and walked up to Richie's mother. Packrat waited on his horse in the distance. Melody began to take Rain from Richie's mother, but neither of them let go. Rain had her fingers intertwined behind Richie's mother's neck. Melody gently pulled Rain's fingers apart and pulled at Rain. Finally, Richie's mother released Rain to Melody. Melody looked at the dismembered doll.

"Oh, we didn't do that. I mean *I* didn't do that. It was broke anyhow."

Melody carried Rain over to her pony and lifted her into her saddle. "We have to be going before it gets dark," Melody said. She mounted her horse. "We'll write."

Richie's father grabbed my hand again. We watched them as they turned their horses and headed toward the Sangre de Cristo Mountains. I walked with Richie's parents to the bench in front of my home. From there, we watched Melody and her crew disappear behind some ponderosa pine trees. Only when they were out of sight, did Richie's parents let go of my hands. Then, without a word more, they got up and slowly stumbled to their car.

I imagined for one last time that I would see Springflower come riding down that trail, on her way to Canada. She was coming to get me...

But Springflower never returned...

## The End

In writing and publishing this book, I only used open source software. For an operating system, I used the Ubuntu Linux version 13.04. For a text editor, I used Libre Office. For graphical design, I used GIMP. For the book formatting and publishing software, I used Scribus and PDF Chain. For final printing and distribution, I used Amazon's Createspace.

I think that all of the software programs listed above were simply superb with their quality, functionality, and reliability.

Made in the USA
Charleston, SC
14 January 2014